PYRAMIDS

PYRAMIDS

THE REAL STORY BEHIND EGYPT'S MOST ANCIENT MONUMENTS

JOYCE TYLDESLEY

VIKING
an imprint of
PENGUIN BOOKS

VIKING

Published by the Penguin Group
Penguin Books Ltd, 80 Strand, London WC2R ORL, England
Penguin Putnam Inc., 375 Hudson Street, New York, New York 10014, USA
Penguin Books Australia Ltd, 250 Camberwell Road,
Camberwell, Victoria 3124, Australia
Penguin Books Canada Ltd, 10 Alcorn Avenue, Toronto, Ontario, Canada M4V 3B2
Penguin Books India (P) Ltd, 11 Community Centre,
Panchsheel Park, New Delhi – 110 017, India
Penguin Books (NZ) Ltd, Cnr Rosedale and Airborne Roads,
Albany, Auckland, New Zealand
Penguin Books (South Africa) (Pty) Ltd, 24 Sturdee Avenue,
Rosebank 2196, South Africa

Penguin Books Ltd, Registered Offices: 80 Strand, London WC2R ORL, England

www.penguin.com

First published 2003
I

Set in 11½/13½ pt Monotype Bembo
Typeset by Rowland Phototypesetting Ltd, Bury St Edmunds, Suffolk
Printed in Great Britain by Clays Ltd, St Ives plc

A CIP catalogue record for this book is available from the British Library

ISBN 0–670–89322–6

The mighty pyramids of stone
That wedge-like cleave the desert airs
When nearer seen, and better known,
Are but gigantic flights of stairs

Henry Wadsworth Longfellow:
The Ladder of St Augustine

For Eleo Gordon, whose idea this was.

Contents

List of Plates

All photographs, unless otherwise credited, are by Steven Snape.

List of Figures

Where not otherwise credited, all figures are by Steven Snape.

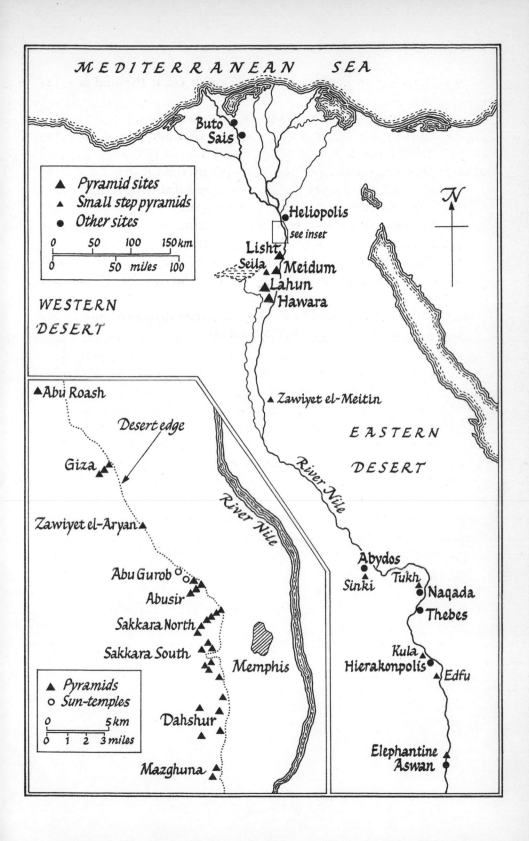

MEDITERRANEAN SEA

Buto
Sais

▲ Pyramid sites
▲ Small step pyramids
● Other sites

0   50   100   150 km
0   50 miles 100

WESTERN
DESERT

Heliopolis
see inset

Lisht
Seila   Meidum
Lahun
Hawara

N

▲ Zawiyet el-Meitin

EASTERN

DESERT

River Nile

▲ Abu Roash

Desert edge

Giza

Zawiyet el-Aryan

River Nile

Abu Gurob
Abusir
Sakkara North
Sakkara South

Memphis

▲ Pyramids
○ Sun-temples

0   5 km
0 1 2 3 miles

Dahshur

Mazghuna

Abydos
Sinki   Tukh
Naqada
Thebes

Kula
Hierakonpolis   Edfu

Elephantine
Aswan

Introduction
First Impressions

I think that it is the experience of most that it is only after repeated visits that any real appreciation of Pyramid or Sphinx is developed, and that their impressiveness increases with continued familiarity. The first visit is fatiguing; and so much is found to do, that emotion succumbs to physical exhaustion . . .[1]

In 1883 R. Talbot Kelly, respected artist and travel writer, was making his first visit to the Great Pyramid of King Cheops, who is today better known as King Khufu. He can perhaps be forgiven for failing to appreciate fully the grandeur of his surroundings. Just one year after Cairo had suffered the indignity of British occupation, tourists were rare and the locals had grown greedy for foreign *baksheesh*. Talbot Kelly and an unnamed male friend had enjoyed a strenuous morning scrambling over and crawling inside the monuments before retiring to their carriage for a well-deserved luncheon. Here, resting in the shadow of the Great Pyramid, they attracted the attention of a vociferous crowd of importuning beggars. Most alarmed by this development, they ordered their driver to start at once for Cairo. Their hasty departure inflamed the rabble, and things quickly turned nasty. A full-scale assault on the carriage followed. It was a dramatic scene. While the driver fought to control his frightened horse, lashing out at all and sundry with his whip, Talbot Kelly and his friend rose to beat off their assailants with stout sticks. They escaped with their pride battered but their wallets intact, fleeing amidst a hail of hostile stones.

Almost a century later I too was visiting Giza for the first time and feeling not fear – I did not anticipate attack by a swarm of angry locals – but a warm sense of excited expectation. As an archaeology student I had spent years learning about the pyramids. I had read books, studied diagrams, attended lectures, written essays and sat, even occasionally slept, in a darkened lecture theatre watching slide after slide of pyramids, pyramid enclosures, pyramid temples and pyramid texts. In theory, I knew just about everything that anyone could teach about the pyramids. Now, with a fellow student to act as my guide, second-hand knowledge was about to become first-hand reality.

And yet, as our taxi sped along Pyramids Road, blaring out Western pop music, belching out fumes and dodging through the dense Cairo traffic, it was difficult to suppress a niggling feeling of disappointment. Like many another visitor I was approaching Giza with a head stuffed full of preconceptions. The pyramids of my imagination were the pyramids promoted by sympathetic travel brochures and soft-filter photography; awesome, austere symbols standing isolated and proud in the golden desert sun. A quick glimpse out of the taxi window was already enough to confirm that this was a hopelessly romanticized vision. Talbot Kelly had driven across twelve miles of cornfields to eat his aborted picnic, but Cairo's ruthless expansion has ensured that today the world's most famous monuments loom uncomfortably close over the suburban streets. Pyramids Road, polluted, crowded and lined with endless rows of hotels, tacky restaurants and souvenir shops – 'your name in hieroglyphs, here, now!' – provides a less than noble introduction to the Old Kingdom royal cemetery.

Things were to get worse. Decanted from the relative calm of the taxi we found the Giza plateau teaming with modern life. It seemed that everyone had chosen that afternoon to visit the pyramids. Guides, souvenir sellers, beggars and tiny children selling water 'bottled' at the nearest pump, vied noisily and persistently for attention. Assorted donkeys and camels waited, bells jingling and plumes waggling, for customers willing to pay an exorbitant amount for a brief, uncomfortable trot across the sands. Straggling groups of overheated tourists, their enthusiasm dimmed by the sheer number of antiquities on offer, followed uninspired guides and filmed everything in sight without really seeing anything.

Close up, the three pyramids appeared so huge that it was impossible to appreciate their size, or even their shape. Outside there were flies, fumes and hustle. Inside, the narrow passages breathed a stifling atmosphere of dust and sweat tinged with more than a hint of urine. The ascent was uncomfortable; the heavy stone slabs seemed to press down on the constant stream of visitors. There was no time to pause and reflect, no peace, no calm, and certainly no feeling of awe. Only in the burial chambers did it seem possible to realize, for a fleeting moment, the true enormity of the structures and all that they stood for. Restored to the outside world, I scratched my flea bites and pondered the dilemma of reality versus illusion.

So much for first impressions. Fortunately, Talbot Kelly is right; when it comes to pyramids, familiarity breeds increasing respect, even love. Somehow the pyramids manage to overcome all the indignities that the modern world throws at them. By the end of that day I had scrambled inside all three Giza pyramids, paid my respects to the Sphinx, ridden a bad-tempered camel, discovered a new enthusiasm and become engaged to be married. By the end of the week I had explored every pyramid within driving range of Cairo. I had stood in the soft desert rain to admire Djoser's Step Pyramid. I had descended beneath the Sakkara pyramids of Unas and Teti, had inspected the rubble-strewn interior of Sahure's Abusir pyramid and travelled to Dahshur to see the military zone which forbade entrance to the Bent Pyramid of Snefru. I had returned to Giza at night, to see the Great Pyramid at peace with the modern world. Back in Liverpool the enthusiasm grew stronger and I stood, in harsher rain, to admire the small-scale pyramid which ornaments the Victorian grave-yard on Rodney Street.

My enthusiasm for pyramids has lasted some twenty years, and it seems unlikely that it will leave me now. Nevertheless, I hesitated when it was suggested that I might write a book about the origins of Egypt's Old Kingdom pyramids. Many forests have already been sacrificed to pyramid selling. There are so very many pyramid books, some excellent, several bizarre and a few downright bad. Could there really be room for one more? A prolonged bout of reading convinced me that there could. My book, however, would take a different approach to the vast majority, which tend to concentrate either on pyramid technology or on what may loosely be described as 'pyramid theory' while ignoring wider aspects of early Egyptian culture. I did not want to write another stone-by-stone analysis of pyramid architecture.[2] Instead I wanted to write a book which would set the pyramids into their historical, even pre-historical, context. A book which would present the pyramids as an integral and eminently achievable part of Egyptian life. By tracing the pyramid-building society back to its roots, I wanted to show not only how and why the Egyptians were able to build their pyramids, but how the pyramids helped to build Old Kingdom Egypt.

But where to start? The first pyramid, the Step Pyramid built for King Djoser at Sakkara, appeared early in Egyptian history, only a few hundred years after the unification of the country. But it did not spring, fully formed, out of a technological void. It was built by a society accustomed to monumental building. Egypt's distinct beliefs – theories of kingship, of religion and of life beyond death – were already firmly in place and a clear evolution can be traced from the mounds which covered the graves of the Predynastic elite, through the splendours of the Giza plateau, to the miniature pyramids which topped New Kingdom private tombs. To understand the skills and beliefs of the earliest pyramid builders we must look backwards, to the time before Egypt was a united land. I have therefore chosen to devote the first section of this book – Conception – to the prehistoric, Predynastic and Archaic periods which precede the pyramid building age. At the other end of the timescale the final section – Variation – continues the pyramid story from the end of the Old Kingdom into the modern era.

Egypt's prehistorians and her historians inhabit very different worlds. The prehistorians are first and foremost practical archaeologists. Disregarding modern boundaries they consider Egypt, in her wider north African/eastern Mediterranean context, as a corridor linking Africa with Europe and Asia. Faced with a paucity of information, they spend their days searching out minute scraps of evidence. Their excavations are slow and painstaking; to the eagle-eye of the prehistorian, flint debris, pot sherds and the smallest of plant seeds rank as important finds.

Egypt's historians are concerned with a far shorter time-span but are faced with a superabundance of riches. Preserved beneath her sands, 3000 years of Dynastic Egypt have left a legacy of copious writings, stone-built temples, rock-cut graves and abandoned villages. Eerie animal-headed gods, ghoulish funerary rituals, dark tombs lit by flickering candles and the ever-present glint of gold add a definite glamour to Egyptology; a glamour which has been boosted by the film industry. Secretly, more than one staid professor believes himself to be the 'real' Indiana Jones.

With a few notable exceptions Egyptologists have been linguists and historians first, archaeologists and anthropologists second. In consequence, their excavations have traditionally been swift and brutal affairs, with small-scale evidence being rejected in the search for texts and commercially valuable artefacts. Today this treasure-seeking approach is unacceptable, and archaeological digs are conducted with the utmost scientific rigour. Meanwhile, much irreplaceable evidence has been lost. The re-excavation of the rubbish dumps left by early missions has become a standard, rewarding procedure. But re-excavation, while useful, is never ideal. Archaeological sites are fragile entities; they remain relatively safe while hidden, but once exposed can never be restored. The excavator of a virgin site becomes its destroyer, and s/he carries a great responsibility to both past and future generations.

To the Egyptologist, ancient Egypt has become a well-defined nation and the Egyptians are real people. As the Dynastic periods develop we start to meet the personalities of the past; those whose names, deeds and thoughts have survived to illuminate their long-vanished societies. Here, too, we find the official records which allow us to divide Egypt's long history into dynasties, or lines of connected rulers. The Egyptian dynasties stretch from Dynasty 1 (c. 3000 BC), the time when the disparate lands of the Nile were first united under one king, to Dynasty 31 and the invasion of Alexander the Great (332 BC). This dating convention is followed by modern Egyptologists who further subdivide the dynasties into periods and Kingdoms:[3]

    Predynastic period (Badarian – Naqada III/Dynasty 0)
    Archaic period/Early Dynastic Period (Dynasties 1–2)
    Old Kingdom (Dynasties 3–8)
    First Intermediate period (Dynasties 9–11)
    Middle Kingdom (Dynasties 11–14)
    Second Intermediate period (Dynasties 15–17)
    New Kingdom (Dynasties 18–20)
    Third Intermediate period (Dynasties 21–25)
    Late period (Dynasties 26–31)

Immediately preceding the Archaic period we experience a clash of terminologies as the Egyptologist's ill-defined Predynastic era is the equivalent of the prehistorian's Late Neolithic; a time when society practised agriculture and made pots, but had no real metallurgy. To this time belong Egypt's earliest, most shadowy kings, consigned to Dynasty 0. To add to the confusion, the very end of the Predynastic age, being literate, belongs to history rather than prehistory.

Prior to the Neolithic (New Stone Age) comes the immensely long Palaeolithic (Old Stone Age), which is conventionally subdivided into Lower, Middle, Upper, Late and Epi- phases. Although the final Palaeolithic offers evidence of good social organization, complex burial rituals and advanced stone-working technologies, it is not possible to prove continuity of tradition across the Palaeolithic/Neolithic divide. It is with the Neolithic that our story truly starts.

A note on calendar dates for the unwary. Egyptologists usually present calendar dates as dates BC (Before Christ), although a few now use the non-Christian term BCE (Before the Common Era). BC and BCE dates are interchangeable. However, prehistorians, who derive their dates by scientific analysis, use the convention BP (Before Present, i.e. before 1950). Caution is needed when comparing the two as BP dates are obviously not interchangeable with BC or BCE dates.

Measurements, too, need to be considered. I quote all measurements in metres, but many of these measurements are not as precise as I would wish. This is unavoidable. It is difficult to obtain accurate readings from a pyramid which is today a collapsed ruin, and quite impossible to measure the height of any pyramid, intact or collapsed, to the nearest centimetre. Pyramid heights can never be as accurate as measurable base-lengths.

SECTION ONE
Conception: Before the Pyramids

The operations of the mind no doubt find their noblest
expression in the language of speech, yet they are also eloquent
in the achievements of the hand. The works of men's hands
are his embodied thought, they endure after his bodily framework has passed into decay, and thus throw a welcome light
on the earliest stages of his unwritten history.

W. J. Sollas, *Ancient Hunters and their Modern Representatives*, 1911.

1

The First Egyptians

Now to describe the everyday life of prehistoric man is difficult, because there is not any history to go on. That is why we talk about these times as prehistoric.[1]

Three hundred and fifty thousand years ago national boundaries were unknown and the deserts which today border the Nile had not yet formed. Hunter–gatherer bands roamed the fertile African savannah, building temporary camps as they followed the herds of large mammals – rhinoceros, elephants, antelopes and horses – which served as their larder. In the region today known as Egypt, a more humid Egypt than we would recognize, her verdant lands irrigated by copious springs, oases and a faster flowing Nile, the hunters found good supplies of stone which they worked into tools, used and then dropped. Many millennia later these discarded artifacts, discovered along the Nile Valley, in the Sinai peninsula and the Western Desert, allow archaeologists to deduce the presence of the otherwise ephemeral nomads. On the basis of their tool kits, rich in multi-purpose bifaces and thick flakes, Egypt's Lower Palaeolithic peoples are classified as belonging to the Acheulian techno-logical phase.

As the climate became increasingly arid the oases were abandoned in favour of the Nile Valley. Improved conditions saw the return of the hunters who camped by newly formed lakes, bringing with them a modified kit of lighter tools. This technological development marks the change from the Lower Palaeolithic to the Middle; a phase which flourished in Egypt from approximately 200,000 to 30,000 BC. Now at last we find our first Egyptian. At Taramsa Hill, not far from Denderah, was found the burial of an anatomically modern child.

Nazlet Khater 4, a specialized mining site, is Egypt's earliest Upper

Palaeolithic settlement. Although occupied for approximately five thousand years, the site has yielded only two burials. One, a badly damaged grave, housed a shattered skeleton of unknown gender plus fragments of foetal bones and splinters of ostrich egg. The other, protected by its covering of stone slabs, held an almost complete male skeleton. The deceased lay on his back with his head pointing towards the west and a biface – the earliest known Egyptian funerary artefact – resting by his head.

While the people of Nazlet Khater quarried their stone and buried their dead, Europe was experiencing its final glaciation. With much of the land lost beneath the ice sheets the hunter-gatherers withdrew to the security of the river valleys, where they widened their diets to include smaller mammals and large amounts of fish. Conditions in Egypt were much kinder, but the country had again grown arid and we see the same enforced dietary changes. Alongside large animal bones Egypt's Late Palaeolithic sites have yielded the remains of small animals and birds, fish hooks and vast quantities of fish bone. Now, for the first time, we start to find the grinding stones which imply the preparation, and perhaps storage, of plant foods. The flooding which coincided with the ending of the European Ice Age washed away much of the evidence for the Late Palaeolithic occupation of the Nile Valley. There is, however, good evidence from further south to suggest that climatic fluctuations were stressing a population forced for the first time to compete for resources. The Nubian Late Palaeolithic cemetery of Gebel Sahaba Site 117, Wadi Halfa, has yielded fifty-nine skeletons, a mixture of men, women and children, twenty-four of whom appeared to have been brutally murdered. Their remains preserve evidence of broken limbs, savage knife cuts and flint flakes embedded deep in the bone.

The groups who roamed the Western Desert in 9300 BC were transient pastoralists. Their cattle were at best semi-domesticated and the relationship between the herders and their food supply was a symbiotic one with the cattle depending on the people for survival in an unfriendly environment, the people caring for and feeding off the cattle while continuing to hunt and gather plants. By 5100 BC the herding communities had adopted a more settled way of life and, while the cowboys who herded the now-domesticated cattle camped in temporary huts on the desert grasslands, their families lived in permanent villages beside the lakes. The herding communities prospered in the Western Desert until increasingly arid climatic conditions forced them to retreat to the Valley.

Meanwhile, from about 7000 BC onwards, we find traces of human occupation both in the Nile Valley and in the Faiyum. These groups, officially classified as Epipalaeolithic, were nomadic hunter-gatherer-fishers who made small-scale stone tools, hunted both small and large game and used their grinding stones to process plant foods and prepare ochre for use as a paint and a cosmetic.

In just six brief paragraphs we have dismissed over 300,000 years of Egyptian development. Now, with the appearance of agriculture and pottery, we enter the Neolithic phase. Time seems to slow down and we start to recognize – albeit through a glass, darkly – the anonymous peoples of our study. The term 'Neolithic Revolution', often encountered in older prehistories, is overly dramatic, suggesting as it does an immediate, irrevocable abandonment of the old hunter-gatherer lifestyle. In Egypt the move towards farming was neither a sudden nor an unexpected change and the old ways would persist alongside the new for thousands of years so that we find the Dynastic Egyptians continuing to hunt, fish, gather wild plants and work stone tools.

Agriculture – the raising of crops – dictates more or less permanent settlement. It is possible to sow seeds and then move on, returning to the fields at harvest time, but this is a haphazard way of life which leaves crops unprotected for much of the year. Permanent settlement enables the farmer to prepare the fields, to deal with pests, thieves and weeds and, thinking ahead, to store surpluses against times of need. But settlement leads to inevitable changes in social structure. Farmers invest their labour in their land. They have larger families both through choice, children being a valued resource, and due to lifestyle changes as decreased mobility and a carbohydrate-rich diet lead to increased female fertility.[2] The ability to store food, or anything which can be exchanged for food, becomes increasingly important in a settled community, and ever-increasing families hoarding limited resources can soon find themselves in conflict.

Arable agriculture was already being practised in the Fertile Crescent, an arc of archaeological sites stretching from Anatolia to south-western Iran, where we find the world's first farming communities dated to c. 8500 BC. Slowly the idea, the seeds and the domesticated animals spread outwards. They were to take some three thousand years to cross the three hundred miles of the Sinai peninsula and make their way to the Nile Valley; a rate of progress so slow it suggests that the Egyptians lacked the incentive to abandon the hunter-gatherer way of life. Farming may be safe but it requires forethought and a great deal of hard work. Hunting, in a land of plenty, offers an immediate large reward for relatively little, albeit dangerous, effort. The first domesticated Egyptian crops of wheat and barley, and herds of goats and sheep, are species indigenous to south-west Asia. They appear at sites whose stone tools and other artefacts are obviously African in origin, a strong indication that farming spread through Egypt by cultural contact rather than by independent development or invasion.

Egypt's oldest farming communities can be seen in the region of the Faiyum, where they are dated to c. 5450 BC. Here developed a substantial lakeside settlement whose residents took full advantage of their fertile environment – hunting big game, gathering freshwater mussels and fishing in the lake – but who also herded cattle and the newly arrived pigs and sheep/goats. Wild plants were gathered, and crops of domesticated emmer wheat and barley were harvested and stored communally in basket-lined pits. The Faiyum artisans adapted their wares to the changing world. The flint-knappers made small-scale arrowheads and sickle blades designed to be fitted into wooden handles, while the weavers created sophisticated reed baskets suitable for grain storage. The potters made plain, rather crude utilitarian vessels using silt mixed with straw temper.

Now, in every hamlet or village, there were choices to be made. There were lucky and hard-working farmers living alongside the feckless and unlucky. There were those who derived their living directly from the land, and those who developed complementary full-time skills; potters, weavers, painters, carvers, jewellers and stoneworkers who traded their specialized labours for food and who were essentially supported by their neighbours. Their differences would soon translate themselves into 'richer' and 'poorer'. The inheritance of material wealth, impossible in a hunter-gatherer community, would eventually allow the formation of a social elite.

The new way of life spread. It is typified by the settlement at Merimde Beni Salama, on the very edge of the Delta to the north-west of modern

Cairo. Here an extensive farming settlement flourished, with occasional breaks and a series of horizontal shifts in occupation, between 5000 and 4100 BC. The earliest Merimde peoples lived in simple round huts furnished with hearths. Here they made flake tools and burnished and herringbone-patterned pottery while practising mixed agriculture, hunting, gathering and fishing. Almost a thousand years later the final Merimde inhabitants dwelt in a well-organized village whose oval, semi-sunken mud-brick homes, thatched with branches and reeds and equipped with ovens, were set along narrow streets. The villagers farmed, hunted and gathered, penning their animals in a reed corral and storing their surpluses in the sunken granaries attached to each house. Spacious workshops allowed the potters to make large polished red/black vessels, the textile workers to convert flax into linen cloth and the craftsmen to make luxury artifacts of bone, horn, ivory and shell.

Upper Egypt, too, had her Neolithic settlements. The region of el-Badari, on the east bank of the Nile near modern Asyut, provides the first glimpse of Nile Valley farming culture, a successful fusion of local, African and Near Eastern traditions.[3] The Badarian phase flourished between 4500 and 4000 BC, and may have existed up to a thousand years earlier. Today we recognize some fifty Badarian settlements and cemeteries, stretching as far south as Hieraconpolis (modern Kom el-Ahmar) and as far east as the Wadi Hammamat. The Badarian sites are generally considered to be technologically and aesthetically superior to the contemporary northern culture. Their best pottery is certainly more accomplished, consisting of thin-walled simple shapes – cups and bowls – with a brown or red polish and often a black rim. The finest examples are pebble polished and decorated with a ripple patterning made by dragging a comb across the clay surface. A cruder rough-ware was produced for everyday use; this more basic pottery belongs to the living and is found in the settlements rather than the cemeteries.

The Badarians lived in small villages on the edge of the fertile land bordering the river. Here they grew wheat, barley, lentils and tubers, kept cattle and sheep/goats in circular pens, hunted gazelle and fished in the Nile. Their grain was stored in basket-lined pits and their rubbish was dumped outside their flimsy round huts. From time to time the settlements would up-sticks and relocate a short distance away; this horizontal shifting was perhaps a response to changing Nile flood levels, but may simply have been a means of controlling the fleas, flies, rats and snakes which would have feasted off a long-established community.

Establishing a tradition which was to last for centuries, the Badarians buried their dead away from the cultivated land. Already, funerary rituals were important. Children not yet mature enough to be considered a full member of the community might be interred within the settlement, but they were the exception. Everyone else was buried in shallow, oval, pit graves, where the vast majority of the contracted bodies lay on their left sides with their heads to the south, looking towards the west. While the poorest graves held only bones, the elite dead, dressed in linen clothing and wrapped in basketry or animal skins, were provided with a wide range of pottery, chert tools, rectangular or oval cosmetic palettes, ostrich eggs and feathers, female figurines and a variety of personal ornaments including combs, beads, bracelets and rings of ivory, shell and bone.

Already we are encountering differential preservation; a phenomenon which has dogged Egyptian archaeology, causing untold bias in our perception of the past. The Nile Valley is a narrow corridor which today cuts through uninhabitable mountains and arid desert. In damper Predynastic times the desert was not yet fully formed, and was in part an uncultivatable savannah with occasional woodlands watered by seasonal wadis. It made good sense for the ancient Egyptians to live close by, but not on, the narrow band of fertile soil – the Black Land – which lined the Nile and its wadis. It made equally good sense for them to bury their dead away from the living and, of course, away from the cultivated fields and pastures which were prone to flood. It was perhaps inevitable that the desert – the Red Land – should became irrevocably linked with death so that the Western Desert, the land of the setting sun, eventually became the kingdom of the dead, a scary place haunted by ghosts and unhappy spirits.

The Upper Egyptian desert burials, shorn of their superstructures, have survived relatively unscathed beneath their burden of sand. The contemporary Delta graves, dug into damper soil, have fared less well and have lost much of their organic content; we rarely recover wood, papyrus and bone from Delta burials. Egypt's mud-brick and reed settlements, her cities, towns and villages, have vanished almost without trace, dissolved by the rising Nile waters, ploughed into modern fields and lost beneath urban development. Stone cult temples may well be preserved as at Luxor (ancient Thebes), but cult temples made wholly of stone were a rarity before the New Kingdom. Egyptologists are therefore faced with a society largely represented by southern graves and their goods, although it has to be said that they have often compounded this bias by choosing to excavate cemeteries rather than search for the more complex settlement sites. Today, with a greater interest in daily – as opposed to funerary – life, Egyptian settlement sites are in vogue. The damage, however, has already been done.

The dangers of basing an understanding of any society on its graves and funerary rituals are obvious. How much valid information would we obtain from an excavation of our own cemeteries and crematoria? Egyptologists are in many ways fortunate. The graves which they study were equipped with a wide range of goods intended for use in the Afterlife; they therefore offer the chance to assess many of the technologies of the past. Nevertheless, grave goods must always represent a biased sample; at best they tend to be atypical, purpose-made, archaic-style artefacts selected by society's elite according to some long-lost rule.

The extensive Naqada cemeteries were excavated by Jacques de Morgan and Flinders Petrie in the last decade of the nineteenth century. Here Petrie, encountering graves like no known others, instinctively classified the Naqada people as Dynastic invaders; foreigners, 'the Falcon Tribe', imposing a totally new way of life represented by a new material culture on the Nile Valley. In this he was following the reasoning of his age. Living in imperialist times, late nineteenth-century archaeologists tended to see all cultural change in terms of conquerors and conquered. He was, however, wrong, as he somewhat grudgingly admitted later. The Naqada people were not foreigners:

The great surprise of the place [Naqada] was the immense prehistoric cemetery, from which that age is commonly called in France the Naqada period. Gradually we extended our work until we had cleared nearly two thousand graves. As the pottery and other products were different from what we knew in Egypt, they were provisionally referred to a 'New Race', and some indications here and at Ballas suggested that these people were invaders in the dark period after the VIth dynasty. De Morgan, who found similar graves, put them to predynastic times, though by a happy guess without any evidence.[4]

De Morgan's 'happy guess' was confirmed by Petrie's own work; the unusual graves in the New Race cemetery actually belonged to a prehistoric cultural group which had its roots in the region of Naqada, on the west bank of the Nile to the north of modern Luxor.

Initially contemporary with the Badarian culture, but soon overwhelming it, the Naqada phase lasted for approximately a thousand years from 4000 to 3050 BC. Naqada sites, both settlements and cemeteries, have been found in the Nubian Nile Valley, and as far north as Minshat Abu Omar in the north-eastern Nile Delta.

Just as prehistorians use tool typology to classify and date, so Petrie devised a pottery typology which could be used to divide the Naqada culture into successive phases. Although excessive reliance on typology is open to valid criticism – it is always important not to confuse artefacts with people, and Petrie's work disregarded the fabric of the pots while paying little attention to geographic and functional preferences – beggars cannot be choosers. This was the only dating system available and, indeed, somewhat modified and partially supported by radiocarbon dating, it is still in use today:

Naqada I, also known as the Amratian (after the type-site of el-Amra), is dated to between 4000–3500 BC and, not strikingly different to the Badarian, is characterized by burnished black-topped ware, and by red polished pots with a white painted decoration.

Naqada II, the Gerzean (after the type site of el-Gerza) is dated 3500–3200 BC, and favours red on buff painted pottery with wavy handles and a higher proportion of mass-produced coarse ware.

Naqada III (once, but no longer, known as the Semainian, after the site of Es-Semaina), is the final Naqada phase which, dated 3200–3050 BC, may also be classified as Dynasty 0. Decorated pottery is now out of fashion and the craftsmen are manufacturing plain, drab vessels similar to those which will be recovered in early Dynastic contexts. Tall, cylindrical jars, often included within the elite graves, appear to be a cheap substitute for the costly carved stone vessels which are also found in Naqada III graves.

While the majority of the Naqada I graves were similar in style to their Badarian predecessors, some were both larger and better equipped.

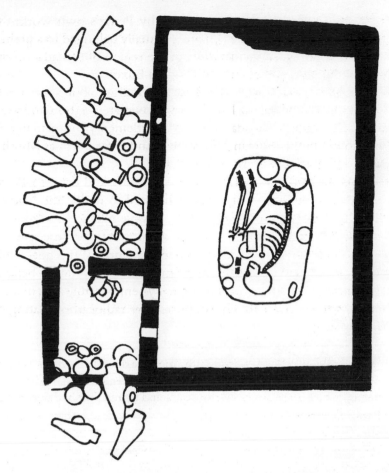

Figure 1.1   Predynastic burial with simple offering chapel.

Already we can detect an emphasis on ritual rather than everyday grave goods. The Naqada deceased are buried with purpose-made artefacts, often slightly distorted, larger- or smaller-than-life, as well as the humdrum objects used during their lifetimes. Alongside the new pottery we find a variety of stone cosmetic palettes. Some elongated rhomboidal specimens have now grown so large as to be severely impractical. Others have an animal theme, being either carved into an outline animal shape, with water-based fish, turtles and hippopotami particularly popular, or having animal motifs carved into them. A wider range of animals decorate the bone and ivory trinkets, the combs, pins, bracelets and rings, and feature either in white paint or in three-dimensional moulding on the pottery vessels. Here, alongside the usual riverine animals, we find such oddities as scorpions, ichneumons and giraffes.

Humans appear on the pottery as featureless, aggressive stick-men who use their harpoons and bows and arrows to slaughter wild animals. More ominously, they also fight and subdue their fellow men. These images of brutality, of dominance and conquest, are intended to impress; in the absence of formal writing they mark their owners out as men who have earned respect. Of less obvious significance are the carefully carved bone and ivory figurines, both male and female, which are found in some of the adult graves. These are not toys, nor are they confined to the richest graves. They have well-defined breasts and pubic regions which to modern eyes suggest a link with sexuality, fertility and perhaps even rebirth, but this may be an analysis too far.

Stone vessels make their first appearance in the Naqada I graves; there are two-handled vases, many made from basalt, a stone so hard that it challenges modern workmen, and smaller cylindrical vases made from softer limestone. Stone vessels will continue to play an important role in the funerary assemblage for many centuries, persisting well into the Dynastic age. For the first time the tool kit includes flat, disc-shaped, hard-stone maceheads designed to be hafted on a wooden, ivory or horn handle. Again these appear to be symbolic rather than functional weapons; some are simply too small and too light to have been of any real use on the battlefield while others, cheap pottery and soft limestone imitations, would have shattered upon impact.

From about 3500 BC the contents of the Naqada graves undergo an obvious change as we enter the Naqada II phase. Enough of the old-fashioned goods persist to indicate that we are not looking at an entirely new culture, but the influx of new styles is obvious enough to suggest the arrival of new ideas in the Nile Valley. This is a time of developing urbanization in southern Egypt. Naqada and Hieraconpolis have grown into sophisticated towns complete with temples, craftshops and rectangular mud-brick housing kept safe behind a crenellated mud-brick wall. The wall forms a symbolic boundary, defining the limits of the town, its ruling elite and its gods, but it also offers a real protection against outsiders who might be tempted by the wealth concentrated within. Life is becoming increasingly materialistic and, as the climate grows more arid, both Naqada and Hieraconpolis are creeping closer to the river which serves as Egypt's main trade route.

Within the town wall are concentrated the elite who control the economy and the specialized craftsmen, servants and labourers who service them. Outside lie satellite villages and hamlets whose peasants farm the land and whose surpluses are traded with, or taken by, the town dwellers. With fewer peasants supporting growing numbers of townsfolk, and a reduction in pastureland leading to a reduction in pastoralism, there is an increasing dependence on cereal production. The farmers are having to work hard to feed their masters; artificial irrigation, until now unnecessary, may suddenly seem an attractive proposition. The peasants are not, however, Egypt's most wretched workers. Far away, on the very fringes of civilization, are the desert mines and quarries whose unfortunate work gangs toil under the most difficult of conditions to extract the precious stones and minerals which are fuelling the economic boom.

In the cemeteries the difference between the richest tombs and the poorest pit graves has become very obvious. Upper-class corpses are now routinely wrapped in linen strips and housed in coffins made of basketry, clay and wood. Their tombs, like their houses, have mutated from oval to rectangular with some of the grander examples incorporating a mud-brick lining. These mud-brick walls offer unprecedented opportunities for decoration, but just one painted Naqada II tomb, Tomb 100 at Hieraconpolis, has survived. This remarkable tomb was robbed in antiquity, but its pale ochre plaster-coated walls are still dominated by red, black and green and white painted images.

Here we see six large-scale boats complete with cabins and occasional crews but, curiously, no oars. Five of the boats are white, and have been identified as river boats; the sixth is black, and is perhaps a funerary boat. The river appears as a safe, controlled environment but the river bank is chaotic; there are wild animals and hunters, fierce fights, and vivid images of bound and dying men. In a scene which seems to have been borrowed from contemporary near-eastern art, one brave hunter wrestles two lions, supporting both with his bare hands. In another vignette a warrior raises his arm to smite an enemy. In Tomb 100 violence and physical domination are clearly linked with earthly power.

Scenes of daily life – or what is generally taken to represent daily life

– are used to decorate the new-style red-painted pink pottery. Here the images are more peaceful. Again water and boats feature prominently; there are animals, birds and hunters while ships, complete with multiple oars, cabins, crews and regional flags, sail on rivers of wavy lines. Occasionally, on board, we see a plump, dancing female figure accompanied by smaller-scale men. This woman is paralleled by the small terracotta female figurines included in many of the early Naqada II graves who, with rudimentary, even birdlike faces, but well-defined breasts and hips, dance an incomprehensible, timeless dance with their arms curved above their heads.

As the Naqada elite were buried with ever-increasing quantities of copper, silver and gold, thieves were drawn to the graveyards like flies to a corpse. While painted pottery and distinctive stone palettes might prove difficult to store and dispose of, precious metal (and it was all precious) could be beaten into anonymity, and could re-enter the economy almost immediately. Jewellery, portable, valuable and easily recycled, was another prime target. By now the craftsmen were making fine wires of gold and silver which could be threaded with colourful semi-precious beads of ivory, faience, gold, silver, shell, turquoise and even lapis lazuli, an exotic stone imported from faraway Afghanistan. The dead were buried in all their finery, decorated with valuable bracelets, necklaces, rings and diadems. No wonder the robbers were tempted.[5]

As the Naqada cultural influence slowly but surely spread along the Nile Valley, what was happening in Lower Egypt? Many of the more northerly Neolithic sites managed to resist the creeping Naqada-ization, retaining their own distinctive cultural identities while indulging in vigorous trade with both valley and Delta sites. Evidence recovered from the Cairo suburb of Maadi, the type-site of the northern Predynastic age, shows just how extensive these trade networks could be.

The people of Maadi grew cereal, raised animals, made pots, carved stone, hunted and fished. But their town was first and foremost a trading post. Equipped with impressive storage facilities – her stone cellars offer one of the earliest known examples of Egyptian stone architecture – Maadi did brisk business with her southern neighbours, acquiring Naqada-style palettes, maceheads and pottery in the process. The Delta, too, traded through Maadi, supplying vast amounts of grain which was hoarded in large vats. Most important of all were the eastern trade links which gave the Maadi merchants access to copper ore. For centuries the Egyptians had been using copper nuggets to fashion beads and small tools by beating and hammering the natural metal, much as they worked flint nodules into bifaces and flakes. But true metallurgy, the melting and casting of copper ore, was becoming increasingly important throughout the eastern Mediterranean world, and this increased use of copper had a knock-on effect. Copper tools led to improved wood- and stone-working skills; carved statues, intricate inlaid furniture and large-scale boats were all now achievable. The larger boats in turn led to more long-distance trade and the importing of good quality timber which allowed the building of even larger boats and even more trade. Maadi profited by importing copper from the Sinai mines and either working it into added-value artefacts, or trading it onwards as ingots or unworked ore. At Maadi the pins, needles, fish hooks and adzes were made of copper rather than bone or stone. However, the merchants did not take their riches to the grave. Their understated cemetery of simple oval pit burials holding contracted inhumations wrapped in matting or shrouds has yielded little in the way of precious goods.

The opulent merchants counting their profits in Maadi, and the anonymous rulers whose soldiers patrolled the fortified towns of the Nile Valley, were part of a powerful elite who had come to monopolize local resources. The land that was to become Egypt was dotted with rich, independent towns and their satellite villages linked together by riverine trade. Anyone with the political vision and military might to expand his sphere of influence would win the most glittering of prizes. He would control the Nile from her most southerly navigable point, the rapids which formed the First Cataract at Aswan, to the Mediterranean Sea.

2

River of Life

*The Egyptians report that, at the beginning of the world, the first
men were created in Egypt, by both reason of the happy climate of the
country, and the nature of the River Nile. For this river, being very
fruitful and apt to bring forth many animals, yields, of itself, likewise
food and nourishment for the things produced.*[1]

The Nile – known simply as 'The River' – was a mysterious being
controlled by the gods. No one, not the ancient Egyptians nor the
classical authors, not even the first Egyptologists, could explain where
she originated.[2] Her annual routine of flooding in the heat of summer
and retreating in the damper winter seemed inexplicably perverse. No
one could trace the river past the modern Sudanese city of Khartoum,
the meeting point of the White and Blue Niles. When, in 1652, Gian
Lorenzo Bernini sculpted his *Fountain of the Four Rivers* for the Piazza
Navona, Rome, he was forced to show his Nile as a veiled, anonymous
figure.

   The source of the Blue Nile, the Ethiopian Lake Tana, was discovered
by James Bruce in the 1770s, but it was not until 1858 that a British army
officer, John Hanning Speke, resolved the issue of the White Nile.
Travelling through equatorial East Africa with the explorer Richard
Burton, Speke embarked on his own private mission to investigate a
large lake known locally as Nyanza. Glimpsing the vast expanse of water,
he jumped to an immediate conclusion: 'I no longer felt any doubt that
the lake at my feet gave birth to that interesting river, the source of
which has been the subject of so much speculation . . .'[3] Two years later,
having traced the rivers which flowed from Nyanza, now renamed
Victoria, Speke could confirm that 'The Nile is settled'.

   Today the geography of the Nile Valley is distorted by the Aswan

High Dam. But if we look backwards, to pre-dam times, we see the united Nile flowing northwards from Khartoum, passing through mile after mile of Sudanese desert, its stately progress occasionally interrupted by rapids or cataracts. A final rapid just to the south of Aswan forms a barrier which can only be navigated at times of high water level, and then only by the smallest of boats. This, the first cataract, forms Egypt's traditional southern border with the ancient kingdom of Nubia. Beyond the first cataract, the broad river continues northwards through Egypt, passing limestone cliffs and over six hundred miles of desert before branching, just to the north of modern Cairo, to form a wide, flat Delta with an extensive coastline. In ancient times there were seven strong Delta rivers, each emptying into the Mediterranean. Now only the Damietta (eastern) and the Rosetta (western) branches survive to irrigate the land via a system of canals.

Modern Lower Egyptians tell jokes – the equivalent of England's Irish jokes or America's Polish jokes – laughing at the supposed stupidity of their southern compatriots. This north/south cultural divide is nothing new and, although frequently exaggerated, does reflect definite differences in lifestyle, stimulated by the differences in geography which we would expect in a long, thin country. Throughout the Dynastic age we find the population concentrating in the area around Thebes (modern Luxor: Upper Egypt) and in the area around Memphis (modern Cairo: Lower Egypt) with the transitional area in between – today known as Middle Egypt – lacking any real regional pride or definition. The Egyptians considered their country to be a land of two very different halves, and they classed themselves as belonging to either Upper or Lower Egypt.

Northern, or Lower (downstream), Egypt is the lush, moist, flat Mediterranean Deltaland, home, in the Predynastic and early Dynastic age, to a varied and tasty wildlife. Here there were swamps, fields, orchards and vinyards. Herds of cattle grew fat on the rich Delta pastures and papyrus flourished in the marshes. Surplus grain, and there almost always was surplus grain, financed profitable trade. The Delta, with its near-eastern land bridge and its coastal links to the wider world, was in contact with all the important eastern Mediterranean trade centres. This led to a constant mingling of traditions and blood. In times of peace and prosperity this was a good thing; the Delta dwellers became cosmopolitan sophisticates, their magnificent cities the envy of the civilized world. But in times of international stress her exposed geography made the Delta highly vulnerable to the foreigners – either armed invaders or economic migrants – who would always be attracted by the promise of Egyptian prosperity and security.

The Southern, or Upper, Egyptians inhabited a narrower, hotter and altogether more constricted world bound by the sterile Red Land and the mountains beyond. Here the contrast between the living and the dead was immediate and unavoidable. Nature, in the valley, seemed uncompromising; hippopotami grazed beside the rivers, crocodiles lurked in the water, and lions and jackals roamed the desert. Although the valley was hundreds of miles long the Black Land, the strip of rich soil which lined the river bank, was only a few miles wide so there could be little expansion to east or west. The most valuable resources were inanimate; there was a seemingly inexhaustible supply of gold and precious stones in the Eastern Desert. Better protected against invasion, less open to eastern and Mediterranean influences yet more exposed to central African and Nubian culture, it was perhaps inevitable that the Upper Egyptians should become a self-referential, inward-looking people. While the north seemed eager to embrace change the south drew on its own deep resources and developed its own traditions.

It would always be stressed that Egypt was a union of two equal, complementary kingdoms. Symmetry, the opposition of two carefully assessed elements, was seen as an aesthetically pleasing device which brought an immense comfort, while the cancelling out of two balanced elements was understood to strengthen weakness which might otherwise prove dangerous or unstable. Egypt's unique geography, which was full of obvious opposites or symmetries, suggested this way of thought. The cultivated Black Land was dramatically opposed by the sterile Red Land, and visitors marvelled as they stood with one foot in the fertile soil, one in the barren desert. The dry land itself was opposed by the wet river which played such an important role in daily life. In heaven Horus was opposed by Seth, while on earth life was opposed by death which could come with remarkable swiftness just as night followed day. Pharaoh would always be styled Lord of *Tawy*, Upper and Lower Egypt, even if circumstances dictated that he only actually rule a fragment of the whole land. Simultaneously protected by the Upper Egyptian vulture goddess

Nekhbet of el-Kab and the Lower Egyptian snake goddess Wadjyt of Buto, his dual role was emphasized by the ceremonial double crown which combined the white crown of Upper Egypt with the red crown of Lower. In times of cohesion and prosperity this system worked well. Upper and Lower Egypt merged into a seamless whole and the united land flourished. In times of stress old prejudices quickly re-emerged, local loyalties surfaced and north and south invariably drew apart.

Some of the earliest known civilizations developed in the world's more arid zones where they were forced to practise intensive irrigation in order to survive. While there has been much debate over the precise order of things – did the need for a national water management system lead directly to the development of the state? Or did the already extant state take over the independent local irrigation systems? – we know that Egypt, at least, had no need to invest in expensive, extensive schemes. The predictable behaviour of the Nile made agriculture a relatively easy science, with abundant crops virtually guaranteed each year. Egypt did practise a non-intensive irrigation which involved the digging of canals and the raising of dykes to encourage her natural basins to fill with water, but this was very much a local operation designed to enhance rather than substitute for nature's own generous provision. The more labour-intensive shadoof, used to lift water to small-scale private gardens and vegetable plots, was never used in the fields. In Egypt, national irrigation was a by-product, rather than a cause, of unification.

Now the Nile, when it overflows, floods not only the Delta, but also the tracts of country on both sides, in some places reaching to the extent of two days' journey from its banks. In some places it even exceeds that distance while in others it falls short of it . . . Concerning the nature of the river I was not able to obtain any information, either from the priests or from others . . . they could not tell me what special virtue the Nile has which makes it so opposite in nature to all other rivers . . .[4]

What caused the Nile to flood in late summer, when every other river flooded in the wet of winter? The answer lay thousands of miles away. From June to September each year the Ethiopian highlands and, to a lesser extent, the White Nile Basin, experience torrential monsoon rains which quickly swell their rivers and lakes. The Nile, carrying its extra burden of water towards the sea, would rise and flood its valley, covering the low-lying agricultural land with a sheet of dirty, reddish water and transforming the settlements into islands linked by raised pathways. This regular flooding was already well exploited in later prehistoric and Predynastic times. One of our earliest Egyptian texts, the 5th Dynasty Palermo Stone (so called because the major part of the shattered basalt stela today resides in the Palermo Archaeological Museum, Sicily), records details of Nile floods stretching backwards through the reigns of known kings into mythological times.

The annual Nile cycle – the flooding of the fields in August and September, the retreat of the waters in October and November and the re-emergence of the land above the water – was to give birth to one of the most enduring of religious beliefs, the Egyptian creation myth. At the very moment of creation, or so it was told, a mound rose out of the swirling waters of chaos. On this mound the sun god created himself; he went on to generate life, first divine, then human. This belief was translated into an association of mounds and islands with life and rebirth. Eventually, inside the Dynastic temples, the ground would rise upwards as the supplicant approached the sanctuary. Here, in the gloomy half light of the clerestory windows, surrounded by papyrus-styled pillars, was the primeval mound made real. Already, inside the mud-brick casing of the elite Predynastic graves, a symbolic mound of earth was being heaped over the deceased.

The Nile gave Egypt her three seasons: the time of inundation (when the land was covered with water), the time of coming forth (when the crops sprouted in the fertile fields) and the time of summer (when the harvested ground baked beneath the hot sun). In so doing, she set the timetable for agricultural and public works. It is natural to regret the loss of this natural rhythm, particularly when we hear of the downside of the Aswan Dam project; the loss of the fertile silt, the increasing salination of the land, the destruction of valuable archaeological sites. But we should be careful not to over-romanticize the past. The ancient Egyptians were reluctant to admit it – they rarely admitted that anything was wrong with their perfect land – but enforced dependence on the Nile did bring its own problems. Every year there was an anxious wait for the river to perform her miracle. The flood might rise too high, damaging the settlements, destroying the canals and delaying the planting

so that the growing crops burned in the summer sun. Or the Nile might
be too low, leaving the irrigation basins unfilled and the fields too dry to
plough and plant. Times of stress and civil disruption tended to coincide
with times of erratic flooding. Little wonder, then, that the Egyptians
became obsessed with storing food against lean times.

The season of inundation, the weeks when their land was transformed
into a giant lake, left Egypt's peasants with time on their hands. It was
impossible to work the submerged fields, and so a vast workforce was
freed to labour for the good of the state. This often translated into
working on the royal building sites for the good of the king. Pharaoh
did not have access to vast numbers of permanent state slaves; he did not
need them. His ability to summon thousands of workers for months at a
time without disrupting the national economy, and without needing to
pay anything more than a basic subsistence allowance, was to prove
crucial in the raising of all Egypt's monuments. Naturally the system of
corvée, or temporary forced labour, was hated by those compelled to take
part; naturally it was supported by a system of harsh punishments designed
to deter those who might be tempted to desert. Scribes, exempt from
the indignity of manual labour, wrote with horror of the fate of the *corvée*
worker:

The field-worker cries more than the guinea fowl. His voice is louder than the
raven's voice . . . When he is taken away to be enrolled in Delta labour he is in
tatters . . . When he returns home from the marshes he is exhausted, for the
corvée has wrecked him.[5]

While the peasants toiled for their king the fields, lost beneath temporary
lakes, absorbed enough water to last an entire growing season. Slowly,
as the faraway rains subsided, the water level would fall and the Nile
would return to its normal course leaving behind a thick layer of fertile,
mineral-rich and disease-free silt and a useful stock of stranded fish.
Careful land management, the rotation of crops alternating with fallow
periods and the occasional use of fields for grazing, would ensure that
the soil remained in tip-top condition.

By early November the irrigation basins had been drained and the
peasants set to work; it was crucial that the fields be ploughed and sown
before they baked hard. After months of weeding, bird-scaring and

routine maintenance, the late spring would bring a magnificent harvest of cereal (barley and emmer wheat, which could be used to make bread, cakes and beer), vegetables (beans, lentils, onions, garlic, leeks, lettuces and cucumbers) and fruits (grapes, figs and dates). When added to the abundant wild foods, the Nile fish, the cattle farmed by the wealthy land owners and the smaller animals (sheep, goats, pigs, geese) kept by the more humble households, this provided for a sumptuous banquet. While the elite dined off meat and honey-sweetened cakes enhanced by the finest of wines, the poor tucked into a rather flatulent diet of bread, fish, beans, onions and garlic washed down with a sweet, soupy beer. Although it was possible to plant and harvest a second crop before the Nile flooded this was seldom necessary. Only those with market gardens and orchards used artificial irrigation to reap a double reward. For most the agricultural year ended after the spring harvest with the bare fields left to bake and crack in the sun; a baking which sterilized the land, killing many of the pests and diseases which would otherwise have reduced future yields.

Egypt's neighbours, condemned to till dry stony ground, could only look on with envy. The gods had been kind to Egypt. Her storehouses groaned with food, her river teemed with fish, her marshes with fowl. Flax, pulled from the fields and processed, was used to make strong, coarse rope, refined basketry and matting, and the finest of linen garments. Papyrus, growing wild along the banks of the Nile, could be bundled, bound with flax rope and shaped into a sturdy raftlike boat. Or it could be split, beaten flat and dried in the sun to make a light but strong paper which would contribute much to the success of the civil service. Only tall trees were missing from the landscape. Wood was needed to make the large ships which supported the trade networks, but the date palms which flourished in every village were useless for this purpose. Although acacia, tamarisk and sycamore fig could be used to construct rafts and small boats, the Egyptians had grown resigned to looking eastwards, to the Levant, for supplies of good quality timber. Lower Egypt, blessed with large stores of grain but lacking many of the natural resources of the south, would control this vital trade in wood.

Egypt was rich in inanimate resources, her greatest asset being perhaps her most simple. The thick mud which lined the Nile, a sticky mixture of clay and sand, made an excellent building material highly suited to the dry climate. Western readers may be tempted to dismiss mud-brick buildings as basic, even primitive structures, but this is far from the truth. Anyone who has ever lived in a mud-brick house will confirm that they are highly efficient; cool in summer's heat, and a warm refuge in winter. These properties would be appreciated for thousands of years, and mud-brick remained the building material of choice until the advent of the Aswan Dam halted the annual deposition of silt.

The 18th Dynasty Theban tomb of Rekhmire shows the ancient brick-makers at work. Mud, collected from the fields, is broken up with a hoe, then mixed with water and trampled with bare feet until it has attained the desired texture. A binding may be added – perhaps chopped straw, or animal dung – to help the brick to cohere and to encourage its plasticity. The brick-maker slaps the mud into a shoebox-sized mould which he then lifts, leaving the still-wet brick to dry in the sun. Plastered, painted, tiled and enhanced with stone and wood door jambs, lintels, and pillars, a mud-brick palace could be transformed into a dazzling, awe-inspiring if somewhat unsubtle sight as it shimmered and shone in the fierce sunlight.

Mud-brick allowed Egypt's architects to experiment with large-scale structures which could be raised with surprising speed. The pharaohs became prolific builders of domestic architecture and, as mud-brick was both cheap and easily available, several kings founded cities which grew from nothing to fully functional in a mere seven or eight years. The glittering palaces, when properly maintained, outlived their builders and survived for hundreds of years. But eventually all the brick cities dissolved into damp mud or crumbled to dust. By late Naqada times Egypt was already littered with abandoned, corroded ruins. This prospect was distressing to those who wished their monuments to remain visible and for all eternity.

Palaces, however splendid, were only intended to last a lifetime. Tombs and temples, the homes of the gods, should last for ever. The only way to ensure that a monument would survive was to build it in stone. But, while stone had been used to make tools since Palaeolithic times, stone buildings had to remain an impossible dream until Egypt had made certain other technological advances.[6]

While the Western Desert hosted a string of oases, the less hospitable Eastern Desert provided Egypt with stone of all colours and textures. Alongside the relatively soft, easily cut coarse-grained limestone, known

as 'white stone', which lined the Nile from Memphis to Esna there
was hard, course-grained red and black granite to be quarried at Aswan,
red quartzite at Gebel el-Ahmar near ancient Heliopolis and, further
away in the Wadi Hammamat, greywacke (schist). In the Muqattam
Hills, Tura, near Giza, provided a finer-grained fossil-free limestone
which shone with a delicate radiance. The Faiyum offered both basalt
and gypsum which was used to manufacture plaster and mortar; Nubia
offered an unspectacular sandstone, convenient for local building projects. On a smaller scale a beautiful, translucent alabaster could be found
in both the Middle Egyptian Hatnub quarries and the Wadi Garawi, near
Helwan, and there was plentiful turquoise as well as copper in Sinai.
There were jasper, chert and schist suitable for making palettes and vases
and, of course, flint. The gold recovered from the Eastern Desert and
transported along the Wadi Hammamat towards Naqada would later be
supplemented by the more abundant Nubian gold.

This superabundance of stone and gold would have been of limited
use without the Nile, which allowed the masons to transport their
cumbersome blocks hundreds of miles from quarry to building site.
Wheels do not mix well with sand, roads are expensive to maintain, and
it was in any case impossible to build a bridge large enough to link the
east and west banks. Egypt never showed any interest in developing a
system of state-maintained roads. Why should she, when her river offered
a far easier and much cheaper means of transport? Every town had its
port, and barges, boats and rafts were as common as our modern lorries
and cars. Movement northwards, following the current, required little
effort with the oars, while to travel south the oarsmen simply had to
hoist linen or matting sails to take advantage of the prevailing wind.
Where necessary, canals could be cut to link the building sites and the
quarries with the Nile, so that the granite hewn in Aswan could be towed
northwards on a flat-bottomed barge and erected in the Delta as an
obelisk.

Ease of movement was crucial to effective kingship. Egypt was a long
and unwieldy country; it could take two weeks – a very long time in
politics – for a message to pass from north to south or vice versa. No
pharaoh, the eccentric 18th Dynasty Akhenaten excepted, dared to
confine himself to one capital city, because the dangers of isolation
were obvious. An invisible king could so easily become a forgotten or

insignificant king. Pharaoh preferred to see, and be seen by, his people and their local gods. And so we find the monarch constantly on the move, travelling with a select, intimate court slowly up and down the Nile, liaising with local officials, making offerings in the local temples and staying in a series of minor palaces and relatively humble 'mooring places' as he passes from one town to the next.

As the king sailed up and down the Nile the sun god Re steered his solar boat across the sky. The link between boats and earthly power is an obvious one. Only the wealthy can own a large boat; boat ownership brings access to greater wealth and the potential to build more boats; the powerful must be constantly on the move in their boats. But boats are also linked with the rituals of death. Large boats play a prominent role in the Naqada pottery illustrations and, of course, they feature on the walls of Hieraconpolis Tomb 100. From the 1st Dynasty onwards the link between boats and death will be strengthened as boats start to be included in the royal mortuary complexes and private tombs. Are the boat scenes intended to be faithful representations of earthly voyages, perhaps the trading missions which earned their owners their wealth? Or are they connected in some more direct way with funerals and the passage from life? Egyptian religion seldom provides us with neat explanations; we should assume that any and all of these answers are correct.

3

The Horus Kings

The priest said that Men was the first king of Egypt, and that it was he who raised the dyke which protects Memphis from the inundations of the Nile . . . Men, the first king, proceeded to build the city now called Memphis . . . he also, the priests said, built the temple of Hephaestus which stands within the city, a vast edifice, very worthy of mention.[1]

By the end of the Naqada II phase the stage was set for Egyptian unity. Already the classic elements of Old Kingdom civilization were in place. Subsequent centuries would see shifts in emphasis, changes in religion and the adoption of new ideas, skills and beliefs, but Egypt's economy, her art, her very thoughts, would remain essentially unchanged.

The Egyptians thought they knew how their country had become one land. Legend told how, in a long-ago time of fragmented rule, the ambitious southern warrior Menes raised an army and fought his way northwards, conquering town after town until all bowed before his rule. The Palermo Stone lends partial support to this drama by recording a succession of semi-mythological rulers who are eventually succeeded by King Menes. The story is repeated with slight variations in most of the king lists, the lengthy chronologies carved by the New Kingdom pharaohs, and in the Turin Canon, a New Kingdom chronology preserved on papyrus. Here we read how Menes was preceded by a series of semi-mortal kings, the 'Followers of Horus' who were in turn preceded by a series of god-kings, each allocated a specific length of reign so that Egypt's scribes could use their king lists to trace their history back to the very moment of creation. Manetho, the 'father of Egyptian history' was sceptical about the non-mortal kings but picked up the story of the valiant Menes, adding the surprising detail that 'he was carried off by a hippopotamus'. From Manetho the story passed into accepted history.

It pleased the Dynastic Egyptians to think that their unified nation had started with a great and glorious battle. The idea of the king as victor, the ruthless slayer of enemies, was deeply embedded in the Egyptian psyche. However, there is no contemporary evidence to support the existence of a King Men, or Menes, and little evidence for a lengthy civil war at the end of the Naqada period. Indeed all evidence points the other way, suggesting that Egypt enjoyed a long-drawn-out, relatively peaceful birth; a sustained period of cultural, political and commercial consolidation followed, perhaps, by a series of short, decisive skirmishes. Although Menes is almost certainly a real king whose name has become hopelessly distorted by time, the parallel kingdoms of Upper and Lower Egypt are likely to be pleasing symmetries rather than actual, deadly rivals.

Late Naqada times saw Egypt occupied by a series of independent town- or city-states and their satellite farming communities, linked together by a shared dependence on the Nile. We assume that there was also a shared language, perhaps with regional dialects, although in the absence of written texts this is hard to prove. Within each state there lived the elite who controlled access to resources, the artisans who converted raw materials into added-value goods, and the peasants, the vast majority of the population, who worked the land and its resources. Some, those buried in the most elaborate of graves, had become very rich; they had access to gold, semi-precious stones and exotic, luxurious goods traded from far afield. The majority were relatively poor, and were interred with few or no significant belongings. This social differentiation is most obvious in the Nile Valley. Lower Egyptian burials hold far fewer grave goods, suggesting either a more egalitarian society or one with differing funerary traditions.

In the valley increasing aridity, increasing population density and a growing dependence on trade was forcing the settlements inwards, towards the river. More and more the independent communities traded together, exporting not only material goods, but ideas. Slowly, ruthlessly, late Naqada culture spread from southern Egypt. Upriver it extended into Lower Nubia, displacing the local Neolithic A-group culture. Downriver it overwhelmed and replaced the distinctive northern Maadi tradition.

By the end of the Naqada III phase Egypt could boast one broadly homogenous material culture with little significant regional variation. Material homogeneity does not, of course, imply political or religious unity, although it does suggest that unity amongst peoples with a shared culture and a shared language might be possible. Here, at this most crucial point in Egypt's development, the archaeologist is faced with the usual problem. In the absence of written texts and settlement sites, it is the badly depleted cemeteries which must provide evidence for a political process. We must assume that cemeteries yielding increasingly large graves filled with increasingly valuable grave goods belong to cities/ towns with increasing economic and political influence and increasing social stratification; that those with inferior burials belong to settlements of dwindling wealth and importance. Using these criteria, we can detect the concentrating of political power in southern Egypt.

Naqada, situated on the west bank of the river at the very end of the trade route from the Eastern Desert via the Wadi Hammamat, was, in tribute to her wealth, known to the Dynastic Egyptians as Nubt, or 'Town of Gold'. However, Naqada, one of Egypt's largest Naqada II towns and home of some of her richest Naqada II graves, was now losing trade to her more dynamic neighbours. There was a decrease in disposable wealth, a decline in influence and an inevitable relegation to the political backwaters. Even her god, the unruly Seth, was being eclipsed by his local rival, Horus of Hieraconpolis. Naqada was no longer a force to be reckoned with and her elite burials were poor when compared to the splendid tombs being built at Hieraconpolis and Abydos.

Further upstream, the equally ancient walled settlement of Hieraconpolis or Nekhen, home of the falcon god Horus, had swelled into a prosperous, densely populated town centred around an extensive open cult or ceremonial centre, itself surrounded by buildings, shrines, walls and fences. The remains of extensive craftshops and an extensive brewery tell their own tale. Here expensive raw materials, imported from east and south, were crafted into desirable artefacts and traded on at a vast profit. Egypt's demand for luxury items appeared insatiable and Hieraconpolis was cashing-in on the now well-established tradition of providing the dead with expensive goods. Later Egyptian tradition would regard Nekhen as one of its most venerable cities; a major cult centre and the heart of the Upper Egyptian Predynastic kingdom. This rich past is reflected in the extent of the archaeological remains.[2]

Hieraconpolis cemetery area 6 has yielded a series of large, looted, mud-brick-lined tombs topped by wood and reed structures. Here, alongside the diagnostic, drab Naqada III pottery, we find the sadly depleted remains of an expensive, possibly even a regal, lifestyle; there are fragments of jewellery incorporating gold, silver, ivory, obsidian and lapis lazuli plus increasing amounts of copper and faience. The owner of Tomb 11, one of the wealthier burials, was equipped for eternity with a collection of precious beads and amulets, stone and pottery models of people and animals, ivory carvings, and a remarkable wooden bed whose feet were carved into bull's hooves. These are, of course, the less-valuable goods discarded by the thieves who desecrated the burial; we can only guess at the original contents of the tomb. Clearly, there were some very wealthy people being buried at Nekhen. These were not, however, Egypt's richest graves.

Thinis, or This (probably modern Girga) was a small, hitherto undistin-guished Predynastic town whose cemetery was situated on the Umm el-Qa'ab at nearby Abydos. During Naqada I and II times this graveyard was used by all, irrespective of rank or wealth. However, by late Predyn-astic times the Umm el-Qa'ab had evolved into Upper Egypt's most exclusive burial ground, home to her most impressive tombs. The most spectacular of these, a twelve-roomed structure known today as Tomb U-j, measures almost 67 square metres in area, and is far larger than anything so far excavated at Hieraconpolis.

Although U-j was looted extensively in antiquity, painstaking exca-vation has proved fruitful, yielding large quantities of Egyptian and imported Palestinian wine jars, small-scale bone and ivory artefacts, and a series of inscribed labels torn off the vanished funerary goods which represent our first encounter with hieroglyphic writing.[3] Some of these brief texts can be translated – they refer to agricultural estates, and to the Delta sites of Buto and Bubastis – while the cryptic scorpion motif scrawled on several of the pots may also be read as a hieroglyphic label. Traces of a wooden structure, possibly the remnants of a shrine, in the burial chamber plus the discovery of an ivory crook-style sceptre, suggest that this is the tomb of a regional king.

We will revisit the Abydos cemetery again in Chapter 4. Meanwhile, can we deduce that this nameless king, with far more disposable wealth than his fellow rulers at Naqada and Hieraconpolis, is now the foremost southern ruler? Does the king's influence extend outside his own region? We know that he has access to goods manufactured in Palestine; does he perhaps have ambitions beyond Upper Egypt? The questions are endless. Fortunately, the Dynastic temple of Horus at Hieraconpolis has provided two artefacts which can help to make some sense of this confused time.[4]

The extremely large but badly damaged decorated macehead today known as the Scorpion Macehead (Ashmolean Museum, Oxford) features a king wearing the white crown of Upper Egypt. The kilted king stands in a field and wields a hoe. Facing him are two smaller-scale servants, one carrying what is usually interpreted as a sheaf of cereal, the

Figure 3.1
The largest fragment of the Scorpion Macehead

other a basket, while behind the king wait the two fan-bearers who protect him from the hot sun. By the king's head are two small carvings, a rosette and a scorpion, which are generally interpreted as representing the king's name and/or title, although name might be too precise a term in this context; the carvings may with equal validity be classed as emblems or tribal/regional symbols representing the king's position or his power.

As it seems unlikely that such an exalted personage would ever dirty his hands in manual labour, we may guess that the king is here giving his blessing to some civic scheme, perhaps the inauguration of an irrigation ditch, by cutting the ceremonial first sod in the same way that modern royalty are often called upon to plant trees, lay bricks and launch ships. If so, this scene would provide us with our earliest evidence for state-sponsored artificial irrigation. So far it is a pleasant, harmless agricultural vignette. But hoes can be used as weapons of war. The contemporary 'Towns' or 'Libyan palette' shows a series of animals, tribal symbols, attacking walled towns with hoes. And we know from our reading of later documents that the dead *rekhyt*-birds which hang by the neck from military standards ranked above the king's head signify the conquest of an unspecified people.

In Egypt there will always be a confusion between art and writing. Just as hieroglyphs use pictures to represent specific words, so a painted or carved tableau can be read as a sentence. Where exactly, if anywhere, do the words stop and the writing begin? This happens to a certain extent in our own artistic tradition, where a seemingly simple religious painting may be loaded with meaning and symbolism for the initiated and, at a more basic level, a cartoon can speak volumes to a child. In Egypt it is carried to the extreme, with the artists relying on pictures, often at the expense of the text which may be minimal or even absent, to tell a story, so that all formal art becomes capable of more than one interpretation and we can find many layers of meaning woven into every scene.

The Naqada stonemasons intended the Scorpion Macehead to be read as a text. To modern observers it carries a cryptic message, although its most obvious meanings cut across the vast cultural divide. We can deduce, from its extreme size, its detailed carvings and its inclusion in a temple cache, that the macehead is far more than a record of a specific, rather humdrum, agricultural event. It is a piece which has definite sacred or religious value, and it celebrates the role of the king. Scorpion is larger than his companions; in Egypt, size will always convey authority and the king will naturally dominate any earthly scene. The crown speaks for itself; we are looking at a monarch who has already appreciated the advantages of a defining royal regalia. What is surprising is the extent to which the formalities of Egyptian art – formalities which will persist almost unchanging for three thousand years – are already well established. We know, from its style and provenance, that the Scorpion Macehead dates to the very end of the Naqada age, but its profiled image of royalty complete with the instantly recognizable crown would not look out of place in a late Dynastic context.

Proof that the image of kingship has already been formalized is provided by the 'Narmer Palette', found slightly apart from the Scorpion Macehead and now housed in Cairo Museum. This is a large, Naqada III-style slate votive palette which records the victories of a king whose two-symbol hieroglyphic name is presented within a *serekh*, a ribbed, rectangular frame. The *serekh* is a schematic representation of the entrance to the archaic royal palace which would, as it was constructed from reed matting, have required columns or bundles of reeds to strengthen and support its walls. By the time the Narmer Palette was carved Egypt's palaces were built of mud-brick, but the archaic style, which had come to denote royalty, persisted. The *serekh* motif, often shown with a falcon, the god Horus, perched on top, is now used to highlight Egypt's earliest royal names; at its most simple level it represents the king within his palace.

Names would always be of great importance in Egypt, where knowledge of a name conveyed power, and memory of a name prevented eternal death. As we lack all knowledge of Egyptian vowels the signs of the catfish and the chisel should literally be read as *N'r Mr*. But, based on our knowledge of later hieroglyphs, we conventionally read the word within the *serekh* as Nar-mer, or Narmer, an untranslatable name which could also be written in an abbreviated form simply as catfish, or *N'r*. This is identified as the king's 'Horus name' and, as such, is not necessarily the name which the king himself would have used; his mother, at least, would have called him by the nomen, or personal name, which she chose for him at birth.

Narmer, with his meaningless Horus name/title, is standing on the brink of a developing tradition. His successor Aha will have a fully

Figure 3.2
The Narmer Palette – Obverse

Figure 3.3
The Narmer Palette – Reverse

formed Horus name Hor-Aha (or 'Horus the fighter'). The 1st Dynasty king Anedjib will add a *nesu-bit* prenomen or throne name, the name used by his people. By the late 3rd Dynasty reign of King Huni we will find the nomen and prenomen written within the cartouche, the flattened oval which represents all that the sun-disc encircles. At the end of the Old Kingdom, and until the end of the Dynastic age, each Egyptian king will rejoice in a series of five names or titles, four of which are short sentences chosen at the time of the coronation to convey the flavour of the reign. If we take the example of Ramesses II, perhaps Egypt's most easily recognized cartouche, he was officially known as *The Horus King*, Strong Bull, Beloved of Right, Truth; *He of the Two Ladies*, Protector of Egypt who curbs the foreign lands; *The Golden Horus*, Rich in Years, Great in Victories; *King of Upper and Lower Egypt*, Usermaatre [Setepenre]; *Son of Re*, Ramesses II, Beloved of Amen. The last of these names, the nomen or personal name, is the name which Egyptologists use today.

With its organized registers and its incorporation of hieroglyphic text alongside well-spaced images, the Narmer Palette makes a clear statement of royal dominance. A reminder of the Naqada II elite hunting scenes and the walls of Hieraconpolis Tomb 100 painted some two centuries earlier, it conveys a message of unemotional, unapologetic, elite bloodshed. Order triumphs over mayhem. The gods are in the heavens, the king dominates the earth, the enemies are in chaos. The larger-than-life-sized king is very obviously the hero. The defeated enemies whose bodies litter the palette have equally obviously been slain for the common good. Already the king has assumed personal responsibility for the killing of Egypt's foes. This is a responsibility which will never be shirked, for it is a religious as well as a military duty. The king will always triumph, enemies will always perish and, gods willing, chaos will always be subdued. Pharaoh triumphant has become a comforting, timeless, image which successive pharaohs will choose to repeat time and time again.

On one face of his palette Narmer, dressed in a kilt and the animal tail worn by priests, and wearing the white crown and false beard of a southern Egyptian king, raises a club to smite the enemy who has fallen at his feet. Behind him, on a separate register, waits a small sandal-bearer who carries not only his master's footwear but a jug. The king stands tall and proud, a prime physical specimen savouring his moment of victory. The bearded enemy – a curiously non-Egyptian-looking northerner, apparently from the Delta 'Domain of the Harpoon' – cringes with abject fear and averts his gaze. Above the prisoner, in a more stylized image, the falcon god Horus holds a man captive; humiliatingly, the prisoner is bound by a rope which passes through his nose. On a lower register we are shown two more defeated enemies while above the goddess Hathor, shown here in her more ancient guise of Bat, watches proceedings with her calm, cow-eyed gaze.

Hathor/Bat again gazes down on the reverse of the palette. Here we see Narmer, still followed by his miniature sandal-bearer but now wearing the red crown and carrying a mace and flail. The king is marching with a troop of soldiers whose ornate standards may well represent the symbols of the newly unified Egyptian provinces. His scribe – essential to record the king's victories – marches before him. As the scribe is smaller than the king, yet larger than the soldiers, we may calculate his relative social rank; a person of obvious importance, he may perhaps be Narmer's son, or his Vizier, or both. Before the procession lie ten unfortunate victims of war, their decapitated heads lolling between their legs. Below, in a separate scene, we see two fabulous snake-headed, four-legged beasts, 'serpopards', their long necks twined together just as Upper and Lower Egypt are now inextricably linked. They form the central hollow where – in a throwback to the original purpose of the palette, which is by now a purely ceremonial item – cosmetics would be ground. On the bottom register, Narmer takes the form of a bull to gore an enemy outside a symbolic fortified town.

The association of animals and hunting with elite power and death has become a well-developed Naqada theme. Egypt's people are settled agriculturalists, indeed many of them live in towns. The hunting of large or dangerous animals has become a remote, upper-class sport, a rite of passage imbued with a deep, almost mystical, significance. The hunter who kills a lion or a bull is understood to absorb part of the spirit of that animal; he is rejuvenated or empowered by his victory. The king who takes the form of an animal to kill is demonstrating that he possesses the characteristics and inner strength of the vanquished beast. The Battlefield (or Vultures) Palette, an incomplete piece slightly earlier than the Narmer Palette, is a prime example of this genre.[5] It shows an anonymous chief who appears as a large-scale lion to maul a hapless foe. Around him the dead and dying are attracting the attention of a flock of vultures. Above, captives tied to regional standards await their fate. In complete contrast, the reverse shows a peaceful scene, with a central palm tree and two spindly-legged, long-necked creatures which have variously been interpreted as giraffes or gazelles.

The conventional explanation of the Narmer Palette is that we are witnessing the triumphs of a southern king who is engaged in capturing the northern towns and so uniting his land. However, we must question the assumption that Narmer is fighting his fellow Egyptians. The hieroglyphs do indicate that Narmer's enemies come from the north but their non-Egyptian appearance suggests that they are desert invaders rather than native Delta dwellers. Throughout the Dynastic age the various western tribes who may be loosely grouped together as Libyans will threaten Egypt's security as they attempt to settle in the fertile Delta. King after king will be forced to raise troops to repel these unwanted immigrants and the Libyans will be presented to the Egyptian people, along with Nubians and Asiatics (easterners), as the implacable enemies of Egypt. As such they will feature in royal propaganda where, invariably, they will be shown in humiliating circumstances with deliberately ugly faces, pale or yellow skins and goatee beards. When dressed – for Egypt's enemies often appear naked – they will wear long, open-fronted coats, and will have ostrich feathers in their hair.

It seems that Narmer has already been forced to defend the exposed Delta, gateway to the prosperous Nile Valley. By the late Predynastic period Egypt was experiencing the increasing aridity which was to turn her savannahs into desert. The nomadic pastoralists who inhabited the savannah were themselves under strain, and settlement in the Delta was becoming a tempting proposition. The need to unite Egypt's independent towns in defence of their riches may have provided a strong incentive for political unification. However, the violent scenes preserved on the votive palettes contrast with the archaeological data, where we find no evidence of increasing numbers of weapons, no obviously murdered bodies in hastily dug northern graves, no burnt strata suggestive of looting. Instead we start to find royal names, written within *serekhs*, in late Naqada contexts. After a detailed stylistic study Egyptologist Werner Kaiser has been able to rank Egypt's earliest kings in chronological order: Iri-Hor, Ka, Narmer. With this tentative king list, we have entered the confused world of Dynasty 0.

Despite the fact that he has been assigned a tomb in the Abydos cemetery, King Iri-Hor remains an insubstantial, ghostly ruler. King Ka seems more solid; like Narmer he is the owner of a fine Abydos tomb and his name has been discovered as far north as the eastern Delta site of Tell Ibrahim Awad, and as far east as the Levantine site of Lod. However, although Ka undoubtedly enjoyed a wide sphere of influence we cannot state with any certainty that he ever ruled a united Egypt. Narmer, in contrast, is obviously entitled to wear both the white and the red crown. If we are correct in our assumption that these crowns already signify Upper and Lower Egypt, as they will do in Dynastic times, Narmer did indeed rule the two lands.

Where does the mysterious Scorpion fit into this scheme? Scorpion has no recognized tomb, although it is tempting to speculate that he may have been buried in Abydos Tomb U-j, a tomb which has yielded a high incidence of scorpion motifs.[6] His macehead, which on stylistic grounds pre-dates the Narmer Palette, shows Scorpion wearing only the white crown, but the back of the macehead is missing. Following the pattern of the Narmer Palette, would this have shown the same king sporting a red crown? His name, written in the *serekh* but missing the falcon, has been found on Predynastic pottery recovered as far north as the eastern Delta site of Minshat Abu Omar. There is little doubt that, like Ka, Scorpion was known in the north but on present evidence, we can go no further.

We can never expect Egypt's kings to tell an unbiased or even a truthful story. Narmer undoubtedly uses his palette to exaggerate his own personal heroism, but that is his privilege. Pharaoh would always be free to reinterpret history to his own advantage, to claim the triumphs of his predecessors as his own. Whether or not he actually campaigned to unite his land, whether or not he fought to expel the Libyans from the Delta, Narmer has obviously taken the decision to promote himself as a mighty warrior. It is surely Narmer, and his royal propaganda machine, who will inspire the legend of King Menes. It may even be that Narmer, with his *nesu bit* name today unknown, is Menes. Here, with some reservation, we will accept Narmer's version of events, and celebrate him as the first ruler of the unified Egypt. However it is Aha, Narmer's son and successor, who will be credited as the founder of Egypt's 1st Dynasty.

All opposition quelled, Narmer is free to don his double crown, becoming king of Upper and Lower Egypt, the final and perhaps the only true pharaoh of Dynasty 0. He rules over a lengthy land of 1 to 2 million people which, divided into provinces, or nomes, stretches from the first Nile cataract to the Mediterranean Sea.

Such an unwieldy land requires efficient government; a new bureaucratic centre, 'White Walls', is established at the apex of the Delta at Inebhedj near modern Abusir. This city will gradually creep southwards as the Nile shifts its course, until it lies opposite the Sakkara cemetery and becomes known as Mennefer or, in its more familiar Greek version, Memphis.

Narmer has assumed the paternalistic duty of care that all of Egypt's rich hold towards the poor. He offers his people security in exchange for total control over their loyalties and labours. Aided by a select band of well-educated, intermarried elite he administers Egypt, defending her against enemies and monopolizing and redistributing her resources. His is a highly centralized control, focused on White Walls. The provinces are governed by bureaucrats based in the north, and any provincial-born scribe aspiring to high office must first travel to White Walls to receive the correct training/indoctrination. There are towns and cities outside the capital, but these are primarily trade centres engaged in collecting and redistributing produce on behalf of the crown. They may retain religious prestige, but all true authority lies in the north, and the principal economic unit outside the capital remains the village.

Narmer's principal duty is the maintenance of *maat*. *Maat* is an Egyptian concept without a direct English translation, but it may broadly be explained as 'rightness', the status quo, or even justice. It is the direct opposite of the chaos (*isfet*) which the Egyptians so dread. Narmer must always be seen to preserve *maat*. The smiting of enemies and the wrestling with wild beasts so beloved of the Naqada masons, symbolizes the imposition of Egyptian *maat* on foreign chaos.

He is aided in his work by his new-found divinity. For pharaoh, the living Horus, is revered as a living demigod and will be worshipped after death as a fully divine being. The divinity which has settled upon him during the coronation ritual is both an enormous asset and an enormous burden, as only the semi-divine can communicate with the gods who control Egypt's destiny. There has been no attempt to fuse Egypt's diverse local gods into one state-run priesthood, and there is no designated priestly class or caste. Instead Narmer is high priest of every cult and he, via a select band of deputies, takes theoretical responsibility for the daily offerings made in each of Egypt's temples. This is a duty of overwhelming importance as the gods control life itself. Denied their regular supplies, they may well turn on the mortals who have failed them. It is essential that Egypt always has a king able and willing to offer to her gods. Narmer has placed himself in a position of unassailable power. Egypt without a king had become a *maat*-less, unthinkable horror.

Narmer stands head and shoulders – literally, in the case of his palette – above his fellow Egyptians. Already, as he smashes the heads of Egypt's enemies, he symbolizes the power and might of the dynastic monarchy. He is *maat* personified. A third ceremonial piece recovered from the Hieraconpolis temple allows us to see Narmer in a less aggressive light. The Narmer Macehead shows the king seated on a raised and canopied throne, wearing the red crown of Lower Egypt. An unspecified ceremony is in progress; we can recognize bound captives, Egyptian standard bearers and an important, unnamed person of indeterminate gender who is brought before the king on a carrying chair. While some Egyptologists interpret the seated figure as a god and the scene as the celebration of the king's anniversary or jubilee, others have argued that it must be a wedding ceremony.

Weddings were usually regarded as private matters; not even royal nuptials were occasions for public celebrations. Is there then some special significance to this particular union? In 1896 Jacques de Morgan had discovered, in a final flourishing of the Naqada cemetery, the enormous 1st Dynasty mud-brick tomb of Neith-Hotep, a lady who, judging from her name ('Neith is satisfied', Neith being the goddess of the Delta town of Sais) may well have been of northern extraction. Neith-Hotep's monument has yielded objects inscribed with the names of both Narmer and, more plentifully, his successor Aha, and it seems that both played a part in equipping her tomb. The queen's own name appears on a label recording the number of beads in a necklace. Here we must speculate. Can it be that the young Neith-Hotep, a northern princess, was married to the victorious Narmer, so bringing a peaceful end to the north–south feud? More recent Western history is riddled with similar diplomatic marriages where the conqueror marries the daughter of his displaced rival to unite two warring houses. If this is the case their son Aha, with his northern–southern heritage, would be the one Egyptian truly entitled to wear the double crown. But before we leave the rose-tinted realm of romance we must consider an equally valid scenario, that Neith-Hotep is a southern princess from the ancient but impoverished Naqada royal family (hence her choice of burial site) who has married into the more vigorous Thinite royal line.

Narmer's unified land is an increasingly literate one. Already compulsively labelling and dating royal property, the civil service is exhibiting the organizational skills and the devotion to record-keeping which will characterize Egyptian bureaucracy for thousands of years. There was nothing that the ancient scribes liked more than a long, complicated administrative task, preferably one involving record taking in triplicate. It is the zeal of these record-keepers and their determination to commit everything possible to writing which finally frees us from our over-dependence on the evidence preserved in Egypt's cemeteries. It is their organizational ability, too, which permits the coordination of resources and the storage of surpluses which will offer a buffer against famine and prove an essential element in the building of the pyramids. Tax collectors are already the scourge of the land-owning classes as they raise biennial assessments, payable in kind, on Egypt's farmers. Even the gods are assessed. In ancient Egypt, as today, death and taxation were life's only two certainties.

4

Archaic Abydos

No other living creature has ever made any effort to save the body from immediate destruction after death . . . Man, as soon as he began to feel within him the stirring of his immortal soul, developed a reverence for the body which clothed that soul during its sojourn on earth. Nearly all but the earliest and most savage of our ancestors practised some form of burial, so that with the aid of objects found in their graves, we are able to piece together a picture of their lives.[1]

All human societies develop rituals for the disposal of their dead. Our first Egyptian, the Middle Palaeolithic child interred at Taramsa Hill so many thousands of years ago, was accorded a deliberate burial. The Upper Palaeolithic man laid so gently on his back in the Nazlet Khater grave was equipped with a stone tool placed carefully next to his head. Nowhere do these most ancient Egyptians tell us why they are treating their dead with such respect but, while good housekeeping must always have been a consideration – after all, some means had to be developed for disposing of decomposing bodies – it seems that already we are witnessing a concern for the well-being of the deceased.

By the Neolithic period concern for the dead has firmed into a standardized rite of passage. As settled agriculturalists Egypt's people are surrounded by greater material wealth – pottery, stonework, foodstores, metals, bone and ivory trinkets – at least some of which is available to take to the grave. They have acquired a wider range of skills, are experienced builders in mud-brick, and are able to make long-term plans for their property. At the same time they are locked into settled, well-defined communities. Barring accidents away from home they know that they, their children and their grandchildren will be buried alongside their parents and grandparents in the cemetery which has effectively become an extension of the living village. The Badarian graveyards, with their ranks of bodies staring sightlessly towards the setting sun, show a uniformity of convention, of accepted ritual, not previously seen. These are prehistoric times, and we have no texts to guide us, but the provision of grave goods suggests – and we can put it no stronger than that – that life beyond death is now possible.

The later Neolithic is an increasingly worldly age. While the ill-equipped graves seem to indicate an equality of opportunity in the egalitarian Maadi spirit world, the socially stratified Naqada burial grounds confirm that both wealth and geographical location have become key factors in achieving a tolerable southern death. The elite, able to make the best provisions for eternity, choose to be buried beside their equals and betters, away from the common herd. As the Naqada culture spreads throughout northern Egypt their religion/funerary rituals spread too, 'converting' the Maadi people. Whatever the underlying theology, death has become a major economic force and the upper classes are prepared to invest heavily in their graves. An extensive, even ostentatious, well-located and well-equipped tomb has become the ultimate status symbol.

What did the Naqada peoples believe? Unfortunately, our first unequivocal evidence for the Egyptian view of life beyond death comes from the Pyramid Texts, a series of spells and incantations first committed to stone in the 5th Dynasty pyramid of Unas, over five centuries after Narmer's own demise. These should be approached with caution. We know that many aspects of Egyptian thought did stay surprisingly constant over the centuries; the ideal of Egyptian kingship, pharaoh triumphant, for example, remained fundamentally unchanged from Dynasty 0 to Dynasty 31. However, religious beliefs are seldom static, and dynastic writings confirm that Egyptian theology was at all times a complex and constantly shifting matter. Changes in religious belief are not necessarily reflected in changes to the archaeological record, and funerary traditions in particular tend to cling to comfortingly familiar rituals even when they have become essentially meaningless.

Bearing this caveat in mind, Old Kingdom theology can be treated as a valuable guideline, the endpoint to which the earlier theologies were heading. As such it provides us with a useful insight into the minds of earlier tomb builders. The Old Kingdom Egyptians knew that, given the right circumstances, the Egyptian soul could survive death. But not everyone could look forward to an afterlife free of the grave. Only the king could hope to escape, for the king was blessed with a tripartite soul whose three distinctive spirits, the Ba, the Ka and the Akh, would be liberated at his death. As long as these spirits flourished, they would enable pharaoh to live on. The three were ineffably complex spirits, but may be crudely defined as follows:

The Ba represented the personality or individuality of the king. Often depicted as a human-headed bird, the Ba was a strong, intrepid spirit which lodged in the tomb but which was free to come and go as it pleased. It could fly around Egypt, or could leave earthly life behind, soaring to live with the gods.

The Ka, or spirit of life, was created as a parallel to the earthly body at the moment of conception. But the Ka was weak; compelled to remain close to the corpse it could never leave the grave and could not survive without nourishment. For the Ka to survive death, the body had to survive in a recognizably human form.

The Akh was an ill-defined, even more nebulous spirit representing the immortality of the deceased.

His exceptionally powerful Ba allowed the dead king to leave the tomb and revisit the world as a spirit. There were many varied and contradictory theories as to what would happen next, but broadly speaking Egypt's first pharaohs expected to shine as undying stars in the night sky, and they orientated their tombs so that the exit to the burial chamber faced the unsetting circumpolar stars. Later kings, turning their pyramids towards the rising sun yet retaining the entrance on the northern face, never entirely discarded the old stellar theology but inclined more to the belief that they would be reborn to sail alongside Re, crossing the sky by day in his boat and then descending at nightfall for a more perilous journey through the dark hazards of the Underworld ruled by the mummified King Osiris.

Pharaoh's people lacked the Ba and so had no means of leaving the tomb. They were stuck in the grave for eternity. Later, during the less autocratic Middle Kingdom, this inequality would be corrected and commoners would be offered the chance to dwell with Osiris.

Meanwhile, with escape impossible, it became of paramount importance that the non-royal tomb be made as large and as comfortable as possible. No one wanted to dwell for ever in a sand-filled pit grave equipped with a couple of cracked pots and surrounded by lower-class burials. Everyone, even kings who in theory had no need of grave goods as they would be departing soon after the funeral, filled their tombs with the food, drink and luxury items which would sustain the Ka for eternity.

How far can we extrapolate this 5th Dynasty theology back to Dynasty 0? Certainly, many of the material elements are already familiar. The provision of grave goods has long been a regular feature of archaic Egyptian death, and it seems reasonable to assume that the extensive collections of impersonal items found in the Dynasty 0 graves are pro-vided for the use of the deceased. The belief in the grave as a permanent home for the living spirit is probably behind the increasing sophistication of the tomb, as attempts are made to improve conditions for the corpse. Above all, early attempts at artificial mummification suggest that, while the Dynasty 0 people may not yet have the fully developed theology of the Ka, they already believe that the survival of the body is of utmost importance. Our earliest mummies date to Dynasty 1 – we have a selection of flexed bodies from the Tarkhan cemetery, and a detached, linen-wrapped arm from Abydos – but it is of course unlikely that we will ever recover the first experimental mummies.

For many centuries Egypt's dead had been sleeping on, and covered by, animal skins, linen sheets or woven mats. Some Badarian corpses rested their weary heads on comfortable leather pillows. Grieving rela-tives used upturned baskets to guard the vulnerable eyes, ears and mouth from the invading desert. These quickly evolved into lidded boxes which completely enclosed the body. Coffins – squat wooden or clay boxes suitable for holding contracted burials – soon followed and stone sar-cophagi were not far behind. At the same time came the provision of a wooden roof and a plaster or mud-brick lining which transformed the simple oval grave into a miniature, rectangular, sand-free tomb capable of holding multiple grave goods. If necessary, the burial chamber could be subdivided by internal walls to create further, better organized storage; no doors were needed to link these chambers, as the spirit could pass through the solid walls. Above ground, a superstructure – a cairn of stones, a flimsy reed hut or a simple stela – flagged the location of the grave, providing a focus for visitors and a useful marker for future grave diggers.

This evolution brought one huge problem. The most simple pit graves – snug, shallow holes dug into the hot desert sands – held their dead contracted and coffinless, curled as if sleeping beneath a comforting blanket of hot sand. The body was completely covered, and nothing separated the corpse from the desert which now enveloped it. As decomposition set in the sterile sand drew away the seeping body fluids, allowing the corpse to dry quickly and naturally. Desert pit graves have yielded a whole series of desiccated but lifelike bodies, their skin, internal organs, hair and even nails still in place. The Egyptians, occasionally stumbling across ancient burials, knew that their dead did not decompose in the desert.

But as soon as they were separated from the hot sands, the elite started to rot. In most societies decomposition would have been accepted as an unavoidable sign of mankind's mortality. In practical Egypt it was treated as a problem to be solved. Logic dictated that the elite should abandon the new burial practices and return to the simple desert graves but no one wanted to take a step backwards. Instead the elite determined to fight nature and combat decay. The science, art and religion – for the preservation of the body would always be considered a magical, mystical ritual – of mummification was born.

The first attempts at artificial mummification concentrated on preserving shape at the expense of tissue. Layers of well-padded resin-soaked bandages allowed the undertakers to mould the contracted limbs into ghoulish parody of life before burying the dead in a short wooden coffin. The bandaged arm with four gold bracelets concealed beneath its bandages, found in 1900 in the 1st Dynasty tomb of King Djer at Abydos, falls into this category. Petrie, its discoverer, assigned the bejewelled limb to a queen, but it is equally likely that he had found the last remains of the king himself, hidden by an ancient thief who had been unable to return to collect his loot. The limb was soon lost in Cairo Museum but the bracelets, with their turquoise, amethyst, lapis lazuli and gold beads arranged palace façade style, survive:[2]

. . . the arm of the queen of Zer (Djer) was found, hidden in a hole in the wall, with the gold bracelets in place. The lads who found it saw the gold, but left it untouched and brought the arm to me. I cut the wrappings apart and so bared the bracelets all intact. Thus the exact order could be copied when my wife rethreaded them the next morning.

When Quibell came over on behalf of the Museum I sent up the bracelets by him. The arm – the oldest mummified piece known – and its marvellously fine tissue of linen were also delivered at the Museum. Brugsch only cared for display; so from one bracelet he cut away the half that was of plaited gold wires, and he also threw away the arm and linen. A museum is a dangerous place.

The rigid bodies, plastered and painted, looked acceptable enough. But, inevitably, beneath their solid bandages the moist corpses continued to putrefy, generating enough heat to scorch and char their hardened linen. Egypt's elite were soon reduced to skeletons, and skeletons did not count as bodies. This cannot have been totally unexpected. The Egyptians were long accustomed to handling dead animals, and they knew what happened when meat was left to rot. They may not have understood the science, but they knew that gutting, the removal of the soft internal organs, would delay putrefaction in game just as they knew that drying in salt, sun or wind would preserve meat and fish almost indefinitely. Clearly, the undertakers should start to handle their dead in the way that they handled their food. And this is what they did. By the end of the 3rd Dynasty evisceration followed by chemical drying in natron salt was becoming routine and the hollow bodies, no longer contracted, were being bandaged and buried in long rather than squat coffins. Centuries of experimentation would lead to the perfection of the technique summarized by Herodotus:[3]

. . . this is their procedure for the most perfect style of embalming. First of all they draw out the brain through the nostrils using an iron hook. When they have extracted all that they can, they wash out the remnants with an infusion of drugs. Then, using a sharp obsidian stone, they make a cut along the flank. Through this they extract the whole contents of the abdomen. The abdomen is then cleaned, rinsed with palm wine and rinsed again with powdered spices but not frankincense, and stitched up. And when they have done this they heap the body with natron for seventy days, but no longer, and so the mummy is made. After the seventy days are over they wash the body and wrap it from head to toe in the finest linen bandages coated with resin . . . Finally they hand back the body to the relatives who place it in a wooden coffin in the shape of a man before shutting it up in a tomb, propped upright against the wall.

This could never be a pleasant ritual: the morticians were dealing with pints of blood, decomposing flesh, discarded organs, strong chemicals, flies and, we must imagine, a truly horrible smell. It therefore comes as no great surprise to find the embalmers' workshops situated on the desert edge, close to running water and, with a satisfying symbolism, part-way between the lands of the living and the dead. Here, safe from prying eyes, the undertakers could preserve the mysteries which guaranteed their highly respected role in society.

The lifelike Egyptian mummy was required to play a full part in its own mortuary rituals. We do not understand the finer details of the Old Kingdom royal funeral, which is neither recorded nor depicted, but we can glean general information from the scenes which decorate elite tombs from the 6th Dynasty onwards. We know that soon after death the deceased was taken to the undertakers' workshop by boat; this was an important ritual, and a symbolic boat journey was made if it was not actually necessary to cross the Nile. In just seventy days the deceased would be purified and transformed into a mummy – a latent being awaiting rebirth. The journey from the undertakers' workshop to the grave was made by sledge, the body in its coffin being dragged across the sand. The deceased was accompanied by an impressive cortège whose size very much depended upon the funding available. Amongst the party we should expect to find priests, including the Lector Priest who would read out the spells at the funeral, the grieving widow (or a paid substitute) who was known as 'the kite', family and friends, servants burdened with grave goods and the funerary feast, and bands of professional mourners who would throw dust over their heads and toss their hair to express extreme anguish. As the dynasties progressed the kite would be replaced by two women representing the winged goddesses Isis and Nephthys, the sisters who mourned and cared for the body of the dead god Osiris.

A whole series of rituals was performed at the entrance to the tomb by the heir of the deceased who, in serving his dead father, would confirm his own right to inherit. The most important of these ceremonies, the 'opening of the mouth', was designed to allow the eyes, ears, nose and mouth to function again, so kindling the latent force within the mummy wrappings. The mummy, taken from its coffin, was propped upright and touched with various sacred objects while the Lector Priest recited the spells which would make the transformation complete. The body was then placed in the sarcophagus, a final feast was eaten, and the tomb was sealed, the last workman sweeping his footprints away with a brush. Alone in the dark, the mummy now awaited its rebirth.

As the undertakers refined their methods, Egypt's tomb builders became more ambitious. Funerary architecture would always have to vary with local geographical constraints; to take an obviously extreme example, it would never be possible to build a large-scale pyramid in the steep-sided Valley of the Kings as stable pyramids require a wide, flat base. Local traditions and preferences, too, would invariably play a part in tomb design, so we find the early Dynastic tomb complexes of the Abydos cemetery developing along very different lines from the contemporary tombs built at Sakkara. However, throughout Egypt, from Dynasty 0 to the very end of the dynastic age, it would always be accepted that the tomb must serve a double function: it must protect the body and its belongings, and must provide a focus for offerings which the family, friends and employees of the deceased will leave for the Ka.

We should perhaps add a third, unwritten function. The tomb must adequately represent the status of its owner. Ownership of a large tomb in an elite cemetery was an obvious mark of social success. Kings in particular used their magnificent tombs as propaganda to prove their status – both earthly and divine – to their people and their gods. The royal mortuary complex, complete and filled with goods, was a sure and certain sign of a well-regulated state. But its significance went far beyond this. Monumental architecture, properly conceived by the royal architects, built by the royal craftsmen and dedicated by the king, could itself serve as an earthly and permanent representation of divine harmony, of kingship and of *maat*. The royal tombs were first and foremost sacred monuments; the universe in miniature, the place where earthly life met the divine. Everything in the complex was designed for a specific ritual purpose, and nothing was included by chance.

Egypt's elite were facing more practical concerns. Frightened by the need to provide for all eternity, they were attempting to take more and more goods to the grave. Clothing, cosmetics, jewellery, furniture, games, weapons, musical instruments, even in some cases a toilet; all were packed into the tomb so that the provincial cemeteries now boasted unprecedented numbers of rich burials and, of course, unprecedented numbers of robberies. The elite would continue to be buried with vast quantities of grave goods until, at the beginning of the 3rd Dynasty, it was realized that the whole system was simply impossible. An eternity in the grave required infinite supplies of food and drink; nothing less would suffice. Magic, however, offered an attractive alternative. The inclusion of a stela, carved with images of the desired goods, could substitute for the goods themselves. Within the tomb, these images would become both real and permanent. Thus at the end of the 2nd Dynasty we find an abrupt decline in the number of grave goods, and a corresponding decline in the number of inscribed sealings used to label the goods. This is matched by a welcome increase in the number of tomb inscriptions which take the form of offering formulae, or requests for material goods which will benefit the dead.

Egypt's highest ranking civil servants were interred in the western desert at north Sakkara, close by the bureaucratic centre of Memphis and the cult centre of the sun god Re at Heliopolis.[4] So sophisticated were their tombs that for many years Egyptologists believed them to be either the actual tombs or the cenotaphs of the Archaic kings, and this interpretation is still found in the older Egyptological literature. Today, with a greater understanding of the royal cemetery at Abydos, Archaic Sakkara is once again classed as an elite rather than a royal cemetery.

Here the 1st Dynasty burial chambers were gradually cut deeper and deeper until they passed through the desert sand into the underlying bedrock. Lined with precious wood, their ground-level ceilings were topped with a low mound protected by a layer of mud-bricks, and then surrounded by a low, rectangular mud-brick building known as a mastaba after the Arabic word mastaba, or low bench. There was no means of access to the substructure other than through its wooden ceiling; the mastaba could only be built, and filled, when the chamber had been roofed after the funeral. Around the largest mastabas were single rows of smaller, brick-lined vaulted tombs intended to hold the anonymous artisans who worked for the deceased; their grave goods reveal that they belonged to potters, boatmen and carpenters who had taken the tools of their trade to the next life.

Although occasionally solid with sand and gravel, the mastaba super-structures were usually honeycombed with chambers which served as storerooms for grave goods. These could be – indeed, needed to be – extensive. Sakkara Tomb 3357, an extreme example dated to the reign

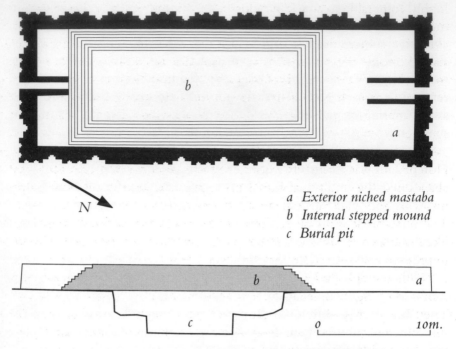

a   Exterior niched mastaba
b   Internal stepped mound
c   Burial pit

Figure 4.1   The 1st Dynasty Mastaba 3038 at Sakkara.

of Aha, incorporated twenty-seven storage chambers in a mastaba built directly above a burial pit which was itself subdivided into four rooms plus a central burial chamber, while to the north of the tomb lay a 'model-estate'; a suite of small-scale buildings including granaries for bread and beer production, a garden and a mud-brick boat burial.

Seen from the outside the mastabas were cheerful buildings, their recessed walls plastered and painted in the *serekh*, or palace façade pattern. This archaic style of panelling, already strongly associated with kingship, is now starting to be associated with death, and may be found on contemporary coffins. False doorways, deep niches painted to resemble doors, allowed the spirits of the dead free passage in and out of the tomb while excluding the living. Tomb 3504, the tomb of the official Sekhemka, included a low bench provided for the display of 300 model bull heads fitted with real horns.

Unfortunately, despite their thick enclosure walls, the mastabas proved highly vulnerable to attack by thieves. By the end of the 1st Dynasty the number of rooms in the superstructure was being reduced in favour of extensive subterranean storage galleries reached by a stairway which started outside the superstructure. Eventually the mastaba would revert to a solid, smooth-walled, rubble-filled mound with two false doors remaining at each end of the eastern wall. The southern door served as an offering chapel; the northern door was provided for reasons of symmetry.

We have already visited the Naqada tomb built for Queen Neith-Hotep. This was essentially a northern-style tomb but here the architects abandoned the traditional burial pit and converted the superstructure into a ground-level burial chamber surrounded by twenty storage rooms. The mud-brick walls of the queen's mastaba were recessed or niched like those seen at Sakkara, and the whole complex was surrounded by an impressive enclosure wall.

Neith-Hotep's husband, Narmer, and her son, Aha, built their own tombs some eighty miles away, in the Umm el-Qa'ab cemetery, Abydos. Their burial ground (known today as Cemetery B) lies to the south of the cemetery used by their Naqada III predecessors. Unfortunately, by the time Flinders Petrie arrived to excavate in 1899, Cemetery B was in a sorry state. Petrie, famously outspoken, did not hesitate to apportion blame:[5]

During four years there had been the great scandal of Amélineau's work at the Royal Tombs of Abydos. He had been given a concession to work there for five years; no plans were kept (a few incorrect ones were made later), there was no record of where things were found, no useful publication. He boasted that he had reduced to chips the pieces of stone vases which he did not care to remove, and burned up the remains of the woodwork of the 1st Dynasty in his kitchen . . . It was the usual French work, but with total indifference to what became of things.

Nothing is more disheartening than being obliged to gather results out of the fraction left behind by past plunderers. In these royal tombs there had been not only the plundering of the precious metals and the larger valuables by the wreckers of early ages; there was after that the systematic destruction of the monuments by the vile fanaticism of the Copts, which crushed everything beautiful and everything noble that mere greed had spared; and worst of all, for history, came the active search in the last four years of everything that could have a value in the eyes of purchasers, or be sold for profit regardless of its source; a search in which whatever was not allowed was deliberately and avowedly destroyed in order to enhance the intended profits of European speculators . . .

One significant band of Abydos despoilers omitted by Petrie are the ancient Egyptians themselves. By the 12th Dynasty the Umm el-Qa'ab was recognized as the burial place of the great god Osiris, and excavations had already been conducted within the 1st Dynasty tombs to try to identify his grave. Eventually Djer's tomb would be converted into a cenotaph for Osiris. As Abydos became one of Egypt's leading cult centres, pilgrims flocked to pay their respects to Osiris, leaving behind the millions of pottery offerings which were to give the site its modern name Umm el-Qa'ab or 'mother of pots'. To further confuse archaeological matters, many of the 1st Dynasty tombs have suffered extensive, ancient, fire damage and all have lost their superstructures.

With one year of his concession still to run, the despised Emile Amelineau, a Coptic scholar rather than an excavator, was ousted and replaced by Petrie. There could have been no greater contrast. Petrie, prudent and painstaking (and perhaps prone to exaggeration), embarked upon a rescue mission, gathering together the surviving fragments, planning the tombs and recording and publishing his discoveries. He found, to his horror, that all but one of the burials had already been ransacked but, through slow, careful work was able to recover much that had seemed irretrievably lost. Against all the odds, some of the tombs still included sealed storerooms and intact subsidiary burials. Working in Cemetery B and the early Dynastic cemetery further to the south, he investigated thirteen royal tombs.[6] To his great joy, he uncovered the missing link which would join his prehistoric Naqada graves to the beginning of orthodox Egyptian history:

Looking at the groups of tombs . . . it is seen that they lie closely together. Each royal tomb is a large square pit, lined with brickwork. Close around it, on its own level, or higher up, are small chambers in rows in which were buried the domestics of the king. Each reign adopted some variety in the mode of burial, but they all follow the type of the prehistoric burials, more or less developed.

The plain square pit, like those in which the predynastic people were buried, is here the essential of the tomb. It is surrounded in the earlier examples of Zer [Djer] or Zet [Djet] by small chambers opening from it. By Merneit [Merit-Neith] these chambers were built separately around it. By Den an entrance passage was added, and by Qa [Qaa] the entrance was turned to the north. At this stage we are left within reach of the early passage mastabas and pyramids. Substituting a stone lining and roof for bricks and wood, and placing the small tombs of the domestics further away, we reach the type of the mastaba-pyramid of Sneferu, and so lead on to the pyramid series of the Old Kingdom.[7]

Today the German Institute of Archaeology is involved in a thorough long-term reappraisal of the site. Petrie, who prided himself on his scientific excavation, would be mortified to learn that their labours have revealed much that he missed.

Cemetery B has yielded three double-chambered tombs dated by their inscribed potsherds and sealings to the Dynasty 0 kings Iri-Hor (B1/2), Ka (B7/8) and Narmer (B17/18) plus the 1st Dynasty tomb complex of Aha. The three Dynasty 0 tombs shared a similar plan; they were large, brick-lined, rectangular pits whose postholes suggest the incorporation of a now vanished wooden lining to the burial chamber. Although the superstructures, too, have vanished, there is evidence to suggest that the pits were roofed with wooden planks and covered with a modest rectangular mound held in place by inward-sloping retaining walls.

The 1st Dynasty kings had greater access to Egypt's resources and, perhaps, a more developed sense of their own grandeur. Aha's complex, five times larger than Narmer's and far more complicated, is nevertheless an evolved form of the same basic plan. Built in three distinct stages and including several separate chambers, it held a series of large wooden shrines. Again, it was topped by a low mound or solid mastaba while to the north-east there was provision for thirty-three subsidiary burials.

The remaining monarchs of the 1st Dynasty built their tombs to the south of Cemetery B. Their tombs cluster together – space is limited on the Umm el-Qa'ab – sharing a similar, gradually evolving plan. Twin stelae, on the east side of the tomb, announced the name of the deceased, while a mud-brick wall separated the royal burial from its satellite burials. The subterranean burial chambers, lined with expensive cedar wood, were surrounded by storage chambers, roofed by wooden planks and topped by a low, brick-clad mound or tumulus itself incorporated in a larger mound. This tumulus, entirely hidden from view, had no obvious architectural purpose and must therefore be assumed to have been of ritual or symbolic importance. Hidden mounds could also be found within the contemporary Sakkara mastabas. Tomb 3038, dating to the reign of Anedjib, incorporated a rectangular mud-brick-cased mound which was later modified to give a stepped appearance,[8] suggesting that the badly eroded mounds of the Umm el-Qa'ab, too, might once have been stepped.

Den's tomb shows the first extensive use of stone in a funerary context; here the burial chamber is paved in dressed red and black Aswan granite. It is also the first to include a stairway leading down to the burial chamber, a development that would have allowed the superstructure to be completed and stocked before the king's funeral. To deter intruders, access to the burial chamber could be blocked with a stone portcullis. Uniquely, a separate annex, reached via its own staircase, housed a limestone block which we may guess once served as the pedestal for a statue of the dead king.

The Abydos tombs lack the detailed writings, the stone carvings and papyri, which would make this period come properly alive to us. In place of histories we are presented with sealings and terse labels. Nevertheless, the ivory tags used to catalogue the tomb contents confirm just how recognizable the monarchy has become. Den, for example, has provided us with a label originally attached to a pair of sandals, which shows the king with his right arm raised to smite the captive Asiatic who grovels at his feet. The caption reads 'the first occasion of smiting the easterners', and fits well with the contemporary smiting of the 'Iwnu' (desert nomads) recorded on the Palermo Stone. A wooden label from the same tomb shows the king celebrating his thirty-year jubilee or *heb sed*; we see pharaoh running a ritual race against time, and in calmer mood sitting on a raised throne. Den, who succeeded to the throne as a child, was to enjoy two such jubilees.

All the 1st Dynasty tomb complexes included satellite or subsidiary graves. These were long, narrow, mud-brick-lined trenches subdivided into individual compartments, whose occupants were provided with their own grave goods and who, having been partially mummified by

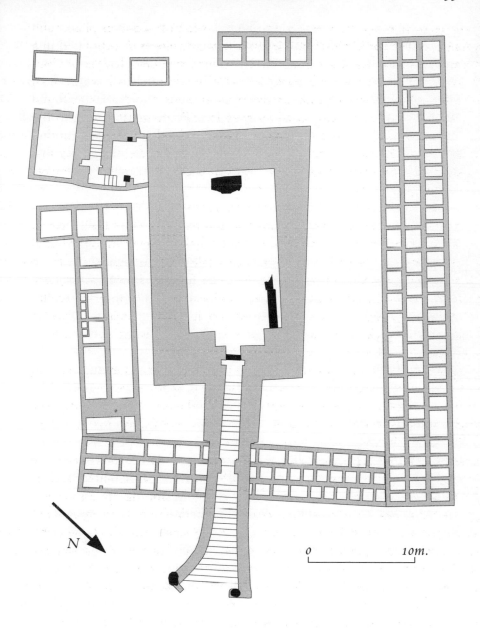

Figure 4.2   The tomb of Den at Abydos. The black areas are granite.

N

0   10m.

wrapping in natron-coated cloth, were buried in wooden coffins. The names of the subsidiary dead were engraved on small-scale limestone stelae which, although crude in comparison to the great royal tombstones, were still an expensive indication of status. Djer's complex included 318 additional burial chambers, some of which were never occupied, and these have yielded 97 stelae. Of these, 76 bore women's names and 11 bore men's. These are not queens, princesses or high-ranking officials; for the moment the elite – even the queen and her children – are kept well away from the royal cemeteries. Nor are they artisans as found at Sakkara. They are the king's personal retinue, his servants, minor officials, favourite women and amusing dwarfs (always a favourite at court; Djer was buried with two), and they are almost invariably young. Some pharaohs gave preferential treatment to animals; Den was interred alongside his hunting dogs while Aha's complex has yielded the bones of several young men plus, buried nearby, at least seven young lions. The lions are unexpected, but the link between strong kingship and powerful animals – bulls and lions in particular – is by now well recognized.

These subsidiary graves, essentially mass graves, are very different in style and far more numerous than the satellite graves found at Sakkara and in some of Egypt's other elite cemeteries. The graves associated with the northern non-royal burials are essentially individual graves which need not have been filled at the same time. As their superstructures are missing we cannot be certain when the Abydos satellite graves were closed, but in many cases they shared a common roof which must imply simultaneous burial. In a few cases the evidence is unambiguous; the subsidiary graves which surrounded the burial chambers of Semerkhet and Qaa, for example, must have been roofed at the same time as the kings' own burials.

The majority of the subsidiary burials were disturbed in antiquity, making it impossible for us to determine how their occupants died. Nevertheless, it is hard to escape the conclusion that the Abydos trenches were filled with attendants executed or persuaded to commit suicide at the time of the king's death. Ethnographic comparisons, drawn across vast distances and timespans, can do little more than open the mind to the infinite variety of human behaviours. From these examples we can see that several societies, at the start of their kingships, believed that their dead and newly divine monarch should not go alone into the unknown. The Mesopotamian death pits of Ur have yielded the bodies of hundreds of attendants who took poison so that they might continue their service by accompanying their master to the next life. Nearer to home, but much later in time, the Nubian kingdom of Kerma has her own mass tombs.

Murder was forbidden in Egypt, yet we know that the king was allowed to kill. He could, indeed must, in the name of *maat*, execute the enemies who threatened Egypt's security, be they Egyptian criminals to be ritually impaled on a stake, or foreign foes to be killed in battle. The Narmer Palette shows the king in the very act of striking the enemy who lies at his feet. As we like to imagine the ancient Egyptians as a tolerant, peaceful people, exotic yet not too far removed in temperament and habit from ourselves, it is generally assumed that this represents a symbolic rather than an actual sacrifice. But, given the unquestioning acceptance of animal sacrifice, it may be that such scenes should be reinterpreted as literal representations of an occasional ritual act. Such practices leave little or no evidence in the archaeological record, although we might expect to find mention of them in Egypt's writings. They are, of course, copiously illustrated in royal art.

The classical authors were divided on the subject, with Herodotus denying human sacrifice but Diodorus Siculus taking the opposite approach:[9]

Red oxen may be sacrificed because it is believed that red was the colour of Typhon [Seth] who plotted against Osiris and whom Isis punished for the murder of her husband. Men also of Typhon's colour, in the earliest days might be sacrificed by the kings at the tomb of Osiris. Now, few Egyptians are red, although most foreigners are and this is why the story spread amongst the Greeks . . .

The tomb of Osiris was theoretically situated amidst the 1st Dynasty tombs of Abydos, but it needs an athletic leap of the imagination to picture Egypt's 1st Dynasty pharaohs going to the grave escorted by an exclusively red-headed band of retainers.

The Abydos satellite burials settle any debate over the strength of the Archaic Period kingship. Pharaoh is far removed from mere mortals and he exerts a control over his people which extends beyond death. He is able to persuade – or compel – the chosen ones to die with him; he can demand, and will receive, the ultimate sacrifice. The chosen ones are, however, people of lowly birth selected for their personal services; we do not find pharaoh persuading his near equals to die. Human sacrifice is a wasteful practice. In Egypt it was a short-lived experiment, abandoned when it was realized that flesh and blood servants could be replaced by wooden and clay models who, through magic, would serve the king efficiently for all eternity. The 2nd Dynasty tomb complexes of Peribsen and Khasekhemwy lack any form of subsidiary burial.

The low-key Abydos tombs came nowhere near to matching the recessed grandeur of Neith-Hotep's mastaba tomb or indeed the brilliance of the elite tombs at Sakkara. But the tombs themselves were merely the private element of the kings' much larger funeral complex. Less than 2 kilometres to the north-east of their Umm el-Qa'ab tombs, on the edge of the cultivated land, the 1st Dynasty kings built massive rectangular enclosures whose now much denuded walls are neatly defined by the trenches of subsidiary graves planted around them.

Aha's, the earliest enclosure discovered, was relatively small (20 × 40.5 metres), had smooth, plastered, mud-brick walls and corner towers and a nearby cluster of subsidiary burials. Subsequent kings built larger, taller complexes featuring niched or recessed facing but no towers so that they must have resembled the fortified towns shown on the late Predynastic palettes. Indeed, early Egyptologists classified these impressive enclosures as fortresses or palaces. More recently they have been interpreted as 'fortresses of the gods'; architecture designed to be used in the next world, when the gods will sail in their boats to visit the dead king.[10]

Here, it was hoped, the cults and rituals of the dead kings would be celebrated long after their deaths. But piety came at a price. Who would pay the priests to conduct the daily rituals – who would care – after the king had gone? Rather than rely on the generosity of his successors, each pharaoh endowed his own mortuary cult with a foundation, a parcel of assets including estates scattered throughout Egypt, which would provide sufficient income to finance a permanent priesthood. The mortuary priests, highly efficient administrators and accountants, managed the land on behalf of their dead king, paying their own wages in kind (grain, bread, beer and meat), making offerings as required and, of course, paying taxes. Any surplus income could be converted into non-perishable goods and stored against lean times. Full warehouses were an important part of Egyptian religious life.

Egyptologist David O'Connor has excavated sections of Djer's mortuary enclosure wall.[11] His work indicates that this was a substantial structure standing some eight or nine metres tall, with three simple, plastered, niched walls and one more complex wall – the north-east – incorporating a deeper and more intricate recessed patterning. It is perhaps no coincidence that this wall faced the rising sun. Around the foot of the walls ran a low mud-brick bench; comparison with the contemporary bench found at Sakkara Tomb 3504[12] suggests that this may have been used to display model bull heads, but as yet no such head has been found at Abydos. Entrance to the compound was through gateways cut in the eastern corner of the north-east wall and the northern corner of the north-west wall, although the north-west entrance was completely blocked soon after its construction. The north-east entrance opened into a small courtyard and then gave access to the main enclosure.

It is unclear what stood within this enclosure. However, excavation of the far larger and better preserved 2nd Dynasty enclosure built by Khasekhemwy, known today as the Shunet es-Zebib (literally the 'Storehouse of Raisins'), has shown that it included an offering chapel, open spaces, brick and more flimsy wattle or reed structures and what O'Connor has described as a large 'sand and gravel mound covered with a mud-brick skin':[13] a proto-pyramid. This feature would have been hidden from view behind the high enclosure walls, but would have been immediately obvious to anyone entering the compound.

The two-dimensional boats of late Predynastic grave art are made real in the elite Archaic cemeteries. Helwan, Tarkhan and Sakkara have each yielded boat graves, each associated with a mastaba, and each with a highly visible boat-shaped superstructure. At Abydos, beside the Shunet es-Zebib, O'Connor discovered a dozen large but very shallow pits each filled with a wooden hull and surrounded by a low mud-brick casing plastered, whitewashed and shaped to resemble a ship. Stone anchors permanently moored this ghostly fleet in place. These are not real boats taken to the grave as part of the Ka's inheritance; these vessels could never have sailed on the Nile. Their purpose is less obvious, and more complex. Are they endlessly waiting for the dead kings to embark and sail to their celestial destiny? Or are they the sacred boats of the gods who are visiting the fortress of the dead king?

By the end of the Archaic Period Egypt could boast a complex and sophisticated pantheon whose gods and goddesses were worshipped in cult temples found in all the major towns and cities. Funerary theology had advanced far beyond a simple desire to make the dead comfortable within the grave, and the royal tombs were being designed to meet specific, not always immediately obvious, religious requirements. As we hesitate on the Archaic/Old Kingdom divide, the time has come for us to meet the deities who were exerting such a strong influence on royal tomb design.

5

The Rising of the Sun

A long, long time ago the sun god Re, also known as Atum, sat on the mound of creation and sneezed and spat. Out of his mouth came two children, Shu the dry air and Tefnut his moist sister. They in turn begat the sky goddess Nut and the earth god Geb. Nut bore Geb two sons and two daughters. Osiris, Isis and Nephthys were good and true but their brother Seth was troubled and angry. Osiris ruled Egypt as a wise and just king, his sister-wife Isis beside him. This so irritated Seth that he decided to murder his brother and take his place. Infinitely cunning, Seth trapped Osiris inside a chest which he threw into the Nile. With Osiris vanished Seth became pharaoh and Isis, despairing, set off to search for her husband.

Isis found the dead Osiris in Byblos and returned to Egypt to bury his body. But Seth discovered her plan and, incandescent with rage, dismembered his dead brother, flinging the pieces far and wide. Transforming themselves into birds Isis and Nephthys searched high and low, recovering the scattered parts until only the penis was missing. Isis, the divine healer, equipped her husband with a replica organ and then recited the spell which would bring him back to life. Her magic was very powerful; nine months later she bore Osiris a son. Isis fled with the baby to the marshes, where she protected him with her magic until he was old enough to defend himself.

Horus grew up to avenge his father. After a lengthy struggle he deposed Seth and took his rightful place as king of Upper and Lower Egypt. Meanwhile Osiris retreated to rule his own land, the Kingdom of the Dead.[1]

This was a creation story born of observation and experience. The very moment of creation, the time that the first mound rose out of the swirling waters of chaos, was repeated every year when the floodwaters retreated to reveal the freshly fertile land. The sun shone all-powerful in the sky, proving Re's unfailing might. Meanwhile Osiris, now a mummy, lived the dark life of an earth god, closely linked with soil, agriculture and rebirth. The two gods complemented each other, and their theologies developed side by side.

The Predynastic deities, each still potent in his or her own local area, were by the dawn of the Dynastic age linked by an increasingly intricate mythology. This was a practical response to an otherwise insoluble problem. Egypt lacked a formal history and an understanding of science; she needed her myths and legends to explain the otherwise inexplicable. In a life full of uncertainty, there were two burning questions. Where did people come from? And what would happen after death? Other questions seemed insignificant in comparison. To address this fundamental need for understanding – to explain creation and the Afterlife – each priesthood devised and celebrated the stories, often contradictory and full of logical inconsistency, which 'starred' their own particular god.

In many ways Egypt's gods were not dissimilar to the gods of Greece and Rome or, indeed, to their human creators. None was all-powerful and none infallible; each had their individual duties to perform; they were free to love, hate, mate and produce children. In appearance, however, the Egyptian pantheon was unique. Here human–form gods could be found in happy co-existence alongside animal forms and bizarre human–animal hybrids, and most deities could be depicted in several equally valid ways. Hathor, for example, could appear either as a beautiful woman or as the cow which symbolized her nurturing nature. If she was required to participate in a set-piece scene, to sit on a throne or shake a sistrum (a holy rattle), she had to have a conventional female body – cows being incapable of sitting on thrones, let alone shaking rattles – but there was no reason why this human body could not be topped by a cow's head complete with horns and a crown. Realism was not an issue: in all their work Egypt's artists set out to convey the essence rather than the physical appearance of their subjects.

Unlike their classical counterparts, Egypt's gods were simultaneously well defined and highly flexible. They could split into several aspects of the same being, so we find Horus worshipped as Horus the child or Horus the elder, as Horakhty 'Horus of the Horizon' or as Horemakhet 'Horus in the Horizon'. Local variation, too, was common, so alongside the famous Horus of Hieraconpolis we find the equally valid 'Horus the

Behdetite' who is specifically associated with kingship and the royal throne, and 'Horus of Letopolis', associated with Lower Egyptian kingship. But this fission, the concentrating on specific attributes within one god, is not unique to Egypt; today we can find the same thing in the Roman Catholic church where the Virgin Mary may be revered in many different aspects. More unusual is the gods' ability to fuse together to create a syncretized deity who lived alongside, and yet was somehow more than the sum of, his component parts. In the Theban-based New Kingdom Amen, the fairly insignificant local god of Thebes, would be joined with the mighty Re to make the composite deity Amen-Re, patron god of the Egyptian empire and inspiration of the great warrior kings. More relevant here is the fusion of Horus and Re to make the powerful solar deity Re-Horakhty, 'the sun god, Horus of the Horizon'; a celebration of Re as the strong god of the rising sun.

Just as mortal Egypt now had a social hierarchy, so a divine hierarchy had developed. Some gods, those associated with the wealthiest towns and those most favoured by the king (usually those who reinforced the idea of divine kingship) had achieved nationwide recognition and were powerful throughout Egypt. The remainder were locally effective – Egypt never banished gods from her eclectic pantheon – but were of little national importance and attracted little funding. The state-sponsored cult temples, prominent features within the walled townships, were already attracting lavish if sporadic royal donations and were slowly but surely being transformed from flimsy reed and wattle structures into substantial mud-brick buildings. There was as yet no real unification of style, and archaic local traditions were still important, but Egypt's shrines were heading towards the homogeneity of architectural thought which characterizes New Kingdom temples.

The cult temple was the one place that the gods could interface with mortals via the king. Here the primary concern was always the welfare of the living Egypt and her pharaoh; a concern which could only be addressed by the offerings, hymns and recitations supplied by the king and his deputies. The new temples, surrounded by high enclosure walls which prevented contamination by the ungodly and which effectively kept the common people out, were very different in nature and design to the mortuary temples and sacred enclosures which were being built to protect the interests of the king both in life and in death. Most kings aspired to build cult temples – an impressive building programme was after all the benchmark of a successful reign – but priority would always be given to the mortuary complex which would ensure the king's own rebirth.

Already the well-endowed fertility god Min of Koptos could boast a series of colossal limestone figures standing in the courtyard of his mud-brick temple. The statues, today broken but originally measuring over 4 metres high, stand as a mute testament to the skill of the early stonemasons and the willingness of the archaic kings to support diverse local cults. If the relatively obscure Min was receiving such generous gifts we may assume that his fellow deities – Horus, Seth, Hathor, Ptah, Re and Neith, to name just a few – were equally fortunate even though their temples have long since vanished. The Palermo Stone lists the carving of cult statues amongst the significant achievements of the earliest reigns, and mentions the erection of a stone temple at the end of the 2nd Dynasty.

Horus the falcon now perched with absolute confidence on top of the *serekh* which defined the royal Horus-name. Horus and kingship had become inextricably linked. In saving Egypt from the disunity which may be crudely equated with Seth, Narmer had become the earthly representative of Horus, king of living Egypt. By the 4th Dynasty Egypt's deceased kings would start to be identified with the equally dead Osiris. Meanwhile, Narmer retained a strong loyalty towards his patron deity and a strong spiritual link with his southern homeland where he chose to be buried alongside his ancestors. In so doing he set a precedent which would persist throughout the 1st Dynasty, as successive pharaohs continued the Abydene funerary traditions which went hand in hand with devotion to Horus. However, with the change to the 2nd Dynasty we can sense a shift in loyalty.

The first five kings of the 2nd Dynasty are remote beings, perhaps the least well known of all Egypt's pharaohs. Their tombs have not yet been identified but there is strong circumstantial evidence to suggest that they were interred at Sakkara rather than Abydos. Here, extensive underground galleries, rooms and storerooms cut in the bedrock to the south of Djoser's Step Pyramid, and a further series of galleries running beneath his pyramid complex, have yielded sealings belonging to three of the missing kings: Hetepsekhemwy, Raneb and Ninetjer. These probably represent all that now remains of their lost tombs – tombs very different in style from those found in the Abydos royal cemetery. At Abydos tomb substructures are relatively simple. At Sakkara the underground chambers mirror domestic architecture, with both private (bedrooms, bathrooms, lavatories) and more public (reception and ceremonial) chambers provided for the use of the spirit.

All trace of their above-ground structures has vanished, but it seems inconceivable that the Sakkara galleries were not covered by impressive mastabas.[2] Where, then, was the equivalent of the northern funerary enclosure, the place where the cult of the dead king was celebrated? An inscription preserved on a statue of the priest Hetepdief indicates that Hetepsekhemwy, Raneb and Ninetjer did build cult centres at Sakkara. And to the west of their galleries there exist the ruins of two large, unexplained enclosures bounded by rubble walls and displaying the sorry remains of stone and mud-brick buildings. But these enclosures (known today as the Ptahhotep enclosure and the Gisr el-Mudir enclosure) are anonymous and undated, and as yet their purpose remains far from certain.

Nowhere are we told why it was felt necessary to abandon Abydos and all that the Abydene traditions represented, but we may speculate that the move coincided with a break in the royal line. The Egyptians seldom recorded challenges to the kingship as rebellion raised uncomfortable questions which were best avoided. If the king had been revealed as a semi-divine being at his coronation, if he was the one super-human in permanent contact with the gods, how could he be deposed by a mere mortal? Here at the very end of the Archaic Period, with writing still very much in its infancy and no tradition of monumental inscriptions, we are left almost completely in the dark. Only the Palermo Stone offers a glimmer of light, indicating as it does a decrease in Nile flood levels which may well have placed Egypt's resources under stress at this time.

It may be that the first kings of the 2nd Dynasty were northerners who, having displaced the ruling southern family, naturally wished to be buried in their homeland. The fact that Hetepsekhemwy's name is found within Qaa's Abydos tomb – a circumstance which strongly suggests that the 2nd Dynasty Hetepsekhemwy buried his 1st Dynasty predecessor – need not rule out this possibility. Throughout the Dynastic age it was accepted that a son (Horus) would bury his father (Osiris), and that a new king should hold a funeral service for his dead predecessor, be he friend or foe, in order to justify his own claim to the throne.

Peribsen, sixth king of the 2nd Dynasty, returned to Abydos where he followed the old ways, building the modest tomb and lavish mortuary enclosure which suggest that he is a king with loyalties to the old traditions. Peribsen is, however, a far from conventional king. In choosing to write his name with a Seth animal rather than a Horus falcon presiding over his *serekh*, he becomes the only pharaoh to boast a Seth- rather than a Horus-name. It is surely no coincidence that his name is not found outside Upper Egypt until after his death. Peribsen's authority is confined to southern Egypt.

Seth was not at first sight an obvious choice of patron for any pharaoh. He was the enemy and divine opposite of Horus. He was anarchic and ill-disciplined, a troublemaker whose unappealing habits included murder, incest and sodomy. His very appearance confirmed his uncomfortable status, being a highly unnatural amalgam of jackal and donkey with more than a hint of aardvark and a curious straight, forked tail thrown in for good measure. But while Seth was a rebel he was still one of Egypt's gods. In any fight between chaos and *maat*, Seth would be firmly on the side of *maat*. The Egyptians were happy to include him in their pantheon, where his presence did much to make the other gods, all of whom were prone to bouts of bad behaviour, look good. Without Seth, Osiris would have been nothing. Two New Kingdom pharaohs would even bear a version of his name, Seti. There was no shame attached to revering Seth and Peribsen, perhaps a native of Naqada, was happy to honour his local god.

Peribsen's successor would revert back to the Horus-title, but would use two forms of the same name. His original Horus-name, Khasekhem or 'The Power [i.e. Horus] Rises', is given on vessels discovered inside the temple of Horus at Hieraconpolis and dated to 'the year of fighting the northern enemy'. Here Horus, restored to his *serekh* perch, wears the white crown of Upper Egypt, never the red crown of Lower. The king's revised Horus-name, Khasekhemwy or 'The Two Powers [i.e. Horus and Seth] Rise' is topped with both Horus and Seth above the *serekh*, and is accompanied by the phrase 'the two lords are at rest in him'. It seems that Khasekhem, originally king of southern Egypt, had managed to reunite his divided land.

Khasekhem had already provided himself with a funerary enclosure, a large double-walled rectangle built on top of a more ancient graveyard at Hieraconpolis. Now, to reflect his changed status, he felt it appropriate to relocate his mortuary complex to Abydos. Here he built the Shunet es-Zebib and, on the nearby Umm el-Qa'ab, an unusual gallery-style brick-lined tomb whose subterranean limestone burial chamber represents one of Egypt's first examples of large-scale stone architecture. His workmen employed fresh, sun-dried mud-bricks which soon proved unequal to their task; collapsing, they fell on, and partially protected, the tomb contents. Therefore, although Khasekhemwy's grave was robbed in antiquity, Amélineau was able to recover an impressive array of stone, copper, bronze and pottery vessels (some with thin gold covers tied in place with gold wire; some still filled with food), copper and flint tools, model tools, hundreds of semi-precious beads, the precious inlays from vanished furniture, tiles, a broken gold and sard sceptre and a few human skeletons.

An incantation for coming forth by day in the royal necropolis:

The word took form, all was mine when I existed alone. I am Re in his first appearance, when he shines forth on the horizon. I am the Great God who took his own form and created his names, the Lord of Enneads who has no rival amongst the gods. Yesterday is mine, and I know tomorrow.[3]

With Egypt reunited and the old traditions firmly back in place, we might expect to see increased devotion to Horus. Instead, as the 3rd Dynasty dawns, we see the gradual emergence of a stronger and more powerful kingship which allows both Horus and Seth to be gradually overshadowed by a third deity, the northern Re of Heliopolis. Re was represented either as a falcon, often soaring with wings outstretched, or as a winged sun disc.

This is by no means a sudden religious revolution, but rather a shift in approach to sun worship. Horus, often combined with Re to form Re-Horakhty, will always be recognized as one of Egypt's most effective deities and pharaoh, now a 'Son of Re', will continue to be a Horus King. The royal tombs, orientated towards the north since the building of Qaa's Abydos tomb, will retain their view of the unsetting circumpolar stars where the dead kings sparkle in the night sky. Nevertheless, as White Walls and Heliopolis grow in importance, as Egypt is increasingly governed from the north, Horus and Hieraconpolis are becoming marginalized. We have entered the Old Kingdom.

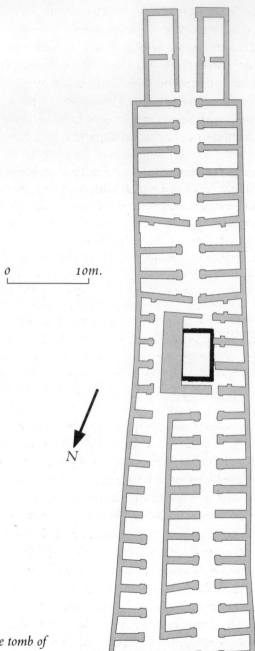

0   10m.

N

Figure 5.1   The tomb of
Khasekhemwy at Abydos.

Hathor, in the form of Bat the divine cow, smiles down on the Narmer Palette. As the daughter, or eye, of Re she is the essence of femininity, associated with motherhood, sexuality and sensuousness in all its forms. She may well be the evolved form of the faceless dancing female figurines recovered from the prehistoric graves. Hathor, however, has two incarnations. Her feared alter-ego, the lion-headed Sekhmet, consistently threatens mankind with an arsenal of war and plagues. Even her father has trouble controlling this wayward daughter:

Re, god of the sun and ruler of Egypt, had quarrelled with mankind. Unleashing the power of Sekhmet, he allowed his daughter to kill all who stood in her way. Egypt suffered. On seeing the horror and the bloodshed Re relented, but it was too late. Sekhmet could not be stopped. He appealed to the wise god Thoth, for help. Thoth made a lake of beer, dyeing it red so that it resembled a lake of blood. The bloodthirsty Sekhmet drank the beer and fell into a drunken slumber. As her rage slowly drained away, she was transformed into the kindly Hathor. Thus mankind was saved. But Re, appalled by what he had seen, retreated to the sky to sail his boat, crewed by the divine trio 'Creation', 'Authority' and 'Farsightedness'. Every day Re and his divine companions sail across the sky, passing from east to west before sinking below the horizon. Transferring to his night ship he spends the dark hours traversing the dangerous land of the dead. Each morning Re triumphs over death, rising to bring light to a grateful land.[4]

Re is the ultimate creator god – he has created himself. Now, with the contradictory logic which characterizes Egyptian theology, he is to be reborn every day. At dawn Re rises a vigorous, shining youth best represented by Khepri, the scarab beetle who pushes his ball of dung (the sun) tirelessly before him. At noon Re is at the peak of his powers. By nightfall he has become an old, spent man and may be represented as Atum, the most ancient form of the creator god. But even in his dotage Re retains his authority over his fellow gods. Re rules over the heavens just as Osiris rules the dead and Horus rules the living, and he gives his authority to the semi-divine king of the mortals.

The sun makes a very obvious, approachable deity. He has little need of a temple or a cult statue, as he shines in the sky for all to see. However, the idea of a democratic or accessible god did not fit easily with the concept of pharaoh as the sole link between the mortal and the divine.

Re would be granted his cult temples – not the usual gloomy buildings provided for Horus, Seth and Ptah, but light-filled temples whose roofs opened to admit the sun's rays – and thus the king would be able to control access to the god. Only the king or his deputies would be given the opportunity to offer the food, drink, clothing, incense and recitations which would persuade Re to continue in his natural rhythm across the sky.

Re was worshipped throughout Egypt, but his principal temple was situated in his home town of Iunu (Biblical On; archaeological Tell Hisn; today Matariya, a suburb of Cairo; more widely known by its Greek name Heliopolis or 'Sun City'). Re's temple, for centuries Egypt's most lavish, allocated space to the cults of Hathor and Iusaas, two fertility goddesses who inspired the sun god in his self-creation. Here the Mnevis bull, the sacred bull of Re, lived a life of total luxury, revered as the manifestation of the living sun god. Here too, kept safe within the 'House of the *Benben*', was the most important cult object associated with sun worship. The mysterious *benben* stone, the sacred ray of the sun made solid, stood in place of a cult statue of Re. There is no surviving illustration of the original *benben*, but we assume that it was a naturally shaped round-topped or conical stone, perhaps even a meteorite. Fifth Dynasty artists depict it formalized into a squat obelisk, while Middle Kingdom scenes show a long, thin obelisk. Akhenaten's New Kingdom *benben*, a crucial element of Aten worship, was variously a round-topped stone, an obelisk, and a free-standing stela.

The same word root, '*weben*', meaning to shine or to rise, is found in the name of the mythical, phoenix-like *benu* bird, a solar being which was able to regenerate itself. Legend tells how Re rose like the sun and assumed the form of the *benu* bird to perch on top of the *benben*; artists conventionally showed the bird as a heron and the stone as a stunted pyramid. Iunu included a 'Domain of the *benu*', possibly a sacred bird sanctuary.

The obelisk, a tall, tapering stone capped with a small pyramid (the *benbenet* or 'stone of the *benben*'; the name also given to the pyramid capstone or pyramidion), carved with royal and religious texts and often covered with sheet gold, also represented a solid ray of sunlight. It was a man-made *benben*, and as such was strongly associated with Re and Iunu. To erect a large-scale obelisk was a magnificent technical achievement, a true sign of devotion and an unmistakable mark of powerful kingship.

Naturally the largest obelisks of all were reserved for the solar deities; obelisks enhanced the temple of Re at Heliopolis and, during the New Kingdom, the temples of Amen-Re at Karnak and Pi-Ramesses. Today just one obelisk stands at Iunu, dedicated to Re by the Middle Kingdom pharaoh Senwosret I.

Iunu had been occupied since pre-Naqada times, her position at the south-eastern tip of the Delta making her a useful trading post whose desert pathways allowed contact with the near east, and whose port allowed links with the south. She was blessed with her own valuable resource: the Red Mountain (Gebel el-Ahmar) which rose to the south-east of the city yielded a quartzite so perfect it was reserved for the best of royal sculpture. Today ancient Heliopolis has disappeared, her stone lost to the nearby Roman fortress-city Babylon, her mud-brick buildings vanished beneath Cairo's north-eastern suburbs and her surviving monuments dispersed. The magnificent Old Kingdom temple of Re, 'The Great Shrine', has disappeared along with the rest, although the discovery of a large platform suggests that it was located at the heart of the city. Evidence for the growing importance of Iunu and the cult of Re at the start of the Old Kingdom is therefore somewhat meagre, and is limited to thirty-six fragments of a limestone chapel dedicated by the 3rd Dynasty King Djoser to the celebration of his *heb-sed* or jubilee, and pieces of both an obelisk and a shrine inscribed with the name of Teti, first king of the 6th Dynasty.

That the priests might, near these Pyramids, make their observations, I in no way question; this rising of the hill being, in my judgement, as fit a place as any in Egypt for such a design; and so fitter by the vicinity of Memphis. But that these Pyramids were designed for Observatories (whereas by the testimonies of the ancients I have proved before, that they were intended for sepulchres) is in no way to be credited.[5]

Modern clerics are dedicated men and women whose destiny has been determined by their religious conviction. They are somehow separate from 'normal' life, and are seldom expected to step out of their own narrow speciality. This distinction between secular and sacred matters did not exist in Egypt where priests were not selected by vocation, or by sect, but were drawn from the ranks of educated men who might be called upon to serve king and country in a variety of ways. Officials switched from religious to administrative posts and back again as required, often holding several offices simultaneously. Versatile men like the 3rd Dynasty Vizier Imhotep or the 4th Dynasty Vizier Hemiunu performed an astonishing range of duties; they were as likely to be found presiding over a court of law or designing and building a pyramid as they were to be found offering to Re. The position of High Priest would not become a full-time, exclusive post until the Middle Kingdom, and even then it would always be awarded to a top-rank civil servant, a career politician rather than a dedicated cleric.

We have already seen the priesthood acting as accountants and administrators. Now we find them acting as scholars, as mathematicians and scientists. Re's priests, led by the Great Seer (literally one who saw), recorded and measured the movement of the sun so that they might make the appropriate offerings at the correct times. Thus the solar temples were observatories and their priests astronomers who charted the sun's progress with religious zeal. Meanwhile, in other temples, darker temples whose stairways lead to open, flat roofs, priests were watching the behaviour of the moon and the stars. The king, as chief priest of all cults, was the master scientist who controlled both light and time. This was a very serious matter. Were it not for the offerings made and the hymns chanted by the king the sun, the moon and the stars would falter, time would stop and all light and warmth would be extinguished. The Egyptians knew that their time-honoured rituals, offerings and timekeeping were highly effective, as their sun never did fail.

The benefits of astronomical study extended far beyond the religious sphere. Navigation would never pose much of a problem in a narrow land where the river flowed from south to north, the wind blew from north to south, and the sun sailed from east to west, but architecture benefited hugely from the study of the sky. Knowledge of the sun, moon and stars allowed the precise alignment of people, buildings or tombs, something which mattered from the earliest of days when the Badarians chose to align their graves to face west. However, a word of warning. Before rushing to re-create the ancient observations, we must always remember that the stars which today shine above Heliopolis do not have the same configuration as the stars that twinkled over the pyramid builders. This makes it difficult for modern observers to relate the stellar map to ancient building patterns. Throughout the pyramid age the never-setting polestar was Thuban in Draco, the constellation of the Dragon, although when the Great Pyramid was built Thuban actually lay some 2 degrees from the celestial pole. Today, due to the 26,000-year cycle of polestars it is Polaris in the Little Bear, while in prehistoric times it was Vega in Lyra, which is today almost overhead as seen from Britain. It was around Thuban that Egypt's dead kings would shine, and it was towards Thuban that they would angle the entrances to their pyramids.

The early astronomers believed that they were looking at a solid yet somehow watery body arched above a flat earth and separated from it by the air. Other mythologies described a sun driven across the sky in a flaming chariot, but in Egypt the sun travelled more sedately, by boat. Egypt, the land of *maat*, lay at the very centre of the inhabited world, and the sky above was filled with stars, the sun and moon, birds, bats, flies, gods and the spirits of the dead. This view of the heavens was personified by the artists who decorated the New Kingdom tombs. In the 20th Dynasty tomb of Ramesses VI we see the lengthy, naked body of the sky goddess Nut stretched over Geb, the earth. This Nut is the sky of the underworld. She swallows the sun's disc in the west, it passes along her body – we are shown ten regularly spaced red discs – and in the morning is reborn between her legs in the east. The ten discs, plus the disc by Nut's mouth and the disc by her legs, represent the twelve hours of the night. In a deliberate symmetry she is stretched back-to-back with Nut the night sky, whose elongated body is decorated with stars. A thousand years earlier, in the pyramid age, Nut was already identified with the sarcophagus which carried the deceased as a pregnant woman carries a living child before birth. Nut had become mother to both Re and the dead king:[6]

You are Re who came forth from Nut who bears Re daily, and you are born daily like Re.

You shall place this lid of the sarcophagus upon its mother

Upper and Lower Egypt developed their own calendars long before they became a unified country. The northern solar calendar was, naturally, centred on the birth cycle of Re. By constructing a false horizon – a perfectly horizontal, circular, mud-brick wall – observing the position of the sun as it rose over the horizon at dawn, and using a plumb-bob to mark its northern and southern turning points or solstices, astronomers had calculated that it took one year or 365 days for the sun disc to return to his birthplace on the south-eastern horizon at the winter solstice. From this knowledge, and from observations of the lunar cycle, there developed a highly complex calendar of twelve months of varying length with, as the year averaged only 354 days, an occasional thirteenth month thrown in to make up the deficit.

Meanwhile southern Egypt employed a lunar calendar based on the regular behaviour of the moon and the annual disappearance of the Sirius, or Sothis, the Dog Star. Sirius was personified in the form of the goddess Sopdet, wife of Sah (Orion) and mother of Soped, and thus was part of a stellar family which paralleled the divine triad of Isis, Osiris and Horus. Every year, for approximately seventy days, Sirius was hidden by the sun's light. Suddenly, in mid July by our own calendar, as the time of inundation approached, Sirius would reappear just before sunrise on the eastern horizon. This helical rising, known to the ancients as the 'coming forth of Sothis', dictated new year's day or the 'opening of the year'.

The southern and northern systems worked well together but they were complex, irregular, and depended upon constant observation. Egypt being a lengthy country, temples situated at Aswan and Heliopolis were likely to obtain slightly different results, and festivals may have been celebrated at different times, and maybe even on different days, at the extremes of the country.[7] The gods did not seem to mind the confusion, but the bureaucrats did. After unification the two calendars were merged and simplified to give a civil calendar which could be used with ease the length and breadth of the land. The year would now be divided into twelve months of thirty days (giving four months per season) plus five extra 'epagomenal' days dedicated to the gods which together gave the necessary 365. There was, however, no leap year and no accounting for the extra quarter day which should have been included each year, so the official seasons slipped imperceptibly out of line with the actual seasons and with the old lunar calendar, which had been retained by the priesthood for the proper celebration of religious festivals. Only every 1,456 years (364 × 4) did the civil new year's day coincide with the new year's day (the rising of Sirius) of the religious and agricultural calendar. This was always a cause for great celebration.

The astronomer-priests went further. Day and night were each split into twelve hours, each hour being named and personified by a deity and each celebrated to encourage Re's solar boat on its hazardous journey across the sky and through the Underworld. But here time had to stop. There could be no subdivision into minutes and seconds as there was no accurate means of measuring such small moments. Without clocks there could be no strict 'Egyptian time' recognized from Aswan to Buto, but this was no great disadvantage; such systems are a relatively modern need and Britain, for example, only synchronized her clocks when the advent of the railways called for a universally applicable timetable.

With the advent of state building projects, timekeeping moved out of the temple and became the responsibility of the scribes who flourished on every construction site, down every mine and quarry, and in the royal dockyards. There could never be an official working day of, say 7 a.m. to 5 p.m. with an hour off for lunch, as this simply could not have been determined. The standard working unit in the Old Kingdom was a ten hour day, but it was an imprecise ten hour day determined by the local timekeeper. Indeed, the 'hours' of the elongated summer's day were always longer than those of winter.

Knowing how many had been summoned to the *corvée*, it was possible to plan the rate at which work would progress, to predict the building materials which would have to be supplied and, of course, having recorded how many days or part days each worker actually did work, to account for the rations which would have to be paid. Nothing was left to chance; every step was carefully monitored. While we lack the written records which detail the planning of the pyramids, we do have some of the records kept by the scribes who supervised the cutting of the New Kingdom tombs in the Valley of the Kings. Here we see the scribes meticulously listing the workers by name, counting man hours, recording excuses, authorizing supplies and inspecting the state-owned copper tools which have to be sealed in the official store every night. Papyrus Reisner I, the record of a Middle Kingdom building project dating to the reign of Senwosret I, is even more explicit: it shows the scribes carefully measuring the exact dimensions of various blocks of stone and then using these measurements as an accurate planning guide:[8]

Given to him in order to erect three interior portals: six workers, two and a half days [i.e.] fifteen [man days] . . .

It is implicit that any significant deviation from budget would be investigated thoroughly. Thus we find an anonymous Old Kingdom overseer employed in the Tura limestone quarry, eloquently querying the amount of time to be wasted distributing clothing when there were blocks to be shipped to the pyramids:[9]

Regnal year 11, 1st month of Shemu, day 23: The commander of the work gang says: An order has been brought to this servant from the Chief Judge and Vizier with regard to bringing the work gang of the Tura quarry to be given their clothing ration in his presence . . . This servant protests against this requirement as six barges are expected.
This servant has become accustomed to spending six days at the palace with the gang before it is clothed; we should waste only one day in clothing the gang.

The same meticulous bookkeeping and obsessive attention to detail is apparent in the records recovered from the ruins of the 5th Dynasty mortuary temples of Kings Neferirkare and Raneferef at Abusir.[10] The priests attached to the mortuary cults which supported the royal tombs and pyramids focused their attentions on the dead. They supplied the needs of the deceased in a well-prescribed routine which included the daily awakening and bathing of the cult statue, the morning and evening food offerings, the regular recitations and hymns, the scheduled sprinkling of the pyramid with cleansing holy water, the pedantic checking of assets (all seals had to have a regular inspection) and the reconciling of income received from the pyramid estates with the offerings and rations dispensed.

Mathematics, then, was the invisible skill which underpinned many aspects of dynastic life from art and architecture to taxation. It was a skill developed early; even the Dynasty 0 Narmer Palette shows an awareness of the canon of proportions, the grid of eighteen squares which dictated the positioning and size of body parts allowing arithmetical perfection to triumph over realism. This system would be applied to all official art from the Middle Kingdom onwards. Plato applauds the Egyptians for their mathematical skills: '. . . the teachers, by applying the rules and

1. Standing high on the desert plateau, above the Nile flood, this 1885 photograph shows the Giza pyramids as they would have appeared to their builders.

2. Today the modern city of Cairo encroaches upon the once remote desert cemetery of Giza.

3. The rectangular enclosure of Djoser's Sakkara Step Pyramid as seen from a Zeppelin in 1931. The pyramid appears the way it was imagined – as a true stairway to heaven.

4. Djoser's Step Pyramid, with the dummy chapels of the jubilee court in the foreground.

5. The serdab, with two eye-holes, which houses Djoser's Ka statue.

6. The immortal king stares out through the serdab eye-holes.

7. Snefru's collapsed Meidum pyramid now stands like a stepped tower amidst a mountain of rubble.

8. Snefru's Bent Pyramid at Dahshur.

9. King Snefru, greatest of the pyramid builders, sits surrounded by his royal titulary.

10. Painted limestone statues of Rahotep and his wife Nofret.

11. Aerial view of the pyramids of Giza taken from a Zeppelin in 1931.
The mastaba cemetery of the elite is clearly visible.

12. An elite Giza mastaba. Like the pyramids of the kings, the tombs of the Old Kingdom nobles were constructed from immense stone blocks.

13. A series of false doors belonging to the modest tombs of the pyramid builders at Giza.

14. Exploration of the Great Pyramid of Giza from *Le Costume Ancien et Moderne* by Jules Ferrario, engraved by Gaetano Zancon.

practices of arithmetic to play, prepare their pupils for the tasks of marshalling and leading armies, and organizing military expeditions, managing a household, too . . .'[11] It was rumoured that Pythagoras learned his geometry from Egypt. Text books such as the Middle Kingdom Moscow Mathematical Papyrus and the 2nd Intermediate Period Rhind Mathematical Papyrus, the somewhat immodestly titled *Correct Method of Reckoning, for Understanding the Meaning of Things and Knowing Everything . . .*, allow us to appreciate this skill first hand.[12]

The use of decimal numbers made the calculation of fractions – always unit fractions with numerator 1 plus the fraction ⅔ – relatively easy, although the lack of a zero seems curious and, of course, the need to write and indeed think (½ + ¼) rather than ¾ seems unnecessarily time-consuming to modern eyes. In the absence of multiplication tables, multiplication and division of both whole numbers and fractions were carried out by a laborious but entirely accurate method of adding and doubling; to take the simplest of examples, 2×2 would become 1×2 doubled, while 5×5 would become 1×5 doubled, doubled again, plus 1×5. This is arithmetic at its most basic level. The Rhind Papyrus poses a series of more taxing questions concerning the calculation of area (triangle, rectangle, circle), volume and pyramid slope alongside complex algebraic equations and problems concerning the sharing of produce. The calculation of the volume of a cylinder, essential for calculating the volume of stored grain, used the 'squared circle' method which gave an approximate value of *pi* of 3.16 (true value 3.1416): the Great Pyramid, whose height is in perfect proportion to its base, demonstrates this early understanding of *pi*.

SECTION TWO

Experimentation: Building in Stone

Yet though the pyramids may fairly claim to be the most famous and the best-known buildings in the world, the ignorance of the average mind with regard to them and the purpose for which they were reared is still just about as general and widespread as the fame of them; and the purpose of this chapter is, first, to tell what and how many, and of what kind they are; next, what was the end for which they were reared in the beginning of history; and lastly, to recount something of the efforts which have taught us what is really known about them.

James Baikie, *A Century of Excavation in the Land of the Pharaohs*: 49.

6

Djoser's Step Pyramid

As for the Pyramid in platforms (which is the largest at Sakkarah and next largest to the pyramid of Khafra) its position is so fine, its architectural style so exceptional, its age so immense, that one altogether loses sight of these questions of relative magnitude. If Egyptologists are right in ascribing the royal title hieroglyphed over the inner door to Ouenephes, the fourth king of the First Dynasty, then it is the most ancient building in the world . . . One's imagination recoils upon the brink of such a gulf of time.[1]

Amelia B. Edwards, journalist, traveller and patron of Flinders Petrie, was indeed standing before Egypt's most ancient stone building. A pyramid some 4500 years old whose door lintel and frame were carved with the royal Horus-name Netjerikhet, the ancient title of the first king of the 3rd Dynasty. Today this king is more commonly known by his Nebty or Nisu-bit name Djoser. The raising of this first pyramid had marked a watershed in Egyptian history. It had brought an unexpected divinity to its architect, the Vizier and Great Seer of Re, Imhotep, who was to be deified as Imouthes, son of the craftsman-god Ptah, and worshipped as a local form of the Greek god of medicine Asclepios. And it had brought a longed for immortality to its owner who would henceforth be celebrated as one of Egypt's most innovative kings.

Khasekhemwy had reunited and strengthened his divided country, and in so doing had restated the ideal of powerful kingship. The self-styled 'Overseer of Foreign Lands' was known and respected throughout Palestine and in Nubia, where a small campaign early in his reign stamped Egypt's authority on her southern neighbours. Back home, Khasekhemwy had proved himself a prolific builder. Not only did he erect the most impressive of the Abydos funerary complexes, he built

extensively at Hieraconpolis while endowing a series of cult temples in
Egypt's most prominent cities. He ordered fleets of ships and even, in
Year 15, commissioned an impressive copper statue to be named 'High
is Khasekhemwy'. His was a hard act to follow but Netjerikhet Djoser,
son of Khasekhemwy and his influential consort Nimaathap, 'Mother of
the King of Upper and Lower Egypt', was more than equal to the task.

It is therefore unfortunate that the glories of Djoser's own reign –
nineteen years[2] of confident prosperity, administrative competence, long
distance trade and mineral exploitation – are almost entirely forgotten as
archaeologists and architects concentrate on the Sakkara Step Pyramid
complex. Lack of space dictates that we too must focus our attention on
Djoser's funerary remains, but we should never forget that his ground-
breaking tomb is but one aspect of a successful, well-rounded kingship
founded on a secure economic base. A weak or bankrupt king could
never have aspired to such an impressive project.

Djoser buried his father at Abydos, including some of his own sealings
within both the tomb and the Shunet es-Zebib. His mother, too, would

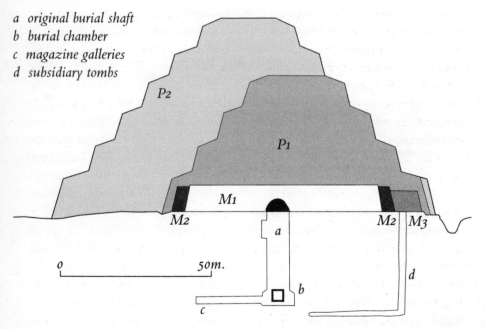

a *original burial shaft*
b *burial chamber*
c *magazine galleries*
d *subsidiary tombs*

Figure 6.1   Cross-section (looking north) of Djoser's Step Pyramid at Sakkara.

be buried in the south; an extremely large mastaba tomb at Beit Khallaf, not far from Abydos, has been assigned to Queen Nimaathap while a series of smaller mastabas in the same graveyard has been tentatively allocated to members of her birth family. But Djoser had determined upon a break with tradition, and now started to build his own mortuary complex on the high ground of the Sakkara cemetery. Shifting religious convictions may have played a part in this decision, although Re, Heliopolis, and the cult of the sun had not yet achieved the importance they would attain during the later Old Kingdom. It seems that Djoser's was first and foremost a practical move. Sakkara, close by White Walls and Djoser's principal palace, was well supplied with limestone quarries, an important consideration for a monarch who had decided to build in stone, and her masons were already experienced in tunnelling through the necropolis bedrock.

Djoser's complex would combine the best of northern and southern funerary architecture. Above ground it substantially replicated his father's Shunet es-Zebib enclosure, suggesting a natural evolution of the old architecture inspired by a new religious approach and, perhaps, by travellers' tales of raised temples in Mesopotamia. Both enclosures boast a pyramid/protopyramid in their north-west quadrant. Djoser's complex may be built in stone, but his ribbed papyriform pillars, rounded log-like limestone ceilings and niched and recessed stone walls are direct copies of the more ephemeral structures erected at Abydos, and most of his building blocks remain inconveniently mud-brick sized. Below ground, the warren of tunnels, galleries and rooms which surround Djoser's burial chamber are a purely northern tradition, highly reminiscent of the Sakkara gallery systems tentatively assigned to the lost 2nd Dynasty kings Hetepsekhemwy, Raneb and Ninetjer.

The decision to build in stone was a logical if ambitious extension of the stone burial chamber employed in Khasekhemwy's tomb and the more local stonework of the Gisr el-Mudir enclosure. Stone offered permanence and the unmistakable proof of powerful kingship. It was therefore very desirable. Technically it was, however, only just achievable. Stone was already the primary medium of official art. It had been used for many centuries in small-scale building projects and, of course, had been used to make tools from palaeolithic times onwards, but it had never been cut on anything like a commercial scale. Efficient quarrying

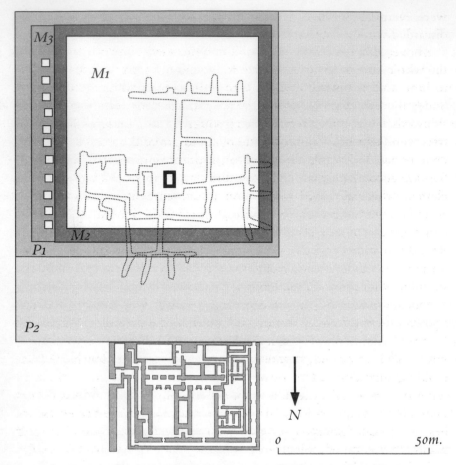

Figure 6.2   Plan of Djoser's Step Pyramid at Sakkara.

demanded skilled manpower, but the manpower was useless without the correct tools and these had to be made from copper, wood and hard stone. As work in the copper mines intensified, Egypt suddenly had to deal with an enormous demand for wood, both good quality imported timber which could be used to build ships and sledges and to make levers, mallets and packing cases, and inferior local wood as fuel for cooking, brewing, smelting and pottery and mortar production. Recycling was common practice; old ships' timbers were fashioned into levers or incorporated into sledges, and all broken or unwanted wooden artefacts were eventually burned (which explains why Egyptologists rarely find discarded wooden objects).

Above all, a large-scale stone monument required firm control over the whole country. Djoser needed to understand the resources available to him, and he needed to be able to claim those resources as his own. Suddenly there was a huge demand for goods and services. The quarries, shipyards, farms, mines, rope-makers, potteries and countless other industries were kept busy supplying the pyramid project and someone – the civil service under Imhotep – had to coordinate and record their efforts. Scribes, accountants, tax collectors and project managers were in their element; this was record-keeping on an unprecedented scale. Efficient, accurate communication was essential. It is highly doubtful that Djoser could have achieved his ambition in a non-literate state, and equally doubtful that the Egyptian civil service would have blossomed into the formidable administrative machine which it soon became without the stimulus of monumental building.

Efficiency in the quarries was a matter of paramount importance. Djoser was not short of manpower – during the season of inundation he could summon every able-bodied peasant in Egypt, should he so wish – and it was only the rate of supply of blocks which limited his building ambitions. The open Sakkara limestone quarries still preserve the traces of ancient stone-working, allowing us to reconstruct Dynastic techniques with a fair degree of accuracy. Here the limestone lies in regular, distinct layers separated by narrow bands of clay. This made the cutting of a block relatively easy. First, the unwanted rubble and sand would be removed from the limestone surface and the block would be marked out with red paint or shallow chisel marks. The masons, equipped with hard-stone hammers, wooden mallets, picks, punches and copper chisels (tools not too far removed from the tools used by all masons and sculptors until relatively recent times), would then cut a wide separation trench around the block. With the block isolated from its neighbours and the separation trench extending past the natural horizontal cleavage layer, long wooden levers could be manipulated to prise the block free.

While rough-cut, coarse-grained local limestone was deemed suitable for the inner parts of the structure – there was, after all, no point in moving stone further than absolutely necessary, and no need to use premium materials for the hidden parts of the monument – shining Tura limestone was to be used for the outer casing. But across the river at Tura the seams of good-quality limestone were hidden below ground and the masons were forced to tunnel into the quarry to reach their stone, creating a network of galleries and caverns within the limestone face.

Below ground, red and black Aswan granite would line Djoser's burial chamber. If life in the Tura limestone quarries was harsh, conditions in the Aswan granite quarries, lying almost 600 miles to the south in a far hotter climate, were much worse. Granite is too hard to be cut with simple stone or copper tools. Again work started with the removal of the inferior upper layers and the revealing of the good quality stone. This was accomplished by repeatedly lighting and dowsing fires to crack the rock surface. Next the block (or slab, or obelisk) was marked out so that its sides and underside could be cut by work gangs incessantly pounding dolerite hammer-stones against the unyielding surface. After weeks of mindless, repetitive, soul-destroying work – but not as many weeks as we might suppose; Hatchepsut's pair of obelisks were apparently quarried in an impressive seven months – and assuming that the block remained free of cracks and flaws, it could be levered free, dressed to its final shape by pounding and rubbing, and loaded on to a barge.

The Aswan granite faced a lengthy journey by boat. On the Umm el-Qa'ab it had been possible to manufacture mud-bricks almost on the doorstep; we may perhaps imagine local villages compelled to 'donate' a specified quota of bricks each week. Now it was necessary to transport and lift blocks which, although many remained mud-brick sized, occasionally weighed a ton or more. The season of inundation, when the water level was at its highest and the canals were brim-full, was the best time to move heavy blocks. However, at any time of year, the loading of a relatively fragile and unstable barge with heavy yet vulnerable stone was fraught with difficulty and there was always a high risk that the precious cargo plus the valuable barge would end up on the canal bottom. As yet, experimental archaeologists have failed to come up with a convincing explanation of how loading was achieved, although it seems reasonable to assume that a canal was cut to link the quarry to the Nile, and that the barge itself was totally surrounded by sand and earth banks to keep it steady. The classical historian Pliny has a suggestion to offer:

A canal was dug from the river Nile to the spot where the obelisk lay and two broad vessels, loaded with blocks of similar stone a foot square – the cargo of each amounting to double the size and consequently double the weight of the obelisks – was put beneath it, the extremities of the obelisk remaining supported by the opposite sides of the canal. The blocks of stone were removed and the vessels, being thus gradually lightened, received their burden.[3]

The transportation of a large block, a triumph of engineering, was considered an eminently suitable subject for funerary and religious architecture. A carving in the pyramid causeway of the 5th Dynasty King Unas shows a barge carrying two large granite columns from Aswan to Sakkara. The columns rest end to end, secured to sledges which in turn lie on wooden scaffolding, and the flow of the river helps the ponderous barge along. Seven hundred years later Queen Hatchepsut would include the transportation of her twin obelisks amongst the celebratory scenes decorating her Deir el-Bahari mortuary temple. Here the obelisks are towed on a vast sycamore barge by a flotilla of smaller boats. With the hard work of loading done, and the equally vexed problem of unloading yet to come, the moving of the obelisks becomes a colourful pageant – an excuse for people to watch and cheer from the riverbank. The question of how such unwieldy barges were returned to the quarries has not yet been solved, although it seems unlikely that they sailed back against the current; perhaps they were dismantled at the building site and returned in pieces.

Although the blocks would be moved as far as possible by water, all would eventually have to cross land. At Deir el-Bersha, in the early Middle Kingdom tomb of Djehutyhotep, we are shown a colossal statue being dragged from the Hatnub alabaster quarry to the river bank. This statue, 7 metres tall and probably weighing just under 60 tons, has been lashed by ropes on to a wooden sledge and is being pulled by teams of workers over a temporary road of wooden planks. The planks are placed in front of the sledge and then gathered up to be repositioned; the provision of a firm roadway is essential to prevent the heavy load sinking in the soft desert sand. Rollers are not used; modern experiments have confirmed that rollers actually increase friction and thus decrease efficiency. Here, to avoid friction and the overheating of the wood, water or liquid mud is being employed as a lubricant. The team is being encouraged in its work by a foreman who stands on the statue's huge knee and claps out a rhythm for his men. The use of sledges to tow heavy objects to the cemeteries will persist throughout the Dynastic age until sledges themselves acquire a magical mortuary significance. Tutankhamen's Canopic chest, a delicate and valuable object not intended to be dragged anywhere, was by no means the only item of New Kingdom funerary furniture to be equipped with symbolic sledge runners.

Experiments have shown that a team of six men would have no difficulty pulling a 5 to 6 ton block on a wooden sledge across a watered wooden track. With manpower freely available it seems that the main problem would have been to arrange the men – up to 3000, perhaps, in the case of a 1000 ton colossus – around the rope so that they each got a decent pull. The use of oxen instead of, or alongside, men would have alleviated this problem, as 3000 men could be replaced by 300 oxen. An image preserved at Tura does show a team of oxen dragging a limestone block, and this is reinforced by the discovery of cattle bones in the Middle Kingdom mortuary complex of King Montuhotep at Deir el-Bahari.

Monumental construction now dominated every aspect of Egypt's flourishing economy. While the royal workshops embarked on a perpetual mission to fill the royal storehouses, and hundreds of workmen were kept busy laying blocks at Sakkara, thousands more, men, women and children, were engaged in the back-up services which made any form of large-scale stone construction possible. At first sight this is conspicuous consumption gone mad; a dead-end waste of Egypt's prolific resources which would have to be repeated reign after reign as countless treasures and man-hours were buried alongside the defunct kings. However, this is to interpret the past through modern eyes. Djoser, who believed that his pyramid would ensure his own survival beyond death, would certainly not have regarded the project as a waste of resources.

In fact, monumental building – one enormous, continuous, national project – did bring economic benefits. Old Kingdom Egypt experienced the steepest of learning curves as Imhotep demanded that his builders produce stone columns, colonnades, porticoes and life-sized statues. An impressive increase in bureaucratic efficiency was sparked by the immediate need to coordinate the labours of thousands of people over hundreds of miles. Artisans, benefiting from unprecedented training opportunities, made huge leaps in technological ability; having built their first pyramid, Egypt's architects and masons felt with some justification that they could attempt almost anything and their confidence was reflected in the quality of their subsequent work. Meanwhile a constant demand for goods, and access to an unlimited supply of top-quality materials, allowed artists and craftsmen to perfect their skills.

Less easy to assess are the intangible benefits, the sense of national pride and religious satisfaction, which the completion of a pyramid might provoke in an enthusiastic young nation. The craftsmen who built the New Kingdom tombs in the Valley of the Kings have left us their written records; we know that they were accorded great respect by their fellow artisans as they alone were privy to the secrets of royal burial. It may well be that those who built Djoser's Step Pyramid experienced a similar feeling of pride as they toiled to become a part of Egypt's heritage. But as yet we have little knowledge of Djoser's workforce and it is presumptuous to credit them with anachronistic 'feel-good' motivation. Here we must simply mark hidden benefits as a possibility, and move on.

The precious Tura limestone, which allowed the pyramid to glisten and sparkle in the reflected rays of the sun, would prove irresistible to later builders who, before the introduction of recent government legislation, have always had a regrettable tendency to treat Egypt's most ancient monuments as convenient quarries of ready-cut stone. By stripping the cover off the Step Pyramid and exposing its rubble core, their destruction has allowed Egyptologists to examine the interior of the monument and reconstruct the stages in its construction. Today the damage of the past is being painstakingly repaired. The late Jean-Philippe Lauer, architect turned archaeologist, worked at Sakkara for over seventy years and it is thanks almost entirely to his efforts that the Step Pyramid complex glows once again on the landscape.

Imhotep's original design was for an unusual square, solid, stone mastaba-like structure (known to archaeologists as M1) with corners oriented to the points of the compass (or to the flow of the Nile and the rising and setting of the sun) and a burial shaft cut directly beneath. This was subsequently extended on all four sides to form a two-stepped mastaba (M2), again cased in white Tura limestone. A third extension to the eastern side then converted the square mastaba to a more conventional oblong shape (M3) while blocking the original access to the substructure. Proceeding with extreme caution – the courses of bricks were angled

towards the centre of the pyramid to ensure strength and core stability –
yet employing larger blocks, the mastaba then became the bottom step
of a four-step pyramid (P1). Finally the base was re-extended and an
impressive six-step pyramid (P2) emerged. In its final version the pyramid
gave the impression of a series of ever-decreasing mastabas piled one on
top of another in the manner of children's plastic stacking cups. However,
it had not been constructed this way, but was made up of accreted layers
of angled stone wrapped around a central core.

Djoser had built the equivalent of the proto-pyramid found in the
identical situation in the Shunet es-Zebib; a stepped mound which is
usually interpreted as a representation of the primal mound of creation,
a source of regeneration and rebirth, but which can with equal validity
be read as a symbolic stairway to heaven, a large-scale ladder which will
lead the dead king upwards to his destiny in the stars. Stairways are
already strongly connected with royal ceremonial, while easy access to
the heavens was naturally a matter of great importance:

The sky-goddess speaks: open up your place in the sky, for you are the Lone
Star, the companion of Hu. Look down upon Osiris when he governs the spirits
for you are not among them and you shall not be among them.[4]

The constant modification of the mastaba/pyramid plan is confusing.
Did Imhotep intend from the outset to build a pyramid, in which case
his gradual approach may be interpreted as a prudent means of ensuring
that the king always had a suitable tomb available? Or did his monument
evolve as construction progressed, as his workmen grew accustomed to
the stone and he himself became more confident in his abilities? The
casing of the original mastaba certainly suggests that it was intended to
stand as a building in its own right, and that it was extended because it
could be rather than because it had to be. Yet this building, had it been
left unmodified, would have been the only square mastaba in northern
Egypt – a circumstance which argues against it actually being a mastaba!

The failure to let go of an apparently completed project is something
which will be found time and time again in Egypt's history. Once the
builders arrived, they seemed incapable of leaving. The New Kingdom
Karnak temple is the classic example of inability to complete; here the
scaffolding never came down and the hammers were never stilled, as for

centuries every pharaoh felt that he or she could add just that little bit more which would make the complex perfect. The same thing is found at the pyramid sites, where builders repeatedly return to an essentially complete monument to modify an essentially finished design. Only when the pyramid owner dies does work stop – inevitably, the complex is incomplete. Here Djoser was no exception. He would die before his final building phase was finished, leaving the substructure, mortuary chapel and indeed most of the enclosure barely functional. Had he lived another twenty years, would we have seen the pyramid and surrounding complex extended to mammoth proportions? As it stands, the final version of the pyramid measures 60 metres high, has a ground plan of 121 by 109 metres, and holds an impressive 330,400 cubic metres of stone, rubble and fill.

The substructure was accessed, in the final pyramid form, by a shaft descending southwards from the courtyard of the mortuary temple which ran along the lower step of the northern pyramid wall. This temple was the heart of the royal mortuary cult, but its multiple rooms and open courtyard are today ill-understood. Djoser's burial chamber lay 28 metres below ground at the base of a wide shaft, 7 metres square, which dropped from the centre of his original mastaba (M1). The masons who excavated this vertical shaft did not attempt to haul their debris upwards, but removed their rubbish via a long stepped corridor which joined the shaft from the north and whose entrance lay well beyond the mastaba superstructure. However, the extension of the mastaba covered both the burial shaft and its service corridor; these were blocked to deter thieves, and a new access ramp was cut. Passing under the mortuary temple, and allowing access via a pit and stairway in the floor of the temple courtyard, the service corridor now ended in a trench to the north of the mortuary temple.

The claustrophobic granite-lined burial chamber, a mere 2.96 by 1.65 metres measured internally, could only be entered via a hole 1 metre wide in its ceiling. This made for added security but was highly inconvenient. It seems unlikely that the chamber could have held a conventional stone sarcophagus but this may not have been deemed necessary, as the closed chamber itself could have acted as a sarcophagus. The room directly above the chamber was destroyed by the dynastic tomb robbers who emptied the shaft in search of its treasures, but it seems that this must have been a 'manoeuvring chamber'; here the priests could make their final preparations before lowering the king to his eternal rest, and here they could store a massive granite plug. After the funeral this plug, weighing over 3 tons, was lowered into its hole, effectively sealing the chamber beneath. The access shaft was then filled with rubble rendering the king – in theory – untouchable.

The burial chamber lies at the centre of a warren of corridors and storerooms which is today further complicated by the tunnels excavated by determined tomb robbers and Late Period restorers. Here the bedrock is in some places soft, in others very hard, so that the earliest modern explorers were occasionally inspired to use explosives to clear its blocked passages. The ancient builders, denied gunpowder, spent almost two decades excavating their maze, and were eventually forced to abandon it incomplete.

When they left, the decoration of the passages and rooms to the east of the burial chamber was already well in hand. In the so-called 'king's apartment' – a cold, dark, suite provided for the dead pharaoh's soul – over 36,000 small plano-convex blue-green faience tiles had been stuck on to sculpted limestone to replicate the ridged reed walls of Djoser's earthly palace, an echo of the smaller but similarly coloured tiles employed within Khasekhemwy's Abydos tomb. We cannot hope to completely unravel the multiple symbolism of Djoser's underground palace, but we know that blue-green was the colour both of regeneration and of the waters which swirled around the primaeval mound, and it does not take too great a leap of the imagination to detect a reference to the 'Field of Reeds', the magical Afterlife of Osiris promised in the Pyramid Texts.

Here in the blue chambers of the subterranean palace one wall shows four panels surmounted by the *djed* pillar, sign of stability, holding up an arch. Another wall includes three limestone false-door stelae bearing scenes of the *sed* festival ceremonies; in two of the doors Djoser runs hard, carrying the document which entitles him to rule Egypt, in the third he stands proud before his gods. The *heb sed* was Egypt's most ancient ceremony of royal regeneration and rebirth; this made it emi-nently suitable for inclusion within the pyramid where the king himself would be reborn. Djoser is employing images of ceremony and victorious kingship which can be traced backwards through Den's Abydos sandal label to the triumphs of the Narmer Palette and Macehead. It was here that Lepsius discovered the true doorway which bore Netjerikhet's name and protocol. Unfortunately the eastern wall of the chamber was never finished and this part of the pyramid is now inaccessible.

Along the east side of the second phase mastaba (M2) eleven additional vertical shafts, approximately 30 metres deep, dropped to galleries running westwards under the pyramid. These were subsequently rendered inaccessible by the easterly extension (M3). The first five of the galleries were provided for the burial of Djoser's immediate family; his consort, Hetephernebty, their children and, perhaps, his ancestors. In contrast, shafts VI to XI led to storage galleries. These have produced an astonishing number – up to 40,000 – of hard stone vessels, platters and cups including examples carved with the names of Egypt's 1st and 2nd Dynasty pharaohs. Why did Djoser require so many second-hand vessels? Had these been looted from the royal tombs, perhaps during the lawless period which marred Peribsen's reign, and then reclaimed by Khasekhemwy and his son? Or had they come from the old tombs, temples and storerooms which must have been demolished to make way for Djoser's own complex?

Djoser's body has never been found. The Step Pyramid has, however, yielded human remains. In 1821 the Prussian General von Minutoli and his Italian engineer Geronimo Segato reported the discovery of mummy parts within the pyramid, including a gilded skull and a pair of golden sandals, but these were subsequently lost at sea in a storm. All that today remain are a mummified left foot wrapped in fine linen and coated in plaster, a segment of an upper right arm and shoulder and assorted pieces of skin, chest and spine, recovered by various archaeologists from the burial chamber but not necessarily belonging to its original occupant.

The loss of his body was only a minor hiccup in Djoser's quest for immortality. Imhotep had foreseen this disaster, and had provided his king with a substitute body, a refuge for his dispossessed Ka. In the *serdab*, a small, dark, enclosed kiosk resting against the pyramid beside the mortuary chapel, sits an almost life-sized painted stone pharaoh. Dressed in a long robe, bouffant tripartite wig, cloak and striped head-cloth and wearing the false beard which proclaims his kingship, the dead pharaoh stares with unwavering dignity through two eye-holes, gazing not at his subjects but, thanks to a subtle tilting of the front wall which reflects the angled back wall of his kiosk, up at the northern sky. His own eyes, once inlaid with precious rock crystal, have been mutilated and now are blank. Countless tourists queue to peer through the holes and stare at the blind king. What they see is, however, a replica. The original statue is now protected in Cairo Museum.

As all statues were capable of housing the Ka, they were all potential instruments of regeneration and rebirth. Their restorative powers, their ability to substitute for the dead king, and their ability to express the essentials of kingship – the king as victor, the king as upholder of *maat* – made them an appropriate addition to mortuary architecture. Colossal statues, each named, each revered, and each, of course, unimaginably expensive, now start to play an increasingly important role in the royal funerary cults and it is unfortunate that the vast majority of these statues have been lost – smashed, stolen and recarved – leaving only empty niches, hollow bases and vacant plinths to testify to a most important aspect of mortuary ritual. In addition to its serdab statue the Step Pyramid complex has yielded a statue base inscribed for Djoser and Imhotep, an unprecedented honour for a non-royal:

. . . Vizier of the King of Lower Egypt, the first after the King of Upper Egypt, administrator of the Great Palace, noble lord, High Priest of Heliopolis, Imhotep the builder, the sculptor, the maker of stone vases . . .

We also have a base which shows the king's feet subduing the Nine Bows, the traditional enemies of Egypt, and four bases plus feet (two adult, two children) found in a pavilion or chapel, which probably represent Djoser in his dual role as King of Upper and Lower Egypt, and his daughters Hetephernebty and Inetkaes. These two princesses are named on several of their father's stelae, and are shown in miniature kneeling beside their father's throne and embracing his ankle on one of the fragment's of Djoser's smashed limestone chapel recovered from Heliopolis.

The first explorers to investigate the Step Pyramid paid little attention to the ruins of the surrounding buildings.[5] We must not fall into the same trap. The Step Pyramid was just one element – albeit the central, dominant element – in Djoser's wider mortuary complex and should not be taken out of its context. The pyramid was the tomb which held the king's remains; it was the place where his spirit would attain immortality and, as such, it was imbued with a latent magic which would be sparked into life by his burial. The courts and buildings surrounding the pyramid each had their own particular functions, and their own particular magic.

Several buildings, the mortuary temple in particular, were connected in a very practical way with the rituals of death and the cult of the dead king. However, Djoser's complex also served as an eternal palace. To fulfil this role it was provided with inaccessible symbolic buildings, idealized stone replicas of Egypt's most important shrines plus permanent copies of the more ephemeral mud-brick and reed buildings which were erected for use in the rituals of living kingship. It is this aspect of the complex, the fossilized palace, which gives it its unearthly, almost eerie atmosphere. Djoser's stone doors, meticulously equipped with stone hinges, stand either permanently open or resolutely shut. Few of his portals are real. Here, in a narrow courtyard lined with vaulted shrines – shrines with rubble cores barred to the living but open via false doors to the dead – we find the raised platform with a double staircase where the dead king could don the appropriate crown and sit in ritual splendour, facing White Walls, on the twin thrones of Upper and Lower Egypt. Here, too, we find the court where the king's spirit might run the ritual *sed* race – the all-important race which, in theory at least, proved that Djoser was still fit to rule Egypt.

Djoser's pyramid enclosure, built in stages like the pyramid itself, eventually measured an impressive 545 by 277 metres. It stood behind a massive, palace façade-style limestone wall over 1600 metres long, 10.5 metres high, and equipped with fourteen false doors each with its own ritual significance, plus one true entrance. The wall itself may have been encircled by a continuous ditch or dry moat cut into the bedrock, although to date only sections of this ditch have been excavated. The northern area and the three joined mounds of the western massif remain substantially unexcavated, and the best-known and most fully restored buildings are concentrated in the southern and eastern sections of the enclosure, and in the area around the pyramid.

Access to the complex was gained through the door at the southern end of the eastern face of the enclosure wall. This opened into a narrow corridor which in turn led into an imposing entrance – two ever-open doors carved in stone – and a columned hall built alongside a now vanished structure known as the 'oblique building'. Here in the gloom

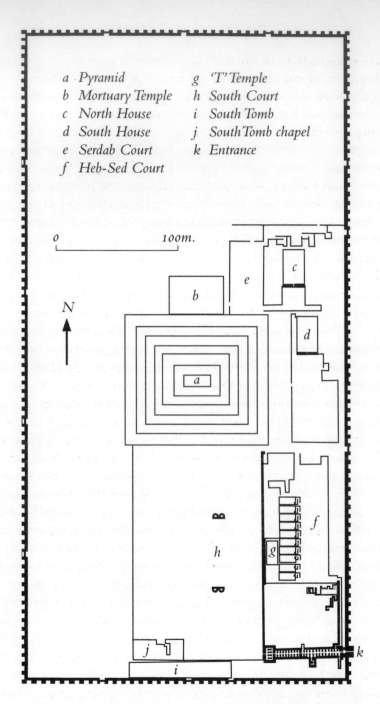

a Pyramid
b Mortuary Temple
c North House
d South House
e Serdab Court
f Heb-Sed Court

g 'T' Temple
h South Court
i South Tomb
j South Tomb chapel
k Entrance

0   100m.

N

Figure 6.3   The Djoser Step Pyramid Enclosure at Sakkara.

of the colonnade it seems that the architect's courage failed him; the twenty pairs of columns, each standing some 6 metres high and each carved to resemble a bundle of reeds or palm stalks are anchored to the stone walls. Imhotep was by no means certain that free-standing columns would prove strong enough to support the heavy limestone ceiling which was itself carved to mimic wooden beams. Flanked by the columns are a series of small rooms or chapels whose precise purpose is as yet unknown.

The South Court (180 by 100 metres) separates the pyramid from the southerly enclosure wall. Here is the petrified replica of the *sed* festival or jubilee arena where pharaoh, donning a tight-fitting kilt and a crown (either the red, white or double crown), and carrying a flail and stick or parchment roll, would run between 'D'-shaped territorial markers to prove beyond doubt his fitness to reign. In his 1971 novella *The Scorpion God* William Golding's god-pharaoh ran a desperate *sed* race to ensure his land's regeneration. In Egypt's more ancient and bloodthirsty past ageing rulers, those who failed in their run, may well have been killed, but by the time Djoser came to the throne the race was no longer a matter of life and death. Indeed Djoser himself, with a reign of nineteen years, may not have been called upon to run the race. In theory, if not always in practice, the jubilee was celebrated after the first thirty years of continuous rule and thereafter with increasing frequency. Den and Qaa, both long-lived kings, are known to have celebrated jubilees.

The South Tomb, situated in the south-western corner of the South Court, has puzzled archaeologists for decades. Above ground, the South Tomb has a conventional mastaba form. Below ground, accessed by a descending stairway, is a burial chamber lined with Aswan granite but too small to hold a coffined body, an intact manoeuvring chamber and a series of corridors and chambers, some of which are decorated with reed-like blue-green faience tiles and incorporating false door stelae showing Djoser running his *sed* race. Who or what – if anything – was buried in this small-scale tomb? Some experts feel that it must have been a provisional tomb made ready in case the pyramid was incomplete at Djoser's death. Others have suggested less practical purposes: it may have been a dummy tomb, modelled on the ancient royal tombs of Abydos and provided for the use of the dead king's soul; it may have been the burial place of the crowns of Egypt, or a statue of the dead king; it may even have been the last resting place of the royal entrails or the royal placenta. Whatever its purpose it was clearly important. Later pyramid complexes would all incorporate a small-scale satellite pyramid, the equivalent of Djoser's South Tomb.

To the north of the entry colonnade is a rectangular suite of chambers of unknown purpose. Further north again lies the *sed* festival complex, the narrow shrine-lined court and throne platform whose symbolic role has already been discussed, and beyond this are found the South House, a ruined complex including an open courtyard and a chapel, and the North House, a smaller version of its southern namesake. The purpose of these pavilions is again unknown, although Lauer, in an echo of the 'fortress of the gods' interpretation of the Abydos funerary enclosures, has suggested that they may have been provided to allow the king's Ka to receive the ghostly representatives of Upper and Lower Egypt. There is some evidence to suggest that these ritual buildings were partially buried in sand almost as soon as they were completed; a deliberate act of concealment and preservation which emphasizes, if such emphasis were needed, the nebulous, living-dead magical purpose of Djoser's pyramid complex.

7

A Brief History of
Failed Step Pyramids

*The pyramids themselves, doting with age, have forgotten the names
of their founders.*[1]

Djoser had set a precedent that his successors felt bound to follow. Such
was the competitive nature of Egyptian kingship that every pharaoh
wanted to outshine the predecessor who was, technically, merely an
earlier version of himself. There could be no turning back to mud-brick
mastabas: nothing less than a stone step-pyramid would do. However, a
successful pyramid builder needed luck on his side. He needed wealth,
peace and an unassailable position, but above all he needed time to
complete his work. Egypt remained prosperous and at peace – indeed,
with the opening of the Sinai turquoise mines, she was wealthier than
she had ever been – but she was entering a phase of short-lived pharaohs
incapable of leaving lasting monuments. In consequence, the history of
the later 3rd Dynasty becomes little more than a list of royal names and
failed pyramid projects.

A piece of ancient graffiti carelessly scrawled on the enclosure wall
suggests that Imhotep, architect of Djoser's mortuary complex, was
retained by his son and successor Sekhemkhet. This is impossible to
confirm, but Sekhemkhet's complex was certainly modelled on Djoser's
own, suggesting that the two shared an understanding of the king's role
beyond death. Sekhemkhet's chosen site lay to the south-west of Djoser's
enclosure. This was not the most obvious building site – it indicates a
strong desire to be buried alongside Djoser – and the uneven land had
to be levelled and terraced before construction could start. Here, as with
Djoser's complex, the basic plan was to be re-thought and expanded in
stages until it surpassed Djoser's own. In its final form the palace-façade
enclosure wall with one true door was to measure 500 by 200 metres; it

was to include a seven-step square-based pyramid which, standing some 70 metres high, was designed to dwarf its neighbour. There was to be a South Tomb topped by a small mastaba, and a series of other buildings of unknown purpose.

Directly beneath the centre of the pyramid, the subterranean burial chamber was to be surrounded by galleries including a royal 'apartment'; this suite of chambers would be surrounded in turn by a set of galleries incorporating at least 132 storage rooms, each packed with precious goods. But Imhotep was thwarted by time. Sekhemkhet's six year reign proved woefully inadequate for such an ambitious project and his embryo pyramid, a mere 7 metres tall, never rose above its enclosure walls.

Sekhemkhet's forgotten complex, totally shrouded in sand, was redis-covered by Zakaria Goneim in the early 1950s.[2] Digging to the north of the pyramid, Goneim was able to locate the passageway leading to the burial chamber; this yielded animal remains, a set of 6th Dynasty papyri and, most unexpectedly, a 3rd Dynasty collection of vessels and golden objects including twenty-one bracelets which must have been abandoned by the ancient thieves who looted the storerooms. Moving downwards, passing under a vertical shaft which led upwards through the body of the pyramid, Goneim discovered vessels whose clay sealings gave the only clue to the pyramid's owner: Sekhemkhet.

The rough-hewn burial chamber lay at the end of the passageway, with its original blocking apparently in place. Here lay an impressive, narrow (too narrow to hold a wooden coffin but wide enough for a mummy), rectangular sarcophagus, carved from a single block of polished alabaster and closed by a sliding end panel operated by ropes. On top of the sarcophagus was what appeared to be a withered funeral wreath, although subsequent analysis has shown the 'wreath' to be decayed wood. Goneim believed that the sarcophagus was sealed with its original mortar; he thought he had discovered an intact royal burial. It is hard to imagine his embarrassed disappointment when, in May 1954, in front of an invited audience of dignitaries and journalists, he raised the heavy end panel only to find the sarcophagus empty.[3]

Unknown to Goneim, hidden beneath its unfinished mastaba the robbed burial shaft of the South Tomb did hold a body; that of an anonymous two-year-old child protected by a wooden coffin and accom-panied by the sorry remains of a once elaborate burial. But what had happened to Sekhemkhet? Goneim's insistence that the alabaster sarcophagus was sealed and the burial chamber blocked when first discovered suggests that the pyramid had served as a cenotaph rather than a tomb. There is a general feeling, however, that Goneim may have been mistaken, and archaeologists tend to refer with tactful caution to the 'apparent' sealing of the sarcophagus. As the excavator is now dead, and unable to defend his opinions, they can go no further. The most widely accepted explanation is that the king's mummy was indeed interred in the sarcophagus beneath his unfinished pyramid but was subsequently destroyed by the thieves who plundered his storerooms. The 'sealing' of the sarcophagus would therefore be a relatively recent accumulation of dust and debris. The fate of the unfinished complex after the king's untimely death is uncertain.[4]

If we know little about Sekhemkhet we know even less about his successor, but it is fairly certain that Khaba, too, set out to build a stepped pyramid. While there is no evidence to link Khaba directly with the so-called 'Layer Pyramid' built at Zawiyet el-Aryan, a part of the Memphite cemetery approximately 4 miles to the north of Sakkara, a series of inscribed stone bowls recovered from a nearby, contemporary, mastaba suggest that he was its founder. Khaba's monument, although smaller than those of his predecessors (had he learned from Sekhemkhet's failure?) was definitely more showy; situated on the edge of the floodplain rather than set back in the desert, it could be seen by all. However, man proposes, the gods dispose. The Layer Pyramid is today represented by the accreted or 'layered' lower levels of its core which are angled inwards to give strength to the whole structure. It would have eventually risen to a height of 42 to 45 metres, in perhaps five steps. The substructure, a simplified version of Sekhemkhet's tomb, was incomplete at the king's death and did not include a stone sarcophagus. We have no idea where Khaba was eventually buried, although it is tempting to speculate that he did make use of his pyramid. This is a site which would clearly repay further exploration;[5] unfortunately Zawiyet el-Aryan, at the heart of a prohibited military zone, is today inaccessible.

The Horus King Sanakht – who is probably to be identified with the *nesu-bit* Nebka recorded by Manetho at the start of the 3rd Dynasty – probably succeeded Khaba. Again, evidence for his brief reign is scarce, and in the absence of any known tomb, Sanakht's most impressive 'monument' is a pair of inscriptions carved in the Wadi Maghara, Sinai.

Huni, the last king of the 3rd Dynasty, proved more durable than his predecessors, and the Turin Canon tells us that he enjoyed a reign of some twenty-four years. Egypt at last had a pharaoh capable of completing impressive building projects, and build Huni certainly did. Not satisfied with one stone monument, he ordered a chain of small-scale three- and four-stepped pyramids stretching throughout his land: the examples at Zawiyet el-Meitin (near Minya, Middle Egypt; the only one of the series built on the west bank), Sinki (south Abydos), Tukh (near Naqada), el-Kula (near Hieraconpolis), south Edfu and Elephantine West Isle still survive, and a seventh example, at Seila (Faiyum), may be added to the list although the recent discovery of a limestone stela and offering table indicates that this pyramid was completed if not built by Huni's successor, Snefru. Uninvestigated remains at Athribis, in the Delta, suggest a tentative eighth. Huni's ownership of the granite pyramid built at Elephantine is confirmed by the discovery of a large inscribed cone bearing his name, and the pronounced similarity of the five southern pyramids suggests that they were all built in the same reign. Much smaller than the Sakkara funerary monuments, the step pyramids are none the less impressive; the largest surviving example, the four-stepped Seila pyramid, still stands almost 7 metres high. Although constructed from a variety of local materials by differing bands of local workmen, it seems correct to consider the pyramids as one project built under royal authority.

None of these pyramids is precisely aligned to the compass points, none has a burial chamber, none has a full mortuary complex although they do have their own compounds, and none has yielded a body. While their purpose is nowhere explained, they do make one important point. Pyramids are already strongly associated with the rituals of dead kingship, but they are not always tombs – they can be taken out of their mortuary context. It remains, of course, entirely possible that the provincial pyramids were built to serve as cenotaphs either for the king or his queens, but the lack of a recognizable mortuary complex renders this theory unsatisfactory. So far pyramids have been confined to northern Egypt, while stone architecture has rarely been seen outside the royal necropolis. Had Huni and Snefru determined to erect a chain of easily identifiable territorial markers – perhaps one for every province, or nome, one outside each regional palace, administrative centre or tax collection point, or one beside each important temple – which would serve as obvious reminders of pharaoh's nationwide power? Were the provinces themselves raising pyramids – under royal command – in tribute to their king? In either case the pyramid would have served a multiple purpose. It would have been a unifying, easily recognized symbol of the king's extensive power – a form of royal logo – and, after the king's death, could have served as a cenotaph and as the focus of the regional royal mortuary cults. If this was the original idea, it was a short-lived one. By the end of the 4th Dynasty the Elephantine pyramid precinct was being invaded by workshops, and during the 5th Dynasty it was substantially lost beneath the town cemetery.

Huni's own tomb has yet to be discovered but, given his longevity and his fondness for pyramids, it seems highly unlikely that he would have been satisfied with an old-fashioned mud-brick mastaba. Archaeologists have long believed, with little real evidence to support their belief, that he started to build the Meidum pyramid which was to be finished by his successor, Snefru, and which is discussed in detail in Chapter 8. An alternative suggestion that he may have built the unique mud-brick-cased 'pyramid' identified by Richard Lepsius to the north of Giza at Abu Roash, should be discounted. This structure, ruined at the time of its discovery, is a collapsed mound of mud-brick lying over a natural rocky outcrop which is itself riddled with later Old Kingdom tombs. In its present form it bears little resemblance to any known 3rd Dynasty royal tomb.

8

Snefru, Master Builder

Inside his sumptuous palace the elderly King Snefru was bored. He wandered from room to room, seeking the elusive something that would amuse him. Finally, almost overcome with ennui, he summoned the high priest, Djadjaemankh, and sought his advice. Djadjaemankh knew his king well: he proposed a wonderful plan. Twenty of Egypt's most beautiful maidens – each blessed with a curvaceous body, well-rounded breasts and elaborately braided hair – were to row on the palace lake. In a refinement added by the king, they were to dress in garments made entirely of netting.

Snefru sat beside the lake entranced; never had he been so happy. The sun shone, the water sparkled, the reeds waved lazily in the gentle breeze. Out on the water the maidens rowed up and down with a slow, steady stroke, their skin glistening with sweat, their net dresses tracing exciting patterns on their naked flesh. Suddenly the tranquillity of the moment was broken. The leading maiden gave a cry of distress; a precious turquoise ornament had fallen from her hair and was lost in the water. The rowers stopped in confusion. The king promised to replace the trinket but the maiden could not be comforted and it seemed that the happy spectacle was over.

Again Snefru summoned his high priest. Djadjaemankh, possessor of an awesome magic, spoke one secret word and the waters became solid. Carefully folding one side of the lake back on to the other, he reached down to collect the jewel. A second command restored the lake to its watery form. The king was mightily impressed, and Djadjaemankh's triumph was celebrated with a great feast which lasted well into the night.[1]

The scribe who preserved the legend of Snefru's fabulous court approved of the king and his all too understandable penchant for semi-naked women. Although this is by no means a contemporary story – the anonymous writer wielded his paintbrush almost a thousand years after Snefru's death – nor, presumably, an entirely truthful one, it does reflect a strong folk tradition. Like Djoser before him, Snefru was regarded as a good and wise king and an eminently suitable god. His cult would be celebrated in the valley temple of his Bent Pyramid for many centuries.

Snefru had inherited a healthy country. The southern border was firmly established at the first Nile cataract where Aswan and Elephantine, once heavily fortified garrisons, were evolving into prosperous towns. Now a series of military campaigns allowed him to push back the frontier and establish a useful trading settlement at Buhen. He returned home in triumph, bringing with him an impressive seven thousand prisoners and many thousand cattle. Military strikes to the east and the west reinforced Egypt's authority, kept the Bedouin and the Libyan nomads under control and protected the turquoise and copper mines which were crucial to Egypt's economy. The grateful Sinai miners would later deify the king who had guaranteed their safety. Nowhere does Snefru admit that these missions were designed to capture an unsalaried workforce – pharaohs preferred to promote their battles as glorious crusades against the forces of chaos – but the snatching of prisoners to 'help' on building sites, down mines and in quarries, was a welcome fringe-benefit of war.

Back home things could not have been better. The Nile was behaving in exemplary fashion and there was food for all. Snefru's civil service thrived while his priests were kept busy managing the land, observing the sky and offering to the gods. Arts and crafts blossomed, stimulated by the demanding funerary industry, and writing became more accessible. Wealth and power were increasingly centralized in the person of the king, and as White Walls flourished the provincial cemeteries, a good indicator of regional status, were entering a genteel decline. Snefru himself, however, remains something of a cipher. Once again we are facing a pharaoh who is almost entirely represented by his funerary monuments.

Snefru's chosen name, 'to make beautiful', neatly summarizes his ambitions and achievements. The Palermo Stone tells us that Snefru commissioned ships, imported timber – forty vessels packed with cedar wood – opened quarries and built a magnificent but unfortunately long-vanished wooden palace. His greatest claim to fame is that he built the first true or straight-sided pyramid. In fact Snefru, inheriting his

throne as a relatively young man and enjoying an enviably long reign –
the twenty-four years suggested by the Turin Canon and the twenty-nine
years recorded by one version of Manetho is contradicted by the contemporary graffiti found inside his Dahshur pyramids which indicate a rule
of up to fifty years – had both the time and the resources to substantially
complete three large pyramids plus the small Seila pyramid already
discussed. Together these monuments hold more than 3.5 million cubic
metres of stone. The Great Pyramid complex may have been larger and
technically more advanced but it is estimated to hold a 'mere' 2.7 million
cubic metres of stone; in terms of sheer weight, Snefru was the greatest
builder of the Old Kingdom. In recognition of his prodigious architectural achievements, and despite the fact that he had demonstrably close
links with the preceding pharaoh Huni, Manetho chose Snefru as the
first king of his 4th Dynasty.

The scribe Ankhkheperresenb, son of Amenmesu the scribe and reader of King
Tuthmosis the justified . . . came here to see the beautiful temple of the Horus
King Snefru . . . He found it like heaven within when the sun god is rising in
it . . .[2]

The moment that Egypt changed from the step to the true pyramid is
captured, like a fly in amber, within the collapsed mound of the Meidum
pyramid.[3] Meidum, 30 miles to the south of Memphis, was perhaps
Huni's chosen site, but Huni had died before his pyramid started to rise.
Now Snefru took over, determined to make the project his own. This
made good sense. So far only one pharaoh, Djoser, had managed to
complete a pyramid-tomb, and even his complex was unfinished at his
funeral. By usurping a prepared site, Snefru was giving himself a head
start on the construction work. Soon Huni's role was forgotten and
Meidum town was, until the 12th Dynasty, known as Djed Snefru,
'Snefru is Steadfast' or 'Snefru Endures', the name of the village built to
house the priests and servants of the pyramid complex.

Royal tombs no longer started as a mastaba. At Meidum the initial
plan was for a seven-stepped pyramid (E1) constructed in angled, accreted
layers. But, as this neared completion with the fourth step built and the
outer casing in place, it was extended upwards and outwards and a more
impressive eight-stepped pyramid (E2) was born. The new pyramid was

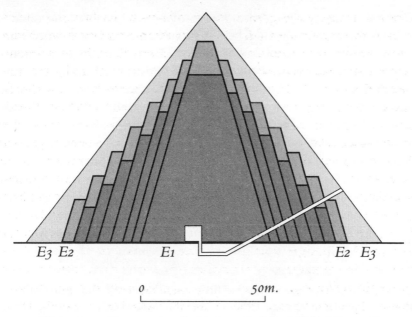

Figure 8.1   Cross-section (looking west) of the Meidum Pyramid.

tied to the old framework, its blocks too were laid in angled accretions and it was cased in fine Tura limestone. Either to save time, or to reflect changing religious beliefs (or both) the interior had been vastly simplified. Gone were the extensive subterranean galleries and storage rooms – Snefru did not intend to be buried with all his worldly possessions – and gone too were the 'royal apartments' provided for the comfort of the Ka. Art, magical art, which would function when his tomb became fully empowered after the funeral, could substitute for real goods and ritual buildings. The entrance was, however, still situated on the northern side so that it faced the circumpolar stars, and the burial chamber remained orientated on the north–south axis.

A long, sloping passageway led from a doorway above the first step, down through the body of the pyramid to a subterranean chamber. Here two small rooms stored the blocks that would eventually seal the burial. Beyond this a shaft rose upwards to the tiny burial chamber (a mere 5.9 by 2.65 metres) which lay at ground level within the superstructure. A corbelled limestone ceiling, used for the first time inside a pyramid, ensured that the weight of the pyramid would not flatten the deceased.

There was no stone sarcophagus within the chamber. This is a curious omission. Although it would have been possible to hoist a full-sized sarcophagus up through the entrance shaft, and indeed ropes and beams have been recovered which might have been used for this very purpose, this would have involved much hard work which could easily have been avoided by placing the sarcophagus within the chamber as it was being built. It may therefore be that, as in Djoser's pyramid, the snug, stone-lined burial chamber itself served as a sarcophagus.

After fifteen years the site was abandoned, unfinished, as Snefru started to build elsewhere. But towards the end of his reign the workmen returned to convert the step pyramid into a true pyramid (E3). This they did by extending the sides – building not on rock foundations, as the old base had been, but on layers of limestone blocks – and filling in the steps with a packing of local stone laid flat rather than inclined inwards. The whole edifice was then re-cased in Tura limestone. In its final form the pyramid was intended to stand approximately 95 metres high, with a square base whose sides measured 144 metres, and a base angle of between 51° and 53°.

The original seven-stepped structure had not been properly bonded to its eight-stepped successor, and both had been cased in slippery limestone. This eventually caused the heavy outer layers of the pyramid to slide downwards, leaving a square, three-stepped, tower-like core standing amid a mountain of sand and rubble and the ruins of the pyramid complex. We should not assume, as many older references do, that this collapse was caused by the theft of the pyramid's outer casing as sections of lower casing survive beneath the rubble mountain to prove that the pyramid was never fully stripped.

Although Kurt Mendelssohn[4] has argued on theoretical grounds that the pyramid must have collapsed while it was being built, there is neither archaeological nor textual evidence to support this thesis and as yet we have found no pathetic tomb-builders crushed with their tools beneath the rubble. Given the survival of Djed Snefru well into the Middle Kingdom, it seems reasonable to assume that the disaster occurred long after Snefru's death. As there are New Kingdom tombs incorporated in its rubble we know that the pyramid had at least partially collapsed by the New Kingdom. This collapse continued into modern times. When Taqi ad-Din visited the site in the fifteenth century he saw a five-stepped structure.

Frederick Norden, visiting three centuries later, sketched only three steps.

Snefru's pyramid had not been properly finished. Ramps still rested against the pyramid face, obscuring and protecting the lower casing. The sarcophagus-less burial chamber was undressed and the tiny mortuary chapel was incomplete; its round-topped stelae, the focus of the funerary cult, were to remain eternally blank. The open causeway which stretched from the mortuary chapel, across the desert, ended not in a stone temple but, we assume, as all trace has now vanished and the high-water level makes investigation difficult, in an ephemeral mud and reed structure. With Snefru dead and buried elsewhere, Khufu had no interest in completing his father's abandoned monument.

Yet Meidum, in its final form, provides the blueprint for the 4th Dynasty pyramid complex. The pyramid, invariably now a true pyramid, stands in the desert, orientated east–west to face the rising sun. The mortuary chapel, which is built against the eastern rather than northern face, is linked by a lengthy causeway to a valley temple built on the edge of the cultivation. A small-scale satellite pyramid is sited to the south of the main pyramid. The valley temple, joined by canal to the Nile, serves as the gateway to the funerary complex. It is here that the boat will moor when it delivers the king's body for burial. Although the complex is a linear one, the intricate architecture and narrow doorways of the two temples make it difficult to process straight towards the pyramid.

The practical purpose of the complex is hard to assess, although there is general agreement that the pyramid served as a tomb, and that the mortuary temple acted as the focus of offerings for the soul of the dead king. The function of the valley temple, the interface between the lands of the living and the dead, is harder to define. Suggestions that the king may have been mummified within his complex, either with the valley temple serving as the place of ritual purification (*ibu*) and the mortuary temple as the embalming workshop (*wabet*), or with the valley temple as a combined *ibu* and *wabet*, lack any supporting evidence and, of course, assume that the king will die close to his pyramid. As illustrations in non-royal tombs invariably represent the *ibu* as a flimsy reed structure, it seems more reasonable to suggest that both *ibu* and *wabet* took the form of temporary shelters erected beside the valley temple and ritually destroyed after the funeral.

We may be tempted to dismiss Snefru's straightening of the stepped

pyramid sides as a simple cosmetic exercise, an attempt to obtain a more
satisfactory sparkle from the polished white casing. This is in fact what
happened; the limestone acted as a mirror to reflect the sun's rays and
the pyramid was transformed into an awesome, dazzling source of light
and heat. But while this enhanced beauty added to its appeal, the change
in pyramid shape had a more fundamental importance and is just one of
the changes which are now apparent in the wider pyramid complex.
Gone are the large rectangular enclosure, the north–south orientation,
the fossilized palace and the ritual buildings favoured by Djoser and
Sekhemkhet. The orientation of the entire complex has been twisted
from north–south to east–west, although the entrance to the burial
chamber remains on the northern side of the pyramid, and the pyramid
is no longer central but stands at the end of a line of sacred buildings.
The literal stairway to heaven has been replaced by a smooth ramp – a
streamlined mound of creation which mimics the spreading rays of the
sun in the way that the *benben* and the obelisk represent the power of light
made solid. Snefru does not expect his Ka to waste eternity replicating
meaningless earthly rites; he is prepared to abandon the trappings of
mortal kingship and move on. Without entirely rejecting eternal life as
a circumpolar star – he still takes the precaution of facing north – he is
preparing to align himself more firmly with his gods. He will sail for ever
in the solar boat of Re and, as a pharaoh reborn after death, will assume
many of the attributes of Osiris, King of the Underworld.

To the north of the Meidum pyramid complex, beyond its limestone
wall, a series of mastaba tombs housed Snefru's favoured sons and courtiers. Later, a well-organized cemetery would be established, but never
properly completed, to the west of the pyramid. Proximity in death to
the royal tomb was a highly prized privilege, a privilege reserved for
Egypt's elite.

Snefru had an extensive family. From the very beginning the pharaohs,
unlike their subjects, were both polygamous and prone to favour inces-
tuous marriages which mirrored the brother–sister union of Osiris and
Isis. While he only had one consort – Hetepheres, the queen who acted
as mother to the nuclear royal family which, under ideal circumstances,
would furnish his heir – Snefru's harem housed a series of lesser queens
and these in turn produced large numbers of children, all of whom
required tombs. The prospect of many children brought a virtual guaran-

tee that there would always be a son (Horus) available to inherit his dead father's (Osiris's) crown, but not all princes were born equal and, in the enclosed world of the harem, the status of the child depended upon the status of the mother. Sons born to the consort outranked their brothers. Sons born to secondary queens found themselves in an uncertain position with just a faint possibility that one of them might inherit the throne. At times of dynastic uncertainty the harem became a hotbed of plotting and intrigue. It is not, therefore, surprising that the king housed his harem away from the court. Only the immediate royal family plus a few favourites actually lived alongside pharaoh.

Buried beside Snefru's pyramid, but outside the complex wall, we find some of the sons who learned their royal business first-hand by serving as high-ranking priests, soldiers and officials. One exceptionally large mastaba was built of mud-brick but packed with limestone chips, a useful by-product of pyramid construction. As the mastaba completely covers the limestone-lined burial chamber, we know that its owner must have died and been buried while Snefru's pyramid was under construction. It has yielded an impressive granite sarcophagus housing a plundered male mummy, its bones defleshed and wrapped separately in finest linen. The tomb is anonymous but, given its size and location, must have belonged to someone of utmost importance. While there remains the faint possibility that this is the lost burial of Huni, interred beside his own, unfinished pyramid, the fact that the neighbouring mastabas belong to Snefru's courtiers suggests that this was the tomb of the crown prince who had predeceased his long-lived father. Today there is a police observation post perched incongruously on top of the mastaba (and two more in the rubble of the collapsed pyramid).

Nearby, the Vizier and 'Eldest Son of the King' Nefermaat, another lost heir, was interred in a large and elaborately decorated mastaba. Nefermaat's wife, Atet, was included in the same mastaba although a system of separate entrances, both located on the eastern side of the superstructure, ensured that their twin burials and limestone-lined cruciform funerary chapels remained entirely separate. Atet's chapel includes colourful scenes of daily life; we see offering bearers carrying wine and figs, men building a papyrus boat, a naked child playing with a monkey and two men – the courtiers Serefka and Wehemka, sons of the deceased – netting fowl. Here too we see Atet's husband, curiously described as 'he who made his hieroglyphs in writing that cannot be removed'. This cryptic remark suggests that Nefermaat invented the new, and short-lived, method of decoration employed on the earlier sections of their chapel walls.[5]

Although the colourful geese who walk in a demure line across the painted plaster north wall of Atet's chapel are counted amongst the most natural and lifelike of ancient Egyptian images, the increasing use of stone within funerary architecture was by now allowing the production of incised or raised relief and this, infinitely more durable than plaster, quickly became the preferred means of decoration. It was not until the 6th Dynasty that simple painted plaster was again popular within the tomb.

. . . Of all known Egyptian statues those of Prince Ra-hotep and Princess Nefer-t (sic) are the most wonderful . . . the princess wears her hair precisely as it is still worn in Nubia, and her necklace of cabochon drops is of a pattern much favoured by the modern Ghawazi. The eyes of both statues are inserted. The eyeball, which is set in an eyelid of bronze, is made of opaque white quartz, with an iris of rock crystal enclosing a pupil of some kind of brilliant metal. This treatment – of which there are one or two other instances extant – gives the eyes a look of intelligence which is almost appalling. There is a play of light within the orb, and apparently a living moisture upon the surface, which has never been approached by the most skilfully made glass eyes of modern manufacture.[6]

The double mastaba built for Rahotep, 'Priest of Heliopolis, Overseer of the Task Force, King's Son of his Body and Director of Bowmen', and his wife Nofret, yielded two beautiful, almost life-sized painted limestone statues recovered from the cult temple hidden within the mastaba core. Today these are housed in Cairo Museum. Although entirely separate the seated figures form a pair. Egypt's upper classes put much effort into making themselves look as different as possible to the rest of the population yet as similar as possible to each other. Cleanliness was the luxury which most obviously distinguished the rich from the poor. The elite appeared clean in body, teeth and clothing, they were perfumed and hair-free. Their faces were adorned with cosmetics, their heads topped by wigs, their nails were manicured and their clothing glittered with colourful jewellery. Individuality, in dress or appearance, was not appreciated and is rarely found in two- and three-dimensional art. Here, for once, it seems that we are looking at people, not stereotypes. Husband and wife are extraordinarily lifelike, the inlaid eyes adding an uncanny appeal to their faces. While Rahotep's cropped hair and dashing moustache give him a contemporary, almost debonair look somewhat reminiscent of Clark Gable, Nofret appears a typical Egyptian lady, stolid and pale in her bushy bobbed wig and tight white sheath dress covered with a stole.

While the masons laboured in stone at Meidum, Snefru had built himself a new mud-brick palace. White Walls remained the bureaucratic capital but the court was now based at Dahshur, some 25 miles to the north. Inevitably, perhaps, Snefru determined to be buried alongside his new capital. The Meidum step pyramid was abandoned at stage E2, and work started on the virgin site chosen for Egypt's first true pyramid. This, 'The Southerly Snefru Shines', is recognized today less poetically as the 'Bent', 'Rhomboidal', 'Blunt' or 'Double-Sloping' Pyramid because of its obvious change of angle two thirds of the way up.[7]

Snefru's architects were still feeling their way. They were working with a relatively new medium at a new site whose workers had no tradition of monumental building, and they were now expected to build upwards, at an untested angle. The true pyramid required far greater accuracy of measurement and alignment than a step pyramid. To make matters worse, the quarrymen had started to supply larger stone blocks which increased quarry efficiency but which were far harder to transport and lift in place, while the old-fashioned desert clay mortar had been replaced with gypsum mortar which required careful preparation if it was to function correctly. Mistakes were costly, and could be dangerous; time was of the essence as the king was getting on in years. Building works started, but all too soon it was realized that the chosen angle of approximately 60° was far too steep for safety. This was quickly modified to a more achievable 54° by extending the base of the pyramid.

There remained, however, a problem with stability. The pyramid was being built on soft, silty clay rather than on firm rock, and only its outer casing rested on an artificial stone base. The core, which would be hidden beneath the casing, was a mess, its courses uneven and disjointed, its mortar ill-prepared. Even though the masonry was angled inwards there were huge subsidence problems and cracks were appearing in the partially complete internal chambers. The masons filled the cracks with gypsum plaster, shored up the walls with wooden beams, gritted their teeth, and worked on; meanwhile the architects went back to the drawing board. The angle of the pyramid was to be adjusted to a flatter 43° 21′ some 45 metres up the face and, as it was realized that the angled courses and the carelessly laid core were contributing to the instability, the masons were to start laying their blocks flat. Stability was restored, even if dignity was lost, and the reduced angle brought the added benefit of lowering the finished height and therefore reducing the amount of stone needed to complete the pyramid.

Like its Meidum cousin, 'The Southerly Snefru Shines' was provided with an entrance part way up its northern face. From here a steep passageway led downwards to an underground, corbelled room; above this lay the corbelled burial chamber, accessed via a hole in its floor. However, this pyramid had a second entrance. Running downwards from the western face a lengthy passageway led past a sophisticated portcullis system, into a second corbelled burial chamber built at a higher level than the first. Eventually, the two systems would be linked by a narrow passage brutally forced through the body of the pyramid.

There may even have been a third system of passages. The 19th-century explorer John Shae Perring tells us that when he first broke through the northern entrance, at a time when the western entrance was still blocked, there was a rush of wind which blew so strongly for two days that 'the lights would with difficulty be kept in': he concluded that 'the apartments must have had some other communication with the outside air'. Ahmed Fakhry, too, has noted a breeze within the pyramid: 'when working inside this pyramid in recent years, I have noticed that, on some windy days, a noise can be heard . . . This noise sometimes continues for almost ten seconds and it has occurred many times. The only explanation for it is that there is still an undiscovered part of the interior . . .'[8] We are therefore faced with the tantalizing prospect of further passages waiting to be discovered.

We do not know why the pyramid had two separate burial chambers. Although the two entrances call to mind the double husband and wife mastabas being built for Snefru's children, a twin burial of king and queen within the same pyramid would have been unprecedented. The provision of a separate burial chamber for the Ka seems a more likely explanation, although this need would eventually have been met by the building of the satellite pyramid. The answer may lie with the structural instability which was always apparent within the pyramid. Perhaps the architects, wary of subsidence and confused by the conflicting demands of the old-style stellar and new solar theologies, were hedging their bets and providing their king with a choice of chambers.

A small satellite pyramid complete with cult temple lay to the south of the main pyramid, within its enclosure wall. We may deduce that this was started after the main pyramid, as its blocks are laid in the new horizontal style. This is a perfect, true pyramid whose internal structure, complete with ascending and descending passageways and a miniature 'Great Gallery', foreshadows that which will be built within Khufu's Great Pyramid. Once again the burial chamber is too small to have housed a human body, and it seems that the pyramid was intended to fulfil the same functions as Djoser's enigmatic South Tomb. Ultimately, however, as the Bent Pyramid was abandoned in favour of the nearby Red Pyramid, the entire Bent Pyramid complex was transformed into a satellite tomb built on the grandest of scales to service its neighbour.

The mortuary temple was, as at Meidum, a surprisingly small and internally simple structure, dwarfed by its pyramid. It held an alabaster offering table and a pair of round-topped stelae bearing the king's image, name and titles. This uncharacteristic simplicity suggests that these were not fully functioning mortuary temples, but chapels built to serve the cults of the two pyramids, which were destined to serve as cenotaphs rather than tombs.[9] Certainly the mortuary temple attached to Snefru's third pyramid, the Red Pyramid, was much larger than its predecessors, although as it was destroyed many years ago, it now survives in ground plan only.

From the temple of the Bent Pyramid a walled causeway ran eastwards passing through the limestone enclosure wall and travelling across the desert to the wadi which housed the valley temple. A further causeway must have connected this temple to the river. The small valley temple was built of white limestone and surrounded by a forbidding mud-brick wall decorated with images of the king. Its rectangular plan was orientated north–south; entering through the doorway in the southern face the priests passed through a series of storerooms and crossed an open court

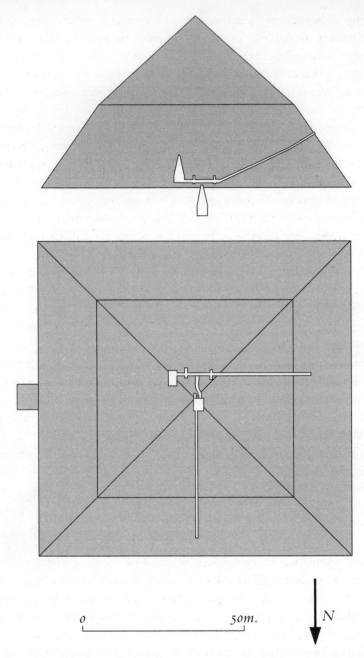

0   50m.   N

Figure 8.2   Cross-section and plan of Snefru's Bent Pyramid at Dahshur.

to enter a portico whose ten carved limestone pillars showed Snefru participating in the *sed* festival rituals. Beyond the pillars, and almost entirely hidden by them, were six stone statues of Snefru housed in niches protected by wooden doors. Each of these statues was an object of worship, and each represented a different aspect of Snefru's kingship.

To the north-east of the pyramid, a second elite cemetery was begun. Here lies the mastaba tomb of Prince Kanefer, another crown prince who predeceased his father. However, Snefru was not happy with the way his blighted now-Bent Pyramid was progressing, and during his 30th regnal year he started work on a second Dahshur pyramid.

Snefru's architects, traumatized by their earlier experiences, had learned some important lessons. The North or Red Pyramid, known to its founder as 'Snefru Shines', was a true pyramid whose prudent slope of 43° 22' makes it the flattest of all pyramids. This flatness undoubtedly aided the robbers, ancient and modern, who have thoroughly stripped its polished exterior, revealing the red stone core beneath. The new pyramid had a square base of 220 metres and a height of 105 metres. It was built on a sturdy limestone platform and its blocks were from the outset laid flat rather than angled towards the core; this meant more work – the masons were required to cut the casing stones to the shape of the pyramid – but increased stability. The one corbelled burial chamber, built within the body of the pyramid, was preceded by two corbelled, ground-level antechambers and reached via a passageway sloping from the northern face. For the first time, the burial chamber had been twisted round, so that it was orientated east–west, and therefore aligned with the pyramid complex.

Against the eastern face of the pyramid the mortuary chapel shows signs of hurried completion, an indication that this one perfect pyramid was chosen as the final resting place of the ailing king. Mummified assorted male human remains – a damaged skull with strips of skin still attached, pieces of rib, part of a left foot, the bandage from the right foot, a hip fragment and a finger – were recovered within the burial chamber and have been identified as belonging to a man just past middle age. Snefru reigned for perhaps as long as fifty years; if these are indeed his remains he must have acceded to the throne as a very young boy.

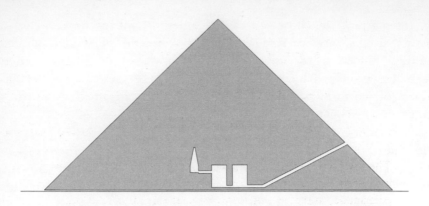

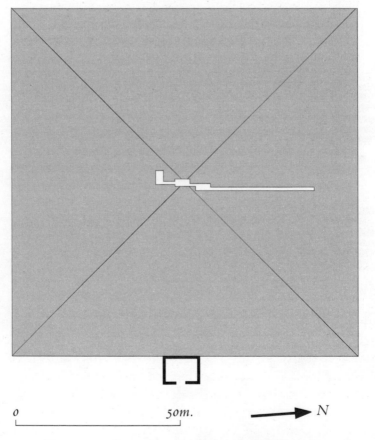

0   50m.   N

*Figure 8.3   Cross-section and plan of Snefru's Red or
North Pyramid at Dahshur.*

Standardization:
The Great Pyramids

The first glimpse that many travellers now get of the Pyramids is from the window of the railway carriage as they come from Alexandria; and it is not impressive. It does not take one's breath away, for instance, like a first sight of the Alps from the high level of the Neufchatel line, or the outline of the Acropolis at Athens as one first recognizes it from the sea. The well-known triangular forms look small and shadowy, and are too familiar to be in any way startling. And the same, I think, is true of every distant view of them, – that is, of every view which is too distant to afford the means of scaling them against other objects. It is only in approaching them, and observing how they grow with every foot of the road, that one begins to feel that they are not so familiar after all.

Amelia B. Edwards, *A Thousand Miles up the Nile*, 1877: 13

9

Khufu's Great Pyramid

Prince Hardjedef, wise son of the great King Khufu, started to tell his story:

'There is a man named Djedi who lives in Djed-Snefru. He is 110 years old yet he eats 500 loaves of bread and half an ox each day, washed down with 100 jugs of beer. He can rejoin a severed head. He can compel a lion to walk behind him without a lead. And he knows the number of hidden chambers in the sanctuary of Thoth.'

Khufu was intrigued. For years he had been trying to solve the riddle of the hidden chambers. He demanded to see the old man at once. Hardjedef sailed to Djed-Snefru and returned with the sage, his children and his books. He brought Djedi to the palace where he was granted an immediate audience with the king.

Khufu asked Djedi if he could rejoin a severed head. When Djedi confirmed that indeed he could, Khufu sent for a prisoner so that he might test the magician's powers. But Djedi refused; surely it was forbidden for even the king to decapitate a fellow man? The king conceded, and a goose was brought instead. The unfortunate fowl was executed and its head placed on the east side of the hall, its body on the west. When Djedi uttered his potent spell the goose and the head moved together and were joined, and the goose started to cackle. Khufu then asked the magician about the number of chambers in the sanctuary of Thoth, but Djedi could only direct him towards the place that the number could be found.[1]

History has credited Khufu with none of the kindly eccentricity of his father Snefru. He is a harsh king, a tyrant happy to execute a man for his own entertainment. Herodotus, about as far removed in time from Khufu as we are from Herodotus, believed that the king whom he knew as Cheops was intrinsically bad; that he had closed the state temples, banned animal sacrifices and exploited his people, forcing them to toil under the harshest conditions:[2]

So wicked was Cheops that, when he had spent all his treasure and needed more, he sent his daughter to work in a brothel, ordering her to earn a certain sum; how much, I was never told. This she managed to do. However, at the same time, having decided to build a monument to her own memory, she asked each client to give her a stone. With these stones she built the middle pyramid of the three that stand in front of the Great Pyramid.

The tale of Khufu's tyranny passed into the writings of Diodorus Siculus and thence, further distorted, into Josephus who declared Khufu the oppressor of the Hebrews.

In fact there is no contemporary evidence to suggest that Khnum-Khufu[3] ever oppressed his people, but then, leaving his prodigious building achievements aside, there is virtually no evidence of his reign, good or bad. His monumental statuary is today all lost and our only near-contemporary view of the king is provided by an ivory carving in Cairo Museum. This, a mere 7.5 centimetres high, shows Khufu seated on a throne and wearing the red crown.[4] The Palermo Stone has little more to offer; it preserves only four years of Khufu's reign, making a vague reference to the carving of statues and recording one solitary Nile level. This meagre detail is eked out by evidence of foreign missions – to Lebanon to acquire cedar wood, and to Nubia to acquire ivory and gold – and by the now standard expeditions to Sinai in search of turquoise and copper.

Snefru had been an exceptionally long-lived monarch. In all too many cases a lengthy reign brings problems for the ageing heir, but in this instance it worked to Khufu's advantage as he survived at least three older brothers to become a long-lived pharaoh. The Turin Canon suggests a reign of twenty-three years, Herodotus gives him fifty and Manetho allows him sixty-three. Khufu was young enough, secure enough and optimistic enough to embark upon an ambitious building project, and he lived long enough to move a considerable amount of stone. In this he was aided by his Vizier and nephew Hemiunu, son of the Prince Nefermaat who had served as Vizier and perhaps architect to his own father Snefru.

Hemiunu's formidable limestone statue, recovered from his Giza mastaba, shows an elderly statesman whose flabby, sagging body and drooping breasts contrast sharply with his small head and somewhat un-Egyptian sharp-featured face; the upper face is in fact a slightly doubtful reconstruction as the original was damaged by the thieves who extracted its inlays. On the statue base we read Hemiunu's principal achievements: he was Vizier, High Priest, Keeper of Sacred Animals, Elder of the Palace, Overseer of the Royal Scribes, Director of Music and 'Overseer of all construction projects of the king'.

Like his father before him, Khufu chose a virgin pyramid site. The Giza Plateau lay 25 miles north of Dahshur, close by White Walls. It was roomy, offered a firm bedrock base and had a limestone quarry close by. Today this quarry displays a chequered design of irregular raised plinths, the bases of vanished blocks separated by the trenches where Khufu's masons squatted to work, removing just under 2.8 million cubic metres of stone.

In the first or second year of his reign the king left his comfortable palace and journeyed into the hot desert to perform the all important foundation ceremony, sacrificing animals, making offerings, wielding a ritual measure and calling on the goddess Seshat, patron of scribes and builders, to support him in his project. As he retreated to the land of the living, work started in earnest on *Akhet Khufu* or 'The Horizon of Khufu', The Great Pyramid of Giza, the earliest and last surviving Wonder of the Ancient World.

Khufu's pyramid holds three chambers linked by a simple system of passageways. From the entrance, 16.5 metres up the northern face and over 7 metres to the east of the central axis, a steep passageway descends first through the body of the pyramid then through the bedrock to level out and enter the incomplete 'Subterranean Chamber' (12 by 7.5 metres) which has a curious, unfinished, blind tunnel leading off to the south. Part-way along the descending passageway, still within the body of the pyramid, is the entrance to the equally steep ascending passageway. This opens into the impressive 'Grand Gallery', a tall (8.7 metres), corbelled corridor whose walls are made from seven layers of overlapping limestone blocks. There are low ramps running along each side of the gallery, their surfaces displaying alternating large and small square holes which coincide with niches in the walls.

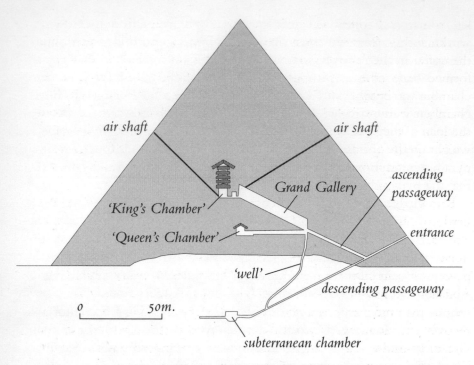

Figure 9.1   Cross-section (looking west) of Khufu's Great Pyramid at Giza.

The lower west wall of the gallery includes the small hole which leads to the 'well', a vent which drops almost to the end of the descending passageway. Here, too, is the entrance to the horizontal passageway which leads south into the ill-named 'Queen's Chamber'. This, almost complete, is built of limestone, measures 5.8 by 5.3 by 6 metres, and includes a corbelled niche which may once have housed Khufu's Ka statue.

The Grand Gallery leads upwards to an antechamber, which in turn give access to the red granite box (10.5 by 5.2 by 5.8 metres) which forms the burial chamber, the so-called 'King's Chamber'. Here lay Khufu's enormous, plain and empty red granite sarcophagus: measuring 2.28 by 0.99 by 1.05 metres and oriented north–south it was, to the seventeenth century explorer John Greaves, 'a narrow space, yet large enough to contain a most potent and dreadful monarch, being dead, to whom, living, all Egypt was too straight and narrow a circuit . . .' To the less romantic Flinders Petrie it was merely a disappointing piece of workmanship: 'It is not finely wrought and cannot in this respect rival the coffer in the Second Pyramid.' The ceiling of the burial chamber is formed from nine massive granite slabs which started to crack as the chamber was being built. To prevent further damage, five stress-relieving chambers were provided directly above the burial chamber; these spread the load of the pyramid which would otherwise have put an intolerable weight on the ceiling. It is here, hidden from view, that we find the only pyramid inscriptions; casual scrawls left by the work gangs which confirm that the pyramid belonged to Khufu.

Knowledge of the internal geography of the Great Pyramid is the hard-won fruit of centuries of investigation by a diverse band of intrepid explorers who, driven by archaeological zeal and a primeval urge to discover hidden treasure, were not afraid to tackle its dark and dangerous passageways, its infestations and ghosts. The twelfth-century writer Abou Abdallah Mohammed Ben Abdurakim Alkaisi[5] tells us that the first serious pyramidologist was the Caliph el Ma'mun. He, determined to recover the fabulous 'pyramid treasure', doused the north face of the Great Pyramid with hot vinegar in a frustrated attempt to crack its blocks. The Caliph eventually forced his way into the pyramid with the aid of a battering ram – his hole forms the entrance used by tourists today – and entered the descending passageway. Here his incessant pounding released the stone which hid the granite plug blocking the entrance to the ascending passageway. Moving upwards, burrowing round the plugs, the Caliph discovered the Queen's Chamber filled with bats and intrusive Late Period mummies, while beyond this 'the higher point of the pyramid was accessible by a passage about five paces wide, but without stairs or steps'. Rumour had it that the Caliph found the gold-encrusted mummy of the king: 'a human body . . . in golden armour, decorated with precious stones, in his hand was a sword of inestimable value and above his head a ruby the size of an egg . . .' However, given that the pyramid had been thoroughly looted by the Middle Kingdom, this seems highly unlikely.

The next significant investigation was conducted by the astronomer John Greaves, whose entertaining *Pyramidographia, or a description of the pyramids in Egypt* was published in 1646. Greaves thrilled his stay-at-home readers, caught in the midst of the English Civil War, with a first-hand description of the perils and discomforts of pyramid exploration:

Having passed with tapers in our hands this narrow straight [the Descending Gallery], though with some difficulty (for at the farther end of it we must serpent-like creep on our bellies) we laid in a place somewhat larger and of a pretty height, but lying incomposed; having been dug away, either by curiosity or avarice of some, in hope to discover an hidden treasure; or rather by the command of Alamoun [el Ma'mun] the deservedly renowned Caliph of Babylon. By whomsoever it were, it is not worth the inquiry, nor does the place merit describing, but that I was unwilling to pretermit any thing; being only an habitation of bats, and those so ugly, and of so large a size (exceeding a foot in length), that I have not elsewhere seen the like.

In 1763 Nathaniel Davison explored the well which dropped from the Grand Gallery. Dangling from a rope held by workmen terrified of the pyramid ghosts, equipped with paper, a compass, a measure and a lighted candle, he made an uncomfortable descent and found himself standing on a heap of stone, sand and rubbish. Like Greaves before him, he was surrounded by bats whose beating wings threatened to extinguish his candle. The bottom of the shaft was blocked and he could go no further, but in 1817 Captain Giovanni Battista Caviglia, undeterred by the foul atmosphere which made several of his unfortunate workmen faint and caused the brave captain himself to spit blood, cleared the well and connected it to the descending passageway, ensuring a flow of relatively clean air through the pyramid.

With Caviglia's discovery that the descending passageway linked to the well, the internal structure of the pyramid was more or less revealed. This caused some incredulity, an incredulity boosted by the tantalizing reference to the hidden chambers of the sanctuary of Thoth in the Westcar Papyrus. Was the bulk of the pyramid really just solid rubble? Surely there must be more chambers, perhaps chambers filled with treasure, or esoteric secrets? Explorers continued their enthusiastic quest for the lost rooms, and it was not until 1837–8, when Colonel Richard Howard-Vyse and his civil engineer associate John Shae Perring conducted the first scientific survey of the internal structure, 'investigating' the revealing chambers with boring rods and gunpowder and filling the Subterranean Chamber with stone in the process, that the truth was more or less accepted. It is ironic that Vyse, a literal believer in biblical history working at the time when hieroglyphic translations were just becoming available, should do much to make the internal layout of the Great Pyramid known, for he himself had no understanding of what he was recording. He believed that he was exploring extravagant tombs made by 'The Shepherd Kings [Second Intermediate Period Hyksos rulers], whose descendants . . . after their expulsion from Egypt, built in Syria, Jerusalem . . .' and he hoped that his work would support evidence gleaned from the Old Testament.

In the late nineteenth century Charles Piazzi Smyth, Astronomer Royal for Scotland and Professor of Astronomy at Edinburgh University, published *Our Inheritance in the Great Pyramid*.[6] Here he explained his belief that Khufu's pyramid had been built under divine guidance using the 'pyramid inch', a unit of measurement (1.001 of a British inch) which the initiated could interpret to predict the future. A mere two sentences will suffice to convey a flavour of his work:

With many of the smaller and later pyramids there is little doubt about their objects; for, built by the Egyptians as sepulchres for the great Egyptian dead, such dead, both Pharaohs and their relatives, were buried in them, and with all their written particulars, pictorial accompaniments, and idolatrous adornments of that too graphic religion, which the fictile nation on the Nile ever delighted in. But as we approach, ascending the stream of ancient time, in any careful chronological survey of pyramidal structures, to the 'Great Pyramid', Egyptian emblems are gradually left behind; and in, and throughout, that mighty builded mass, which all history and all tradition, both ancient and modern, agree in representing as the first in point of date of the whole Jeezeh [Giza], and even the whole Egyptian, group, the earliest stone building also positively known to have been erected in any country – we find in all its *finished* parts not a vestige of heathenism, nor the smallest indulgence in anything approaching to idolatry; no Egyptology of the kind denounced by Moses and all the prophets of Israel; nor even the most distant allusion to Sabaism, and its elemental worship of sun, or moon, or any of the starry hosts of heaven.

Smyth was not the first to develop such theories – he himself acknowledged a large debt to John Taylor's 1859 *The Great Pyramid: why was it built? and who built it?* – but his persuasive books were an instant popular success. Victorian Britain was a land struggling to reconcile the certainties of established Christianity with the scientific developments which were changing life beyond all recognition. The railways had arrived, harsh electric light was poised to replace the more gentle gaslight, and Charles Darwin had already published his *On the Origin of Species by means of Natural Selection* (1858); to many, the 'pyramid inch' seemed as real, or as preposterous, as the theory of evolution and the establishment of mankind's prehistoric past. But, while there was fossil evidence to support human evolution, the 'pyramid inch' could neither be proved nor disproved as there were no accurate measurements available.

Smyth's work bore surprising fruit. The Smyth family were close friends of the Flinders family, and it was at their home that the young Anne Flinders met her future husband William Petrie. Their son, William Matthew Flinders Petrie, known to all as Flinders, read Piazzi Smyth's work as a precocious thirteen-year-old already keenly interested in archaeology, geometry, trigonometry, weights and measures:

. . . one day I brought back from Smith's bookstall, in 1866, a volume by Piazzi Smyth, *Our Inheritance in the Great Pyramid*. The views, in conjunction with his old friendship for the author, strongly attracted my father, and for some years I was urged on in what seemed so enticing a field of coincidence. I little thought how, fifteen years later, I should reach the 'ugly little fact which killed the beautiful theory'; but it was this interest which led my father to encourage me to go out and do the survey of the Great Pyramid . . .[7]

Father and son planned a joint expedition to measure the Great Pyramid and prove or disprove Smyth's theories; by way of practice, they conducted the first accurate survey of Stonehenge. But William, always indecisive, kept delaying their departure until eventually, in 1880, the twenty-seven-year-old Flinders set off alone. His was not a comfortable expedition; throughout his life Petrie scorned anything approaching luxury, and his digs were famed for their primitive living conditions. Now he slept on deck on the engine gratings, feeling too ill to venture inside the ship. On arrival in Egypt he moved into an abandoned tomb where he slept on sand and lived off tins of increasingly rank food. Working conditions within the pyramid were not good, and the despised tourists often got in the way of the survey, causing Petrie to work late into the night when the plateau was deserted. Inside the pyramid he worked naked; outside, he scared off the curious by leaving off his outer garments to reveal pink underwear.

Petrie, aided by Ali Gabri, a local workman who had been employed by both Vyse and Piazzi Smyth, managed to conduct the first systematic survey of the pyramid using a complicated set of triangulations which extended over the entire site. The work was painstakingly slow; it took several hours each morning to set out the survey points, and all measurements had to be checked and re-checked. After two seasons of survey and structural examination the figures were collated in England. The end result was so accurate that Petrie's survey is still used today. His figures flatly contradicted the measurements which underpinned Smyth's work, and so disproved the existence of the pyramid inch:[8]

. . . Instead of a pyramid measuring 9140 inches, as was supposed, it measured only 9069 inches. Hence all theorizing about the days in the year being represented was erroneous. The size of the pyramid was ruled by being 7 × 40 Egyptian cubits (20.6 inches) high and 11 × 40 cubits wide. This is strongly confirmed by the pyramid of Meidum, which preceded it in date, being 7 × 25 cubits high and 11 × 25 cubits wide; it shows the use of the same system of a large number of cubits, 25 or 40, as a unit, multiplied by 7 or 11 for the dimensions. The angle of the slope required for this 7 and 11 proportion is within the small uncertainty (two minutes) of the actual remains.

The theories as to the size of the pyramid are thus proved entirely impossible . . . The fantastic theories, however, are still poured out, and the theorists still assert that the facts correspond to their requirements. It is useless to state the real truth of the matter, as it has no effect on those who are subject to this type of hallucination. They can be but left with the flat earth believers and other such people to whom a theory is dearer than a fact.

We can sense Petrie's frustration as, towards the end of his life, he reviews his most impressive work. He had set out with an open mind to measure the Great Pyramid, and had produced a set of verifiable results. His methods and his calculations were out in the open for all to see. Yet his work did nothing to stem the flow of alternative theories. Indeed, if anything, it polarized the opposing parties so that Petrie's survey may be regarded as the catalyst which caused the acrimonious split between the 'academics' and the 'pyramid theorists' which still exists today.

Petrie's work confirmed what everyone could see. *Akhet Khufu* is a pyramid of astonishing size and impressive geometric precision standing 146.5 metres high, with a slope of 51° 50′ 40″. Its sides, with an average length of 230.33 metres, vary by less than 5 centimetres and are orientated almost exactly towards true north, deviating by only 3′ 6″. Its base is almost completely level, varying by less than 3 centimetres from north to south. Seen from the outside the pyramid once appeared perfect, its Tura limestone casing fitted close together to give the smooth, polished appearance of a stone mirror. Beneath the casing the rough blocks of the core, laid in horizontal courses and packed with stones and copious amounts of gypsum mortar, were far from perfect but this did not matter; these blocks were hidden from view.

Neither the earlier nor the later pyramids were as large or as accurate in their alignment. Size was, to a large extent, a matter of confidence; kings who both anticipated and achieved a long reign left the largest monuments. But alignment is a different matter. We might excuse the earlier pyramid builders their discrepancies on the grounds that they were still perfecting their techniques, but it seems curious that Khufu's successors were unable or unwilling to emulate his precision.

Given the problems encountered at Dahshur and Meidum, Khufu's obsessive accuracy makes perfect sense; everyone knew what would happen if errors crept into a pyramid. But this is ancient Egypt, and it is tempting to see his desire for absolute alignment as something more; as a quest for the perfection which would reinforce his chance of eternal life. For like most things in Egypt, mathematics, essentially a practical skill, could hold a mystical meaning for the initiated. The most obvious example of this is the number sequence which makes up the 'Horus–eye fraction'. When written in hieroglyphs the fractions ½, ¼, ⅛, ¹⁄₁₆, ¹⁄₃₂, ¹⁄₆₄ of the *hekat* (the unit of volume) resembled the components of the symbolic eye of Horus which was torn out and eaten by Seth, and later restored by Thoth, patron god of mathematics, 'who did it with his fingers'. This gave the fractions a curious power while allowing the tale of the eye of Horus to be read as a form of equation. Thoth could have solved the Horus riddle by adding ¹⁄₆₄ to ⁶³⁄₆₄ (the sum of the fractions) to make a whole number, or a whole eye. Eyes, the eye of Horus, and green eye-paint as an offering for the dead king form a frequent theme in the Pyramid Texts:[9]

Utterance 702: The green eye-paint of the king is the stalk of the papyrus and of your eye which is in the fire. The green eye-paint of the king is with you.

As green eye-paint represents rejuvenation its opposite, black eye-paint, represents the darker aspect of renewal; here we have the symmetry of the healed and the damaged eyes.

How was precision achieved on the building site? The Egyptians never tell us; such mundane matters being too obvious to mention. However, there is no need to postulate esoteric, long-lost or alien knowledge. As we have already seen, the Egyptians were accomplished practical mathematicians; builders, carpenters and artists rather than theoreticians. The mathematics involved in planning a perfect pyramid are not difficult, and the preliminary production of scale drawings and models would not have caused the architects to lose

Figure 9.2   The 'Eye of Horus' and its fractional values.

much sleep. It is the conversion of this theory into full-scale blocks and mortar which poses huge technical problems.

The ability to take accurate, universally recognized measurements was fundamental to the developing state – tax collectors, land agents, astronomers and accountants all needed to be able to measure and align. Distances were measured in small cubits (c. 45 centimetres; average elbow to fingertip length in an ancient Egyptian male) or in the slightly longer royal cubits (c. 52.5 centimetres) which could be divided into 7 palms and subdivided into 4 fingers. One hundred cubits measured a *khet*, and the square *khet* or *setat* was the usual unit of land measurement. The cubit was measured using a wooden cubit rod; knotted ropes were used to measure greater distances but, as the rope was liable to stretch, the results obtained were of variable accuracy. In the absence of degrees a slope was measured in *seqed* which expressed angles as a ratio of the horizontal to the vertical measurement (7 palms; the royal cubit): the *seqed*, dependent upon the cotangent of the angle of inclination, decreased as gradient increased. The most common *seqed* of the Old Kingdom pyramids is 5½ or 5¼ palms: the Great Pyramid's base angle of 51° 51′ is the equivalent of a *seqed* 5½.[10]

To experienced star-gazers, the location of true north was relatively easy, and the false horizon used in star-gazing could help to align the pyramid.[11] An observer, standing within the circle and looking north-wards, could use a forked sight (*bey*) and a plumb line (*merkhet*) to note the exact position of the rise and fall of a chosen star on the mud-brick horizon. By extending these points until they met at the centre of the circle, and then bisecting the resulting angle, true north would be revealed.

Egyptologist Kate Spence has recently proposed a variant astral method which involves aligning two opposed circumpolar stars (Delta Ursae Majoris and Beta Ursae Minoris, or Epsilon Ursae Majoris and Gamma Ursae Minoris), one at its upper culmination and the other at its lower, with a plumb line which should pass through the north celestial pole and thus indicate true north.[12] This technique would have given vary-ing accuracy which, as she has pointed out, may well account for the measurable differences in pyramid precision over time. Both methods would, perhaps, have been somewhat impractical on a site where many alignments were required to prove the accuracy of the northern reference line.

Easier in daylight hours, but less reliable again, is the calculation of north from the shadows created by the sun.[13] If a vertical pole or gnomen is erected, its shadow position taken mid-morning serves as the radius of a circle. As the sun continues to rise the shadow will dwindle and then lengthen again; when it reaches the edge of the circle it forms an angle with the original radius. The line bisecting this angle points true north.

Once north had been ascertained, a north–south reference line of rope supported on posts hammered firmly into the bedrock could be established. From this line, the architects laid out their reference grid, a perfect square, its sides aligned and measured and its angles accurate right angles. We can still see the rows of regularly spaced post holes which surround and run parallel to the Great Pyramid. The confirmation of a right angle by the 3–4–5 triangle method formalized by Pythagoras was known to the Old Kingdom Egyptians, who made and used wooden set-squares and who may have had an understanding of the intersecting arcs method of calculating a right angle. It was impossible to check the diagonals of the square reference grid, as the foundation included raised bedrock which prevented the accurate stretching of rope from corner to corner. However, as the pyramid rose above the bedrock, and the square became smaller, this would have become an additional check.

The Egyptians rarely dug foundations for their buildings, and Khufu's pyramid was to rest upon a platform of good quality limestone which incorporated natural bedrock steps, conveniently reducing the number of core blocks needed. This foundation platform had to be levelled with utmost precision. For a long time Egyptologists believed that this could only have been achieved by flooding the entire base with water held within mud-brick dams. This method would, however, have been fraught with practical difficulties: how could vast amounts of water be transported to a raised desert site? Would the masons have cut the rock underwater, measuring down from the surface? As the Egyptians did have the use of the square level, a simple wooden device incorporating a plumb-bob suspended from an A-frame, we can more realistically imagine this being used in conjunction with measurements taken from a limited amount of water held in mud-brick troughs and rock-cut channels. The slight difference in levels observable between the south-east and north-west corners of the Great Pyramid may well have been caused by the prevailing wind blowing across the water in the levelling trenches.[14]

Equally important was the maintenance of the pyramid angle. The diagonals rising from the four corners had to run straight and true or the pyramid would appear to twist, as does Khaefre's pyramid. The corners of the Great Pyramid were built from extra-strong limestone, to give added stability to the whole structure. Their slope could be measured using the *seqed*, and masons' marks on the individual blocks suggest that the slope was calculated and re-calculated as the courses were laid.

It would not have been possible to look down and check the line of sight as throughout its construction the lower part of the pyramid was obscured by scaffolding and ramps, but it may have been possible to align the pyramid edges and diagonals by eye using backsights situated away from the pyramid. The casing blocks, their bases already trimmed, were lowered into position and then dressed top and sides (but not front), so that each block was effectively tailored to its unique position on the pyramid. In the uppermost courses, where accurate alignment was of crucial importance, space was extremely limited. *In situ* cutting was impossible and the smaller blocks had to be pre-cut before being raised. Consequently, the tops of pyramids display the least accurate alignments.

As the core and its casing rose from the base, the core perhaps rising slightly faster, the outer surface of the casing was left untrimmed – another argument against downward sighting – and it was only when the pyramid was complete and the ramps were being dismantled that the casing was cut back, working from top to bottom, to give the pyramid its final smooth slope. Menkaure's pyramid, abandoned unfinished at the king's death, still has its lower layers undressed and, as this undressed stone was less attractive to thieves, these layers survive today.

Herodotus tells us exactly how the pyramids were built:[15]

. . . in steps, some call this technique battlement-wise, or altar-wise. After laying the stones for the base they raised the remaining blocks to their places using machines made of short wooden planks. The first machine elevated them from the ground to the top of the first step. On this there was another machine which received the block and moved it to the second step, where a third machine received the block and moved it still higher. Either they had as many machines as there were steps in the pyramid, or possibly they had a single portable machine which was transferred from layer to layer as the pyramid rose – both accounts are given, and therefore I record both. The upper portion of the pyramid was finished first, then the middle, and finally the part which was lowest and nearest to the ground.

He was completely wrong, but then he had never seen a pyramid being built. The Egyptians constructed their pyramids from the bottom up, and then dressed them from the top down, and they did this with the aid of ramps and manpower rather than complicated lifting devices. Ancient ramps are rare; by their very nature they would be smashed apart and dumped during the final, tidying-up stage of building works. We do, however, have some evidence of ramps left standing against unfinished pyramids; Khaba's Layer Pyramid and Huni's small-scale Sinki Pyramid show diagnostic traces and, of course, it is likely that the mound of sand

and rubble which surrounds the Meidum pyramid includes a substantial percentage of ramp. To the south of the Great Pyramid lies a characteristic debris, a mixture of limestone chips, gypsum and tafla clay, which may well be the remains of the dismantled ramps dumped in the abandoned quarries.[16]

Every Egyptian building site was different and, as we might expect, the builders suited their methods to local conditions. This has provoked intense academic debate. Was/were the Great Pyramid ramp/ramps internal (very unlikely) or external? Was there a single ramp, ramps on the four sides, or ramps on the four corners? Was/were it/they straight (unlikely, as a single straight ramp reaching to the top of the Great Pyramid would require more material than the pyramid itself), zig-zag (but the bends would make manoeuvring difficult), wrap-around (the ramp would obscure the pyramid), or a combination? The most recent theory[17] is that maximum efficiency would have been obtained from a single, straight ramp built up to a third of the height of the pyramid, and then a smaller, wrap-around ramp which would allow the placement of the smaller upper blocks. The wrap-around ramp would have to be attached to the pyramid by limestone supports which could be removed as the ramp itself was dismantled. Controversially, this model would require that the upper portion of the outer casing be added from the top downwards so that the supports might be removed along with the ramp. Undressed casing stones recovered at the base of the queens' pyramids suggest that the Great Pyramid may indeed have been fitted with pro- trusions to allow the suspension of a wrap-around style ramp, but as yet we have no further confirmation of the theory.

Petrie believed that Khufu's architect must have modified his plans as work progressed, as the passages were '. . . certainly altered once, and perhaps oftener, in the course of building'.[18] With our greater under- standing of pyramid architecture it seems more likely that all three chambers were part of the original plan, with the Queen's Chamber built as a *serdab* room and the Subterranean Chamber, whose access passageway is too small to have allowed the introduction of a sarcophagus, perhaps serving as a form of symbolic underworld for the use of the spirit. This would make sense if the Subterranean Chamber was started last, and abandoned at the king's death, and would explain why, contrary to normal practice, the chamber was cut directly into the bedrock beneath the pyramid (normal practice being to build the substructures in a large open trench before the body of the tomb was built on top).

'Air-shafts', long, narrow (20 centimetres square) passageways, not perfectly straight but oriented towards the northern pole star and the constellation of Orion, lead from the King's and the Queen's Chambers. The purpose of these passageways remains a mystery, although it seems that they had a ritual rather than practical function; their role as 'air-shafts' must certainly be questioned, as they would have supplied very little air to the pyramid builders.

The king's shafts run through the body of the pyramid and perhaps pierced the pyramid's now-vanished outer casing. As yet these shafts remain unexplored. The shafts leading from the Queen's Chamber were discovered in 1872 by Waynmann Dixon, hidden behind camouflage stones. These shafts are dummies, and extend only a short distance into the pyramid masonry suggesting that the purpose of the chamber had been revised while construction was in progress. Within the northern shaft Dixon found a pounding stone, a small wooden board and a curious forked copper tool which was probably once attached to a wooden handle; these tools are now displayed in the British Museum. In 1993 a team from the German Archaeological Institute in Cairo led by Rudolf Gantenbrink under the direction of Rainer Stadelmann sent a small robotic video camera, UPUAUT 2, along the southern shaft, but the robot found its way blocked by a stone plug fitted with two copper pins. A second exploration, in 2002, found a second blocking stone behind the first.

Khufu realized that his pyramid would attract thieves. This was the essential paradox of pyramid building. A conspicuous tomb served as a powerful magical object, guaranteeing regeneration to the soul within, but it also acted as a signpost to untold treasures and therefore threatened the safety of the corpse it guarded. Khufu took all sensible precautions and his pyramid was both protected by its priesthood – while the cult survived no one would dare desecrate the tomb – and fitted with physical barriers. The 'trial passages' and 'narrow trench', a series of underground passageways to the north of the pyramid causeway are, at 22 metres in length and 10 metres in depth, a miniature version of the corridors within the Great Pyramid. Vyse and Perring, who discovered the passageways, believed that these were the remains of a fourth, unfinished, queen's pyramid. Petrie, however, argued convincingly that they represent an experimental area where the masons could practise their techniques and blocking skills.

The pyramid had to be sealed from within – how then could the burial party make their escape? The seventeenth-century Counsul-General Maillet had an ingenious theory. After Khufu's funeral, the burial party would secure the pyramid. They would then bury each other in turn, until just one unfortunate attendant was left to conduct his own funeral and bury himself. Needless to say, this is not what happened.

The entrance to the burial chamber was blocked by three now vanished granite portcullis slabs which, after the funeral, were lowered down grooves in the wall. Passing along the Grand Gallery the burial party knocked away wooden props to release three granite blocks which would slide down and seal the ascending passageway. Trapped between the portcullises and the blocked passageway, the burial party then made their escape down the well which allowed them to join the descending passageway just before it entered the Subterranean Chamber. The entrance to the well was camouflaged with stone and, as the party made their way upwards, so was the entrance to the ascending passageway. The burial party emerged through the entrance, and blocks were slid down the descending passageway. Finally the entrance hole was covered with the limestone casing which would render it invisible. This procedure would leave the well open but inaccessible within the pyramid; this fits well with the descriptions of early travellers who found the well filled with rubbish and rubble but not deliberately blocked with granite.

None of these precautions worked. The robbers were able to bypass the blocking stones by tunnelling through the softer limestone which surrounded them, and well before the end of the Old Kingdom thieves had smashed the corner of Khufu's red granite sarcophagus to lever off the heavy lid. Blocks from the complex were being reused in the Middle Kingdom pyramid of Amenemhat I a mere five and a half centuries after Khufu's death, but the pyramid itself survived more or less intact throughout the Dynastic age. Eventually its valuable outer casing was stolen, with many of its blocks being used to build Medieval Cairo.

Khufu's pyramid was surrounded by a narrow courtyard paved with large limestone slabs and defined by a tall limestone wall. Following the Meidum plan, the only access to this private inner area was via the walled causeway, 750 metres long, which linked the low-lying valley temple to the mortuary temple. Today it is hard to imagine the atmospheric splendour of this processional route; the large, almost square mortuary temple has been completely demolished leaving only tell-tale traces of basalt paving, granite pillars and decorated limestone walls plus an intrusive Saite burial shaft. The surviving decorations include scenes of the *sed* festival rituals, and processions of estates bearing offerings for the dead king. But when Herodotus visited Giza the causeway and temples were substantially intact, and tourists were able to walk along the dark, cool passageway towards the shining pyramid:[19]

It took ten years' oppression of the people to make the causeway for the conveyance of stones, a work not much inferior, in my judgement, to the pyramid itself. This causeway is five furlongs in length, ten fathoms wide, and in height, at its tallest point, eight fathoms. It is built of polished stone, and is covered in carvings of animals.

The valley temple is now lost under the modern suburb of Nazlet es-Samman, where present conditions make excavation very difficult.

The Giza necropolis, like Abydos before it, served as a port for ships awaiting divine and ghostly passengers. Five boat-shaped pits were excavated close to the causeway and mortuary temple, but these were empty when opened and are presumed to have had a ritual rather than practical significance.

Two narrow, rectangular pits dug parallel to the south side of the pyramid outside the enclosure wall were entirely different. These pits, roofed with limestone blocks sealed tight with mortar, housed real, dismembered boats. The pits, just over 30 metres long, were too small to hold the lengthy vessels intact and, as it is unthinkable that Khufu's workers could not have excavated a larger pit had they so wished, we must assume that the inadequate pit size and the dismantling of the boats was a deliberate choice. While one boat remains sealed in its tomb, the subject of a conservation project conducted by Waseda University, the easternmost has been fully reassembled by a team lead by master-restorer Hag Ahmed Youssef of the Egyptian Department of Antiquities. After almost twenty-eight years spent rejoining the 651 parts (1,224 pieces of wood), it is now displayed in a glass boat-shaped museum alongside the pyramid. Made out of cedar planks sewn together with fibre ropes, the full-sized (43 metres) vessel is a wooden copy of a papyrus reed boat, complete with curved prow and stern, a central cabin or shrine and five oars on either side. Its restorer believes that it shows unmistakable signs of use and has suggested that this may well be the boat which was used to take the dead Khufu to his tomb. Others believe that the unused boat was built for immediate dismantling and burial. Whatever its purpose, it seems that the boat was buried by Djedefre, Khufu's short-lived successor, as the pit contains his cartouche. Unfortunately the move to the museum has not been good for the boat and, in the absence of proper light, temperature and atmospheric controls, it has started to warp and shrink.

A tiny satellite pyramid was constructed outside the enclosure wall, approximately 24 metres to the south-east of the main pyramid.[20] This has sides 22 metres long, and includes a descending passage and a minia-ture burial chamber whose walls lean inwards, following the shape of the pyramid. Although the superstructure has been flattened, the pyramidion survives to suggest an original slope of approximately 51°45′, almost exactly the same slope as the Great Pyramid.

Far larger were the three pyramids complete with mortuary chapels which lay to the east of the satellite pyramid. These were simplified versions of the king's own tomb built to approximately one fifth its size to house Khufu's closest female relatives. As they have now collapsed, indeed two were never completed, we can see that all three were built around a stepped inner core. GI-a, the northermost pyramid, has been tentatively assigned to Hetepheres, wife of Snefru, whose title 'Mother of the King' indicates that she was Khufu's own mother. GI-b, the middle pyramid, has been allocated to the long-lived Queen Meretetes, another 'Mother of the King' (Djedefre? She was also the mother of Crown Prince Kawab who predeceased Khufu) who outlived Snefru, Khufu and Djedefre to die during Khaefre's reign. GI-c, the northern and best preserved pyramid, has been allocated to the obscure 'King's daughter' Henutsen, possibly the mother of Khaefre. This pyramid was built after the other two, and may not have formed a part of Khufu's original complex. All three pyramids were looted in antiquity.

In 1925 George Reisner's team was busy surveying the area to the east of the Great Pyramid. As they worked to the north of GI-a, a tripod leg sank deep into the desert sand revealing the presence of a shaft hidden beneath a layer of plaster. After weeks of patient excavation – the shaft, known today as G 7000x, proved to be 27 metres deep and was completely filled with limestone blocks – the team entered the simple chamber at its base. Here they discovered the neatly stored remnants of Hetepheres's burial equipment including her alabaster sarcophagus and, in a niche in the western wall, her sealed alabaster Canopic chest complete with linen-wrapped internal organs still steeping in embalming fluid. It was to take almost two years to empty the tomb; only then did it become apparent that Hetepheres's sarcophagus was empty.

Her burial equipment included thousands of fragments of pottery and a precious collection of wooden furniture including a dismantled canopy, a bed, two chairs and a sedan chair which bore the queen's name. The wooden elements of these pieces had long-since decayed but enough of their golden coverings remained to allow Hag Ahmed Youssef to bring them back to life. More personal items included gold razors and knives used for shaving the head and limbs, small alabaster pots containing perfumes and kohl, and a collection of jewellery stored in a wooden box covered with gold leaf and labelled 'box holding rings . . . mother of the King of Upper and Lower Egypt, Hetepheres'. Hetepheres's treasures are today displayed in Cairo Museum.

Reisner, a romantic at heart, believed that his team had discovered the secret reburial of Hetepheres's looted tomb. More recently archaeologists have inclined to the belief that this may have been Hetepheres's intended tomb – a pyramid occupied before its superstructure could be completed – but even looting by the undertakers does not explain the absence of Hetepheres's body.

10

The Pyramid Builders

Our wonder at the mighty mass of the Pyramids of Gizeh, then, is not to be mere wonder at the barbaric power which summoned myriads of slaves and forced them to toil till by sheer brute force they had piled up these mountains of stone. Brute force, unguided and unorganized, would never have built the Pyramids, though millions instead of thousands had been employed, and for centuries instead of decades, but would only have led to disaster and confusion. The wonder of the Pyramids is that five thousand years ago there was found a race whose keen intelligence so clearly understood the need and the marvellous power of organized and trained human labour, architects and engineers who were capable of directing the energies of a hundred thousand men without confusion towards a clearly foreseen end, and craftsmen who were capable of producing, with tools whose material seems to us pathetic in its inadequacy, results which put to shame the best achievements of men using the finest modern tools.[1]

The unprecedented scale of the Great Pyramid leaves archaeologists almost, but not quite, lost for words.[2] Comparisons may be odious but here they seem necessary as bald figures are nowhere near sufficient to describe the sheer size of the monument. Amelia B. Edwards tells us that 'it stands 115 feet 9 inches taller than the cross on top of St Paul's, and about 20 feet lower than Box Hill in Surrey; and if transported bodily to London, it would a little more than cover the whole area of Lincoln's Inn Fields' although she adds with some truth that such comparisons tend to diminish rather than do justice to their subject. Somers Clarke and Engelbach show how the base of the Great Pyramid could accommodate both the Houses of Parliament and St Paul's Cathedral with space to spare; George Goyon gives a similar illustration, this time it is Strasbourg Cathedral which fits neatly within the pyramid's cross section. Baines and Malek provide perhaps the most helpful international illustration; various pyramids appear alongside such modern monuments as the Statue of Liberty, the Taj Mahal and the Saturn V launch vehicle complete with Apollo spacecraft.

While Sir Alan Gardiner tells us that the height of the Great Pyramid is 'exceeded in monuments made entirely of stone only by the tower of Ulm Cathedral', I. E. S. Edwards quotes Baldwin Smith's calculation that Westminster Abbey, St Paul's Cathedral, Florence Cathedral, Milan Cathedral and St Peter's, Rome, could all be squeezed into its interior. Napoleon Bonaparte, fascinated by everything Egyptological, calculates that there is enough stone in the three Giza Pyramids to build a wall 3 metres high all around France; James Baikie adds to this '. . . a town the size of Aberdeen might be built out of the materials which Khufu gathered together for his monstrous tomb . . . if the stones were divided into blocks a foot square, and these blocks placed end to end in a straight line, the line would be long enough to reach two-thirds of the length of the circumference of the earth at the Equator'. Even today, when our horizons are dotted with skyscrapers and towers, when height alone no longer provokes awe, the sheer unrelieved bulk of the Great Pyramid remains a breathtaking achievement.

In a non-mechanical age vast size implies a vast workforce. Herodotus tells us that the pyramid was built by 100,000 slaves who 'laboured constantly and were relieved every three months by a fresh gang'.[3] Diodorus Siculus inflates the number to 360,000, which represents at least 18 per cent of Old Kingdom Egypt's total population.[4] The gripping image of tens of thousands of slaves toiling in the harshest of conditions for Khufu's folly has proved remarkably durable, surviving into the modern age to be reinforced on the celluloid screen. It is, however, wrong on two counts. Khufu did not have a vast body of slaves at his disposal, and even if he had, there was no way that 100,000 could work simultaneously on the building site and associated quarry.

How many, then, did work at Giza? Various archaeologists and construction experts have independently attempted to calculate the minimum number of pyramid and quarry workers, their calculations slightly handicapped by not knowing how long the building site was in operation, or exactly how many blocks were cut and laid. The often quoted total of 2.3 million separate blocks within the Great Pyramid is after all only an approximation; we cannot see beneath the pyramid's surface and the inclusion of bedrock, sand-filled gaps and rubble-filled cavities within the core would have speeded up construction work considerably.

Craig Smith has used modern project-analysis techniques to suggest that the pyramid could have been built in ten years by a workforce of 40,000, with the heaviest workforce required in the middle of the building operation; he assumes that the pyramid would have been built as quickly as possible. Rainer Stadelmann has estimated that the masons must have placed approximately 340 blocks per day, working a maximum ten hour day for at least nineteen years, although of course the rate of block placing would slow down as the pyramid rose and its building site – the flat pyramid top – decreased in area. Stuart Kirkland Wier has calculated that the Great Pyramid could have been built by 10,000 men working for twenty-three years, and compares this to the mere 1790 men he believes were required to build Djoser's Step Pyramid. Mark Lehner and Zahi Hawass, taking account of their own archaeological discoveries, have suggested a total of 4000 primary labourers (quarry workers, hauliers and masons) plus 16,000 to 20,000 secondary workers (ramp builders, tool makers, mortar mixers and those providing back-up services such as food, clothing and fuel) giving a total workforce of 20 to 25,000 working for twenty years or more. They subdivide these into 5000 permanent, salaried employees and up to 20,000 temporary workers. Of course, if we allow Smith's workmen double the time, and halve their number, we reach Lehner and Hawass's figure of 20,000 working for twenty years.

So many workers were bound to leave archaeological footprints in the Giza sand. Egyptologists had long suspected that Egypt's major construction sites were supported by purpose-built villages or barracks but could find no evidence to support their belief. In 1888 theoretical knowledge became reality when Flinders Petrie started his investigation into the Middle Kingdom Faiyum pyramid complex of Senwosret II at Illahun and its associated walled settlement, Kahun. Kahun, virtually untouched by robbers and farmers, yielded a complete town plan and its neat rows of mud-brick terraced houses, interspersed with larger homes and perhaps even a royal palace, provided Petrie with a wealth of papyri, pottery, tools, clothing and children's toys; all the debris of normal, day-to-day life which is usually missing from Egyptian sites.

If we are to make sense of the Great Pyramid as a man-made monument this is precisely the sort of evidence that we need to find at Giza. But with so many splendid tombs on offer, few early Egyptologists were prepared to 'waste time' looking for domestic architecture. Only Petrie gave the matter some thought, identifying a series of buildings as a workmen's barrack. These 'barracks' have, however, yielded no domestic refuse and, being inconveniently sited within the cemetery, away from the valley, are today reclassified as storehouses and workshops.

At Giza the sacred precincts of the royal necropolis were defined by the 'Wall of the Crow', a massive limestone boundary which effectively separated the lands of the living and the dead. It is beyond this wall, rather than in the necropolis itself, that we need to look for evidence of the living. Thanks largely to the ongoing excavations of Mark Lehner and Zahi Hawass, we now know that there was once a substantial pyramid town close by Khufu's valley temple. Unfortunately, this settlement now lies beneath the modern town of Nazlet es-Samman, and is largely inaccessible. The town dead, men, women and children, were buried nearby in a sloping desert cemetery whose varied tombs and graves – including miniature pyramids, step pyramids, small mastabas and beehive-shaped or domed tombs – incorporate expensive stone elements 'borrowed' from the king's building site. The larger and more sophisti-cated limestone tombs lie higher up the cemetery slope; here we find the officials and administrators involved in the building of the pyramid plus those who furnished its supplies.

While the tomb of the master baker supplies us with scenes of industrial bread production, the tombs of the supervisors include inscriptions relating to the organization and control of the workforce. In the absence of official documentation, these writings provide us with our only under-standing of the pyramid-building system. They confirm that the work was organized along tried and tested lines designed to reduce the vast workforce and their almost overwhelming task to manageable pro-portions. This splitting of task and workforce, combined with the use of temporary labourers, was a typical Egyptian answer to a logistical prob-lem. Boat crews were always divided into left- and right-side *phyles* and then subdivided by task; the New Kingdom tombs in the Valley of the Kings would follow this nautical system and be decorated by left- and right-hand gangs.

At Giza the workforce of 15,000 was allocated to crews of approximately 2000 and subdivided into named gangs of 1000: graffiti shows that the builders of the third Giza pyramid named themselves the 'Friends of Menkaure' and the 'Drunkards of Menkaure'. These gangs were further divided into *zaa* or phyles of approximately 200, always named in deference to their nautical origins Great/Starboard, Asiatic/Port, Green/Prow, Little/Stern and Last/Good. Finally the phyles were split into divisions of maybe twenty workers who were allocated their own specific task and their own project leader. Thus 20,000 workers could be separated into efficient, easily monitored working units, gang or phyle loyalty could be developed, and a seemingly impossible project, the raising of a huge pyramid, became an achievable ambition.

Which came first, the organization or the pyramid? It seems impossible that either could have happened without the other. As the bureaucracy responded to the challenges of pyramid building, the pyramid builders took full advantage of the improved administration which allowed them to summon workers, order supplies, and allocate tasks. It is no coincidence that the 4th Dynasty shows the first flourishing of the hieratic script, the cursive, simplified form of the more elaborate and time-consuming hieroglyphic script which would henceforth be used in all documents and non-monumental inscriptions.

To the south of the pyramid town was an extensive, cohesive industrial complex divided into blocks or galleries separated by paved streets equipped with drains, and including some workers' housing. Investigations are still in progress, but the site has already yielded a copper processing plant, two bakeries with enough moulds to make hundreds of bell-shaped loaves, and a fish processing unit complete with the fragile, dusty remains of thousands of fish. This is food production on a truly massive scale although as yet archaeologists have discovered neither storage facilities nor warehouses.

The animal bones recovered from this area and from the pyramid town include duck, the occasional sheep and pig and, most unexpectedly, choice cuts of prime beef. The ducks, sheep and pigs could have been raised amidst the houses and workshops of the pyramid town but cattle, always an expensive luxury in Egypt, must have been grazed on pasture – probably the fertile pyramid estates in the Delta – and then transported live for butchery at Giza. Of course we do not know who was eating the beef; it may well have been reserved for the gods, royalty and higher ranking state employees, but the abundance of meat on the construction site is far removed from the rather pungent slave diet of vegetables suggested by Herodotus:[5]

There is an inscription in Egyptian writing on the pyramid which records the quantity of radishes, onions and garlic eaten by the labourers who built it, and I remember very well that the interpreter who read the inscription to me said that the money spent in this way was the equivalent of 1600 talents of silver.

The many thousands of temporary manual labourers, those who visited Giza to put in a three or four month shift before returning home, were housed in less comfortable surroundings in a temporary camp beside the pyramid town. Here they received a subsistence wage in the form of rations provided by the industrial complex, the standard Old Kingdom ration for a labourer being ten loaves and a measure of beer or its equivalent. We can just about imagine a labouring family consuming ten loaves in a day, but as supervisors and those of higher status were entitled to hundreds of loaves and many jugs of beer daily – food which would not keep fresh for long – we must assume that these were notional rations actually paid in the form of other foods, goods or perhaps credits. In any case, the pyramid town, like all other Egyptian towns, would soon have developed its own economy as everyone traded unwanted rations for desirable goods or skills.

The labourers who died on site were buried in the town cemetery along with the tools of their trade; as we might expect, their hurried graves were poor in comparison with those of the permanent workers who had a lifetime to prepare for burial at Giza.

Within the 'Wall of the Crow' were the richest private tombs of all. Khufu's courtiers and relations were allocated stone mastabas in the two elite cemeteries beside the Great Pyramid complex. The Western Cemetery housed the tombs of the court officials, the Eastern Cemetery the tombs of family members.[6] By the end of the Old Kingdom their regular layout had been disrupted by intrusive later burials – interment close to Khufu's pyramid remained highly desirable for centuries after the king's death – but in their heyday these cemeteries, criss-crossed by broad streets and roads so that they bore an uncanny resemblance to a modern American city, showed the same dedication to precision planning as the pyramid complex itself.

Here in the well-ordered city of the elite dead each mastaba had its own private subterranean burial chamber and, above ground and easily accessible, its own chapel. This, in its most typical form, comprised a mud-brick shelter protecting a delicately carved and painted slab stela set into the south end of the eastern façade. Gone is the intricate decoration found in the Meidum mastabas; these slab stelae are the only decorated and inscribed element included in the austere, early Giza mastabas. The king was generous – he had provided the tombs and stelae – but he only gave so much; anyone who wanted to improve their mastaba was free to do so, and in some instances the original mud-brick chapel was replaced by one of stone complete with a false door. Hemiunu's large, solid mastaba, situated in the centre of the Western Cemetery and built towards the end of Khufu's reign, was eventually enlarged on the north, south and east sides and fitted with a corridor leading to twin serdab chambers cut into the eastern mastaba face.

In the burial chambers and shafts of the Western Cemetery mastabas we find the curious non-royal tradition of 'reserve heads'; of the thirty-one known examples, twenty-seven have been recovered from Giza and are mostly dated to the reigns of Khufu and his son Khaefre. The reserve heads are unpainted, uninscribed sculptures of lifelike appearance – they are, as far as we can tell, the faces and features of individuals rather than symbolic expressions of might or power that we see in royal portraiture, or stereotyped, mass-produced heads churned out by an uncaring factory – but they are cut off at the neck and therefore break a basic Egyptian artistic rule that people should be shown complete in their tombs to ensure that they will be reincarnated as whole beings. Their flat bases allow the reserve heads to stand upright, like modern hairdressers' wig stands, a comparison which appears all the stronger as the heads themselves are bald. While most of the heads have been delicately carved from fine limestone there are some crude examples incorporating a great deal of moulded plaster, and even two made from mud.

While the elite mastabas were plundered in antiquity and excavated in an unscientific age, the workers' tombs were more or less ignored, their rather basic grave goods being of little interest to robbers in search of gold. Consequently many worker skeletons have survived intact, allowing scientists to build up a profile of those who worked and died at Giza. Of the six hundred plus bodies so far examined, roughly half are female, with children and babies making up over 23 per cent of the total: confirmation that the permanent pyramid workers lived with their families in the shadow of the rising pyramid. The elite skeletons are nowhere near as well preserved as those of the workers, but enough have survived to show that the workers died on average ten years younger than the elite. This may in part be a reflection of the samples studied; the elite tombs housed nobles who we may presume died of natural causes while the worker tombs house younger families, some of whom must have died in accidents on site. Nevertheless, it seems that upper-class men, benefiting from good food and white-collar work, and saved from the cramped, unhygienic conditions of lower-class housing, could reasonably expect to reach the grand old age of forty-five. Women in both communities, subjected to the hazards of childbirth, died earlier than their menfolk, with many dying in their twenties.

Many have been happy to attribute Egypt's achievements to outsiders. To take just one example:[7]

. . . the seeds of Egypt's greatness were sown by a few colonists who entered the country peaceably and organized the carrying out of great construction works, the technical and scientific skill embodied therein being in their sole possession, which they reduced to 'rule of thumb' equivalents within the capacity of the native labour to enable these works to be carried out. On completion of these works they left the country, taking their knowledge with them. Hence the rapid falling off in construction work which showed itself after the Great Pyramid had been completed.

After comparing ancient DNA samples from Giza with samples taken from modern Egyptians living the length and breadth of the Nile Valley and Delta, Dr Moamina Kamal of Cairo University Medical School has suggested that Khufu's pyramid was a truly nationwide project, with workers, conscripts rather than slaves, drawn to Giza from all over Egypt. She has discovered no trace of any 'alien' race (either human or intergalactic). Historical racism is unnecessary; the ancient Egyptians built their own monuments. Effectively, the pyramid served both as a gigantic training project and – deliberately or not – as a source of

'Egyptianization' or cultural indoctrination. The workers who left their isolated rural communities of maybe fifty or a hundred people to live in a town of 15,000-plus strangers, returned to the provinces with new skills, a wider outlook and a renewed sense of national unity which was balanced by a loss of loyalty to local traditions. The use of shifts of workers spread the burden of work and brought about a thorough redistribution of pharaoh's wealth in the form of rations while ensuring that almost every family in Egypt was either directly or indirectly involved in pyramid building.

11

Khufu's Descendants

*Although the kings designed these two [pyramids] for their sepulchres,
yet it happened that neither of them were buried there. For the people,
being incensed at them by reason of the toil and labour they were put
to, and the cruelty and oppression of their kings, threatened to drag
their carcases out of their graves, and pull them by piece-meal, and
cast them to the dogs; and therefore both of them [Khufu and Khaefre]
upon their death beds commanded their servants to bury them in some
obscure place.*[1]

Khufu's triumph left Egypt's architects superbly confident. The Great
Pyramid was an engineering and organizational masterpiece – the sun's
rays petrified – while its surrounds, the substantially completed mortuary
complex and the neat social hierarchy of the western and eastern mastaba
cemeteries, were *maat* preserved in stone. No one could doubt pharaoh's
divinely inspired abilities: everyone could look upon their new national
monument with awe and pride. The Old Kingdom artists and sculptors,
inspired by this new confidence, would go on to produce some of the
most beautiful, spare yet expressive, works of the Dynastic age.

With Khufu dead and buried, everything had to start all over again.
But first the succession had to be settled. Khufu had left a large but by
no means united family. With at least twelve children by various queens,
and with the designated heir, Kawab, already dead, a series of sons,
sons-in-law and grandsons competed for the ultimate prize. Djedefre,
husband of Khufu's eldest daughter Hetepheres II and probable son of
Queen Meretetes, emerged the victor and confirmed his right to rule by
burying his father, taking the opportunity to preserve his own cartouche
in one of Khufu's boat pits. Djedefre stressed his loyalty to the sun god
by becoming the first pharaoh to take the title 'Son of Re', but this filial

piety does little to overcome the slight air of unease surrounding his accession. Although he would be included in the Turin Canon and the Abydos and Sakkara king lists, the Greek historians ignored Djedefre's reign – the treatment usually reserved for usurpers – so that they jump straight from Khufu to Khaefre. George Reisner believed, erroneously, that Djedefre was Khufu's son by a blonde Libyan queen, and that he murdered his half-brother Kawab, only to be murdered in turn by a third brother, Khaefre. As we have already seen, Reisner was an incurable romantic. In fact we have no idea how Djedefre's family or people regarded him, and suggestions that his mortuary complex was deliberately attacked soon after his death have proved unfounded.

Djedefre now started to plan his own pyramid complex, which was to be built a few miles north of Giza in an ancient cemetery on the edge of the Delta near the modern town of Abu Roash.[2]

There is a tendency for modern observers to see the Great Pyramid as the ultimate in pyramid design; everything that comes after, being smaller, is automatically perceived as inferior. This is not necessarily how the Egyptians saw things. Although size undoubtedly mattered, with larger buildings, monuments and sculptures being classed as 'better' on several levels (better because they demonstrated greater wealth and control over resources, and better because like pharaoh himself they dwarfed humanity and approached the gods), pyramid building was still an evolving art and the pyramid remained just one element in the wider mortuary complex. While all the Old Kingdom true pyramid complexes share certain features, each was an evolution of those that had gone before, incorporating both changing religious beliefs and new building technologies so that there can be no one absolutely typical pyramid site.

Khufu had concentrated his resources in his pyramid and had been happy with relatively basic temples. Now, perhaps because of his strengthened solar convictions and a drawing away from the image of the pyramid as the primal mound, Djedefre simplified his pyramid's internal structure, reducing its size while replacing Khufu's restrained chapels with buildings of greater complexity. The emphasis was to be on the whole complex as a place of ritual and worship rather than on the pyramid in its role of tomb and gigantic ramp to heaven. At the same time, the pyramid enclosure was remodelled so that it bore a passing resemblance to Djoser's step pyramid enclosure; a large rectangle, it incorporated the pyramid bounded by an inner enclosure wall, the mortuary chapel, boat pit, a small satellite pyramid and workshops and storage areas. A lengthy causeway was to link the mortuary temple to its valley temple.

Djedefre's reign – eight years according to the Turin Canon, at least ten years suggested by the inscription in Khufu's boat pit – proved far too short to complete this ambitious project. At his death his red granite temples were incomplete, and while the T-shaped trench, which was to hold his subterranean burial chamber and antechamber, had been cut and roofed, his granite-clad pyramid – 'Djedefre's Starry Sky' – remained an ill-defined flat-topped limestone mound incorporating a substantial amount of natural bedrock. Although it today stands a mere 12 metres high, with a base length of approximately 100 metres, the pyramid was probably intended to reach 67 metres in height, with a base of approximately 106 metres and an angle somewhere between 48 and a very steep 60 degrees.

Fragments of the king's oval or cartouche-shaped granite sarcophagus, unusual in an Old Kingdom context, were discovered inside the burial chamber, but the pyramid was otherwise empty. The statues which once adorned Djedefre's complex were discovered lying in the abandoned boat pit to the east of the pyramid, where they had been unceremoniously dumped by the Late Period scavengers who stripped the complex of much of its reusable stone. This recycling continued well into recent times, with nineteenth-century observers recording a regular procession of camels – Petrie suggests as many as 300 each day – removing blocks from the site.

Amongst the 120 statues and statue fragments included in the pit, and now housed in the Louvre Museum, Paris, was a superb red quartzite head broken from one of Djedefre's sphinxes. The human-headed, lion-bodied sphinx was an explicit symbol of divine royal power; the awesome combination of animal strength and overwhelming royal might first seen on the pottery and votive palettes of the Naqada age. Its very name, derived from the Egyptian *shesep ankh [Atum]*, 'living image [of Atum]' connected the sphinx with the solar creator god Atum, and it would later be identified with the various forms of Horus-Re. Here Djedefre as sphinx wears the simple *nemes* headcloth and offers our first sculpted view of the royal cobra, or uraeus, which reinforces his kingship.

Djedefre's eldest son, the 'Unique Associate of his Father, Prince

Setka, Lector Priest of his Father, Governor of the Palace, Member of the Elite, Initiate of the Morning House . . .' was proud to be depicted as a scholar and a scribe. His composite red granite, limestone and wood statue, recovered from Djedefre's pyramid complex and displayed in the Louvre Museum, shows him sitting cross-legged holding a papyrus scroll in his lap. Setka, however, was not destined to be king and the throne passed to his uncle Khaefre, son of Khufu.

Khaefre returned to Giza to ally himself as closely as possible with Khufu's memory by building his own mortuary complex to the south of the Great Pyramid. The two pyramids were closely aligned, Khaefre's carefully positioned so that it too was in line of sight with Heliopolis, with its northern face turned towards the still-important pole star. The unsubtle message was clear. Family rifts were now resolved and, with his older brothers dead, Khaefre would take up where his father had left off. Indeed, so closely would Khaefre be associated with Khufu that Herodotus, believing Khufu and Khaefre to be brothers, links the two together as masters of unparalleled evil:[3]

Chephren [Khaefre] imitated the conduct of his predecessor, and, like him, built a pyramid, which did not, however, equal the dimensions of his brother's. Of that I am certain, for I measured both myself . . . The reign of Chephren lasted fifty-six years. Thus the affliction of Egypt endured for the space of one hundred and six years, during the whole of which time the temples were shut up and never opened. The Egyptians so detest the memory of these kings that they do not like to mention them by name.

The second Giza pyramid, 'Khaefre is Great', was indeed smaller than its predecessor. Its square base is 15 metres less and its height of 143.5 metres is approximately 4 metres shorter. However, it is built on higher ground and this, together with its slightly steeper angle (53° 10' rather than 51° 50') makes it appear the larger pyramid. Khaefre had chosen a sloping site – the bedrock in the north-west corner had to be cut down by 10 metres before building could start – but the end result justified the difficulty. Khaefre's complex was looted during the First Intermediate Period; its blocks were used in the pyramid built by the 12th Dynasty King Amenemhat I at el-Lisht, and much later in the splendid New Kingdom temple of Ptah at Memphis. However, Khaefre's cult re-emerged during the 26th Dynasty, when the king was again revered as a god. Today Khaefre's complex remains the most complete of the Giza three and, while Menkaure's is the better preserved pyramid, Khaefre's is the only pyramid to retain some of its upper-casing stones. These, stained the yellow-brown of old teeth by decades of Cairo pollution, allow us a veiled glimpse of its vanished glories.

Khaefre's valley temple lies close by the modern town Nazlet es-Samman, beside the Sphinx Temple.[4] Built inside a thick cube of local limestone blocks, dressed inside and out with polished red granite and paved with alabaster, it had an unusually complex internal structure incorporating large granite columns and colossal statues of the king. In front of the temple, and connected to it by two ramps, were a harbour and canal: traces of less permanent structures, perhaps embalming sheds or tents, of brick walls and canals, have also been identified in this area but are as yet not fully understood.

Two portals in the eastern face – the gateways of Upper and Lower Egypt? – were dedicated to the goddess Bastet and her sister Hathor. Each was guarded by a pair of colossal sphinxes, and each was closed by a massive wooden door hung on copper hinges. The doorways allowed access to a short corridor which opened into a north–south hallway or antechamber. Here two massive statues dwelt in tall, narrow statue niches. From the west wall of the hallway a passage opened into a T-shaped pillared hall, dominated by sixteen granite pillars and twenty-three or twenty-four royal statues and lit by the dim light filtering in through the high clerestory windows. While a corridor in the south-east corner led to six storerooms arranged on two levels, a passageway in the opposite corner led to the limestone causeway, passing a corridor and stairway which allowed access to the roof.

The causeway which rises across the desert to link the north-western corner of Khaefre's valley temple to the south-eastern corner of his mortuary temple is cut from the living rock of the Giza plateau. Although its walls are still partially extant, we do not know if it was originally roofed, or if its walls were decorated with funerary scenes.

The badly preserved mortuary temple was once intricate and impress-ive. Again built with a thick core of local limestone, its walls were lined with granite and Tura limestone, its floors partially paved with alabaster and its chambers and courtyards dominated by images of the dead king.

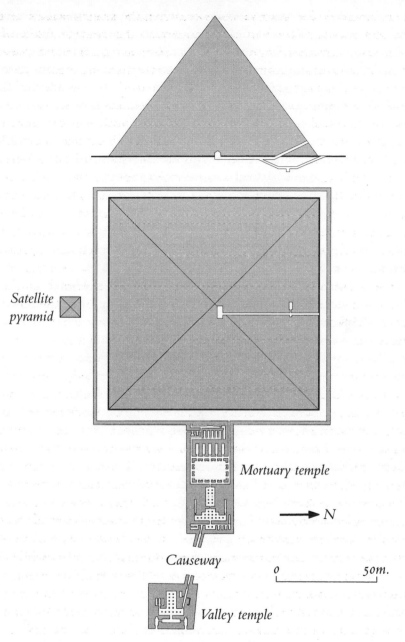

Satellite
pyramid

Mortuary temple

→ N

Causeway

0   50m.

Valley temple

Figure 11.1   Cross-section of Khaefre's pyramid at Giza and
plan of the major elements of his pyramid complex.

The one, rather narrow entry led, via a series of pillared halls and statue chambers, to an open colonnaded courtyard supported by rectangular pillars and surrounded by twelve colossal statues of the king. On the western wall, in a situation comparable to the six statue niches discovered in Snefru's valley temple, five passages led to narrow rooms or niches designed to hold royal and divine statues. Behind these rooms lay five smaller rooms, statue niches or perhaps storerooms employed to hold the statue offerings and paraphernalia. Backing on to the pyramid, the sanctuary, long, dark and narrow, housed a granite stela or false door where offerings would be made in perpetuity to the dead Khaefre. The passageway leading to the pyramid courtyard, a narrow and unceremonious exit, ran from the north-west corner of the colonnade, and stairs to the roof ran from the north-east.

While Khaefre's funeral barge moored in front of his valley temple, a fleet of hidden boats was eternally moored within his mortuary complex. Five boat pits were cut into the bedrock surrounding the mortuary chapel but, although at least two of these were roofed with limestone slabs and have yielded pottery fragments, none have supplied any trace of an actual boat.

Khaefre's pyramid followed the simplified internal structure developed by Djedefre, and his subterranean burial chamber was built, lined and roofed in a large, open trench before the pyramid was erected on top. The entrance, just over 11 metres up the northern face, was well hidden; so well hidden that many archaeologists believed that there was no entrance and it was not until 1818 that Giovanni Battista Belzoni determined to discover its secret. Determined is the right adjective for this ex-circus strongman for, as the intrepid explorer confides,[5] failure was too awful to contemplate: 'I was confident that a failure in such an attempt would have drawn on me the laughter of all the world for my presumption in such a task . . .'

Eventually Belzoni realized that the entrance was not in the dead centre of the northern face, but slightly to the east. Slowly he removed the blocking stones to reveal a granite corridor running downwards, through the masonry. Beyond a granite portcullis, which caused him considerable delay, the corridor opened into a horizontal passageway leading to the burial chamber. Given his struggle with the blocking stones and portcullis, Belzoni had realistic hopes of finding an intact burial. The chamber was, however, bare and the plain, polished granite sarcophagus was open, its heavy sliding lid broken in two. The few bones discovered in the sarcophagus turned out to be bull bones, and the burial chamber wall bore written evidence of at least one earlier visitor:

The Master Mohammed Ahmed, stonemason, has opened them; and the Master Othman attended this and the King Ali Mohammed at first from the beginning to the closing up. ·

Deflated, Belzoni scrawled his own name and the date, and retreated.

With its internal structure revealed it became obvious that there was a second entrance to Khaefre's pyramid. Also on the northern face, the second entrance opened at ground level outside the pyramid, and cut downwards through the bedrock. However, it was completely blocked with granite blocks which Colonel Vyse first attempted to move manually but which he soon, thwarted by 'the unskilfulness of the Arabs', blew to pieces. A passageway led downwards into a horizontal corridor. A subsidiary chamber, perhaps a storeroom, or even a serdab room comparable to the 'Queen's Chamber' in Khufu's pyramid, opened off the corridor, which eventually reached an ascending corridor connecting with the original passageway leading to the burial chamber. The two entrances are unexplained; they may reflect a change of plan, a change in belief; or the provision of access for the builders.

The pyramid courtyard was surrounded by a limestone wall, 2 metres high, which has survived in sections. Beyond this, to the west, lay Petrie's 'barracks', now reinterpreted as workshops and storage rooms. To the south of the main pyramid, outside its enclosure wall, stood a small pyramid which has been identified as the subsidiary pyramid provided for the *Ka* of the deceased. While its superstructure is now largely destroyed, its burial chamber has yielded jar fragments, ox bones, pieces of wood (the remains of a coffin?) and two necklaces which suggest that it may have been a queen's pyramid rather than a true subsidiary tomb. The real subsidiary pyramid is probably represented by a sealed passageway, lacking any sign of a superstructure, discovered to the west. This leads downwards to a niche holding the dismantled components of a cedarwood shrine or box. Khaefre, unlike Khufu and Menkaure, makes no further provision for the burial of his womenfolk.

Statues now feature larger than ever in the royal mortuary cults. Khaefre's mortuary temple displayed a whole series of over-life-sized images of the king, the king and his consort, and the king in the role of a god. His valley temple was even more impressive; when rediscovered it was littered with the fragments of somewhere between fifty and a hundred hard-stone statues. The most celebrated surviving sculpture, a substantially complete polished diorite image of the seated king, is now housed in Cairo Museum. It shows Khaefre dressed in the simple kilt and *nemes* headcloth plus flat uraeus and false beard which proclaim his kingship. Behind his head, not immediately obvious from the front, the god Horus extends his wings and his protection to the king; on the side of his throne the sign of the two lands confirms his earthly kingdom. Khaefre's well-developed upper body gives an impression of controlled power and muscular strength, but his broad face lacks the character which bring's Djedefre's sphinx to life. Khaefre is dignified, majestic and even divine, but he is not an individual; he is an archetypal dead pharaoh.

The most famous representation of Khaefre is undoubtedly the Great Sphinx which crouches beside his valley temple, lazily guarding the entrance to the mortuary complex. This fabulous beast consists of the king's head, approximately twenty-two times life-sized, perched atop a disproportionately massive lion's body carved at a scale of approximately thirty to one. The human head is bearded and wears the *nemes* headcloth which makes an effective substitute for a mane; the lion's tail curls nonchalantly over its back. The Sphinx is today clean-shaven, a circumstance which has led to the popular misconception that it is female. In 1817, however, Captain Caviglia discovered fragments of a long, plaited, curved beard, the type of beard worn by gods and deified kings, buried in the sand surrounding the Sphinx's chest. Although carved from the same rock as the Sphinx, the figures decorating the support which allowed the beard to jut proud of the chest are obviously New Kingdom in style. While some would argue that the beard is an entirely New Kingdom 'enhancement', glued on to the Old Kingdom face with mortar, it seems more likely that it is an original Old Kingdom feature, re-decorated in the course of the New Kingdom restorations.

The Sphinx lies some 72 metres long and 20 metres tall, making it Egypt's largest statue, comparable in scale only to the New Kingdom Abu Simbel temple carved into a Nubian cliff-face by Ramesses II. As it is carved from a naturally occurring rocky outcrop covered in places with a veneer of stone blocks masking structural defects within the rock, the Sphinx shows differential weathering due to the three limestone strata included in its body. Broadly speaking, the base of the Sphinx, including its paws and rump, is carved from hard, brittle rock, the middle section which includes most of the body is cut from bands of softer rock, while the head is made from good, firm stone. The sculptors worked by cutting a giant horseshoe-shaped trench to isolate a rectangle of stone; as they shaped this rock they reused the limestone taken from the head region in Khaefre's valley temple. Meanwhile stone taken from the ditch was being used to build the Sphinx Temple.[6]

The Great Sphinx has enjoyed a colourful history. Abandoned and neglected by the end of the Old Kingdom, its temple was eventually lost beneath the windblown sand. A thousand years on it enjoyed a resurgence of power when the isolated head poking through the dunes was recognized both as a powerful variant of the god Khepri-Re-Atum and as a form of Horemakhet (Horus in the Horizon). In the first year of his reign the 18th Dynasty king Amenhotep II built a new mud-brick temple to the north-east of the Great Sphinx and dedicated a stela to the Sphinx as Horemakhet. His son, Tuthmosis IV, developed an even greater devotion to the Sphinx, for it was in its shadow that he had a life-changing dream.

Tuthmosis visited Giza as a young prince not directly in line to the throne and not particularly interested in Re or the ancient solar cults. Religion was an old man's pastime; he had come to hunt in the desert. At noon, hot and exhausted by the chase, Tuthmosis retreated to the cool shadow and fell into a deep sleep. In a dream Horemakhet appeared before him, imploring Tuthmosis to restore his neglected statue in exchange for the throne. When Tuthmosis woke he carried out the god's wishes, clearing away a veritable mountain of sand and repairing a broken paw and a hole in the chest. He even repainted the Sphinx, using bright blue, red and yellow pigments. Horemakhet must have been satisfied as Tuthmosis did indeed become king of Egypt. And as king, he remembered his patron. In the first year of his reign he had the remarkable story carved on the 15 ton, 3.6 metres tall 'dream stela' (itself carved from a lintel taken from Khaefre's mortuary temple – Tuthmosis's devotion to rescue archaeology only stretched so far) which formed the back wall of a small open-air chapel built between the newly restored forepaws.

The 19th Dynasty Ramesses II enhanced this chapel with two smaller stelae, dated to the first year of his reign and showing him worshipping the Sphinx. Today Ramesses's stelae are in the Louvre Museum and, while Tuthmosis's now-broken stela remains in place, his chapel is almost entirely demolished.

The Sphinx endorsed Tuthmosis's right to rule, an endorsement which would have been welcomed by any second-born son. Tuthmosis returned the compliment by publicizing the Sphinx's powers as a prophet and kingmaker. This stimulated renewed interest in the ancient solar cults which had been relegated to second place by the growing power of the Theban god Amen. While his son Amenhotep III cautiously promoted the cult of the Aten (the sun) his grandson Amenhotep IV, also known as Akhenaten, dedicated his life to Aten worship. Tutankhamen, the post-Amarna restorer, had every reason to be wary of the solar cults yet he built a villa or rest house close by the Sphinx. Ramesses II was to usurp this building and replace Tutankhamen's name with his own. By this time Giza was a popular tourist attraction, busy with New Kingdom buildings and shrines so that it must have resembled, in spirit if not in style, modern Giza.

Tuthmosis chose to illustrate his stela with two mirror-image sphinxes lying on a plinth or pedestal with an open doorway. The pedestal was probably an artistic device used to bring the recumbent beast up to the level of the standing king, and in other contemporary scenes, for example, the stela of the scribes Mentuher and Kanakhet, which shows a large sphinx with two steep pyramids in the background, there is no doorway shown. However Tuthmosis's door has led to centuries of speculation that there might be an unknown chamber hidden within the body of the Great Sphinx. No major chamber has yet been found but there is indeed a passageway leading downwards from the Sphinx's rump. This was discovered by Emile Baraize, the engineer who cleared and surveyed the Sphinx in 1925, but he closed the passageway with limestone slabs and cement and it went unrecorded. Reopened by Mark Lehner and Zahi Hawass in 1980, it was found to be a blind passageway which stops abruptly in the bedrock. There is no indication of when, or why, this was cut.

The Sphinx, looking towards the rising sun, was able to glance down into the open courtyard of his own temple. This, physically close to

Khaefre's valley temple and architecturally close to Khufu's mortuary temple, was open to the sun's rays and therefore contrasted with its roofed and secretive neighbour. A central colonnaded court with twenty-four granite pillars housed a series of colossal statues which are now represented by ten empty sockets set in the alabaster floor. Near this court lay two sanctuaries – one to the east and one to the west, possibly representing night and day, or the rising and setting sun. Whatever its purpose, the temple was incomplete and, as we do not find anyone in the elite cemeteries claiming to be a servant of the cult, possibly unstaffed at Khaefre's death.

The Turin Canon tells us that Nebka succeeded Khaefre. Nebka is otherwise invisible, although he may be the owner of the Unfinished Pyramid built at Zawiyet el-Aryan which has variously been attributed, on the basis of almost unreadable masons' markings scrawled on its blocks, to Nebka, Bakka, Khnumka or Wehemka.[7] Designed to equal Khaefre's monument, its superstructure consists of a platform plus one ruined course of large limestone blocks. Its confident substructure is far more advanced and includes an oval pink granite sarcophagus carved out of one of the floor blocks and similar in style to Djedefre's sarcophagus. Although its lid was sealed in place with clay the sarcophagus was empty, bringing to mind the sealed but empty sarcophagus of Sekhemkhet. The remains of an enclosure wall define the rectangular pyramid enclosure.

A brief list of cartouches carved on a rock face in the Wadi Hammamat during the Middle Kingdom suggests further possible owners for the Unfinished Pyramid by recording the succession Khufu, Djedefre, Khaefre, Hardjedef, Baufre. We have already met Khufu's second son, Hardjedef, sage of the Westcar Papyrus. Could either he, or his brother Baufre have ruled after Khaefre? We know that Hardjedef was eventually buried in a large Giza mastaba. In death Hardjedef was celebrated as a wise man and seer, a 4th Dynasty version of Djoser's architect Imhotep. The fragmented 'Instructions of Hardjedef', written during the 5th Dynasty, preserve the sensible advice supposedly offered by the sage to his young son, Auibre:

Build a good house in the graveyard, make a worthy resting place in the west. For the house of death is for life.

Baufre has left no monument, suggesting that his name may be a distortion or a throne name adopted by one of Khufu's other known sons. But he, too, has a tale to tell: the fabulous story of Snefru's court which precedes Hardjedef's tale of the magician Djedi in the Westcar Papyrus, is narrated by Prince Baufre.

Eventually Khaefre was succeeded by his son Menkaure, born to Khamerernebty I and married to his sister Khamerernebty II. Herodotus[8] tells us that Menkaure (Mycerinus) was a good man beloved of his people, who reopened the temples and allowed offerings to the gods. But Egypt had been condemned to suffer 150 years of bad kings and Menkaure was fated to enjoy a reign of only six years. The king was not prepared to accept this injustice, and so:

. . . perceiving that his doom was fixed, [Menkaure] had lamps prepared, which he lighted every day at eventide and feasted, and enjoyed himself unceasingly both day and night, moving about in the marsh country and the woods, and visiting all the places that he heard were agreeable. His wish was to prove the oracle false, by turning nights into days and so living twelve years in the space of six.

While the Turin Canon allows Menkaure eighteen years, it seems that he may have reigned for considerably longer, perhaps as many as twenty-eight years. Even this was not long enough to finish the mortuary complex which his son and successor, Shepseskaf, hurriedly completed in mud-brick.

Menkaure has attracted a whole host of legends. Herodotus tells the tale of the king's beloved only daughter who, having died young, was entombed by her grieving father in a gold-plated wooden cow. This cow, attended by ranks of colossal wooden female statues, was displayed in the royal palace at Sais where Herodotus inspected it: it is not clear what Herodotus actually saw – he tells us that the 'cow' was lying down and covered by a cloth, and that it was only paraded before the people once each year – but perhaps it was some form of cult statue dedicated to Hathor. He then repeats a less romantic version of this tale which sees Menkaure raping his daughter who, shamed, hangs herself; the queen, believing her daughter to have been betrayed by her serving maids, exacts revenge by cutting off their hands, thus explaining why the wooden attendants at Sais, too, lack hands. But, as Herodotus wisely adds:

All this is mere fable in my judgement, especially what is said about the hands of the colossal statues. I could plainly see that the figures had only lost their hands through the effects of time. They had dropped off, and were still lying about the feet of the statues.

Herodotus also records, but quickly dismisses, rumours that Menkaure's pyramid was built by Rhodophis, a courtesan of outstanding beauty and seemingly unlimited earning power. Strabo based a Cinderella-like tale on this legend: Rhodophis's sandal is stolen by an eagle which flies to Memphis and drops it in the king's lap. Pharaoh, smitten by the shoe's charms, orders an immediate search for its owner. Rhodophis is found, brought to Memphis, and in best story-book tradition, marries the king who builds her a pyramid as a token of his undying love.

The pyramid was also to be assigned to Nitocris, the female pharaoh whose rule was to see the end of the Old Kingdom; her naked spirit is said to haunt the Giza plateau where it is occasionally glimpsed by credulous men but never by women. The ninth-century Arab writer Masoudi tells of further hauntings at Giza:[9]

The king assigned to each pyramid a guardian; the guardian of the eastern pyramid was an idol of speckled granite, standing upright, with a weapon like a spear in his hand; a serpent was wreathed around his head, which seized upon and strangled whoever approached, by twisting round his neck . . .

The guardian of the western pyramid was an image made of black and white onyx, with fierce and sparkling eyes, seated on a throne, and armed with a spear; upon the approach of a stranger, a sudden noise was heard, and the image destroyed him.

To the coloured pyramid he assigned a statue, placed upon a pedestal, which was empowered with the power of entrancing every beholder till he perished.

When everything was finished he caused the pyramids to be haunted with living spirits, and offered up sacrifices to prevent intrusions by strangers, and of all persons, except those who, by their conduct, were worthy of admission.

Still in the realm of Gothic romance, but much later, both Menkaure and his pyramid were to feature prominently in Rider Haggard's

Cleopatra, where the dead Menkaure exerts his revenge on Egypt's last, unfortunate queen.

'The Divinity of Menkaure' was aligned with the pyramids built by Khufu and Khaefre but, as space was by now somewhat restricted, was built at a much smaller scale. This was the smallest pyramid to be built since Khaba erected his Layer Pyramid at Zawiyet el-Aryan, and it was to establish a precedent for all pyramids to come. Never again would Egypt see tombs built to the scale of the Great and second Giza pyramids. To detract from its short stature, the bottom layers of the pyramid were cased in expensive red granite. The finished pyramid had a height of approximately 65 metres, a base of 102 by 104 metres and an angle of 51° 20'. In antiquity it attracted the attention of Caliph Malek al-Azis Othman Ben Youssef who, for no good reason that we know, determined to demolish it. Gangs set to work with levers and wedges but after eight months of little progress the Caliph accepted the inevitable and retreated, leaving only a superficial wound.[10]

The unfinished, roofed limestone causeway runs around, rather than through, Menkaure's valley temple, allowing visitors to the upper temple to bypass the lower. The valley temple, now lost beneath the Nazlet es-Samman cemetery, was built in mud-brick incorporating stone elements (column bases, door thresholds, flooring); a far from ideal situation which suggests its hasty completion during Menkaure's seventy-day embalming period. More open in plan than Khaefre's valley temple, its central doorway leads through a pillared vestibule into a courtyard flagged with a single line of limestone slabs which, somewhat in the manner of the lines drawn in children's playgrounds, directed the visitor onwards. Beyond this courtyard, up a low step, lay a pillared hall, six statue niches and a sanctuary. The temple storerooms have yielded the fragments of over 500 hard- and soft-stone vessels including many whose style dates them to the 1st and 2nd Dynasties; one bears the name Nebre, while others are inscribed for Snefru. Menkaure, like Djoser before him, has raided the warehouses if not the tombs of his revered forebears.

George Reisner excavated Menkaure's pyramid complex at a time when there were only thirteen known statues and statuettes of the 4th Dynasty kings. Suddenly the archaeologist was faced with an embarrassment of riches, as the two pyramid temples yielded an unprecedented series of statues of Menkaure, dyads of Menkaure and his queen, and

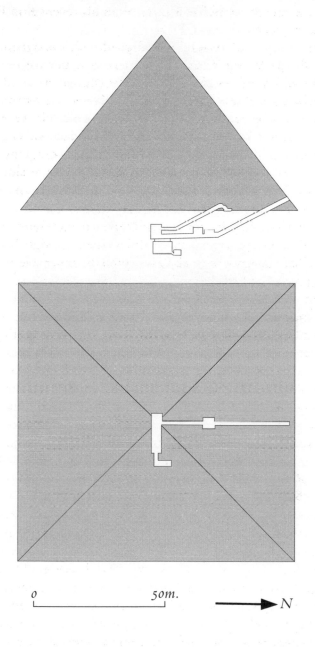

Figure 11.2   Cross-section and plan of Menkaure's pyramid at Giza.

triads depicting Menkaure, Hathor and the various divinities which symbolized Egypt's provinces. From the mortuary temple came a damaged but still impressive over-life-sized alabaster statue of the king which Reisner identified as the focus of the mortuary cult, suggesting that it had stood in front of, as if emerging from, a false door.

From the valley temple came one of the most celebrated pieces of Old Kingdom sculpture. Discovered in a hole filled with sand and debris in 1910, and now housed in the Museum of Fine Arts, Boston, the greywacke piece shows the king standing alongside an anonymous queen, most probably Khamerernebty II. The queen, dressed in a skin-tight sheath and with her bushy wig tucked behind her ears, stands with her left arm across her body so that her hand touches the king's arm, and her right arm encircling her husband in a gesture of support. The king, slightly larger, is dressed in kilt, headcloth and false beard, has his hands by his side and his left leg slightly forward. His squared, firm face is finely chiselled and impassive, the queen's face provides a pleasing contrast, showing the roundness and softness considered more appropriate to an Egyptian woman. The polished stone glows softly and is to modern eyes beautiful and perfect; the Egyptians, of course, painted all their statuary, and there are still traces of paint on the king's face (red) and the queen's wig (black).

One aspect of Mankaure's [sic] personality we know very well, and that is his face. Quite a number of contemporary statues, agreeing most closely in their presentation of his features, have come down to us . . . Their sincerity and truth are manifest; they show us a man who can have had small pretensions to beauty. Except the chin, which is normal, every feature is prominent. The over-development of the frontal sinuses, accentuated by a receding forehead, the protruding eyes, the nose, which not only juts out but is thick at the tip, and the unusually salient cheek bones, make up a face full of character, and by no means lacking in power, but one in which depth and delicacy are subordinated to curiosity and objectivity . . .[11]

Many would feel that Battiscombe Gunn is here being unjustly harsh in his assessment of Menkaure's facial features, although it has to be said that some of Menkaure's other statuary shows the king with an unimpressive round face, prominent eyes and a curiously thin upper lip which might, in the original painted versions, have been hidden by a moustache. Bearing in mind the often-repeated caveat that such pieces are not intended to be realistic portraits, we have to wonder how far these images reflect the style and skills of the royal workshops, how far they are representative of the king himself.

His mortuary temple, substantially complete at Menkaure's death, and relatively well-preserved today, is a simplified version of Khaefre's temple. Again it was designed with a local limestone core lined inside and out with granite; again it was set slightly apart from the pyramid's east face; again, it was to be completed in plastered and painted mud-brick. From the central doorway in the eastern face a long corridor ran to an open courtyard complete with drainage system. Beyond this a hall with six granite pillars led to a long, narrow room or offering hall. To the north-west, a narrow passageway passed a room with five statue niches and opened into the pyramid courtyard. The false door, long vanished, was independent of the mortuary chapel and set in a small offering shrine against the eastern face of the pyramid.

The pyramid entrance, which lay some 4 metres above ground level on the north face, was only discovered after Vyse had employed gun-powder to drive a meandering gallery right through the pyramid masonry proving, albeit by accident, that there are no hidden chambers in this part of the superstructure. From the entrance a partially granite-lined passage dropped downwards through the core and into the bedrock before opening into a horizontal chamber whose walls were carved with false door panels; our first glimpse of internal pyramid decoration since we visited the Step Pyramid. Beyond this a horizontal passage, guarded by three granite portcullises, led to a plain, rectangular antechamber (14.2 by 3.84 by 4.87 metres) whose westerly niched recess suggests that it may have been intended to serve as a burial chamber. A descending corridor dropped from the anteroom floor to both the burial chamber and to a rough room, or 'cellar' provided with six niches, variously identified as statue niches, or niches provided for the four Canopic jars plus the crowns of Upper and Lower Egypt. The burial chamber (6.6 by 2.6 by 3.4 metres and orientated north–south) was considerably smaller than the anteroom. Completely lined with granite, its ceiling was carved to give the impression that the dead king lay beneath a curved vault. From the northern wall of the antechamber, directly above the entrance from the horizontal passage, a corridor led upwards through the bulk of the pyramid before petering out, unfinished, in a rough upper chamber.

Inside the burial chamber Vyse found a beautiful dark basalt sarcophagus carved with elaborate palace façade panelling. He determined to send it to the British Museum, but in 1838 it was lost at sea when the *Beatrice* foundered off the Spanish coast. The sarcophagus had been empty, but the chamber at the end of the blind upper passage yielded a wooden coffin complete with some tattered human remains: a pair of legs, a lower torso, and some ribs and vertebrae wrapped in coarse cloth. These remains did reach London intact, and have been dated by radiocarbon analysis to the Roman period.

The wooden coffin was inscribed for the dead king:

Osiris, the King of Upper and Lower Egypt, Menkaure, living for ever. Born of the sky, conceived by Nut, heir of Geb, his beloved. Thy mother Nut spreads herself over you in her name of 'Mystery of Heaven'. She caused you to be a god, in your name of 'God'. O King of Upper and Lower Egypt Menkaure, living for ever.

But this, too, is an anachronism; dated on stylistic grounds to the Saite period, the coffin is 600 years older than its bones. Menkaure, as the kindest and most compassionate of the three Giza kings, was an especial favourite of the 26th Dynasty restorers, and it seems that in his case 'restoration' extended to providing the king with a new coffin and, perhaps, a new body.[12]

Three queens' pyramids (known today as G III-a, G III-b and G III-c) rose to the south of the main pyramid. G III-b and G III-c today stand as four-step pyramids equipped with mud-brick mortuary chapels; whether this is a deliberate reference to Djoser's pyramid, or whether they are simply unfinished and unclad, is not clear. Both were used for burials, unfinished or not, and G III-b has yielded the remains of a young woman. The easternmost pyramid, G III-a, is the most complete of the trio and is a true pyramid with a granite and limestone casing. As it has a T-shaped substructure, similar to those found in main pyramids, it may be that this was originally built as a satellite pyramid, although its granite sarcophagus and mortuary chapel show that it was eventually used for a burial. Menkaure made no further provision for his family and his sons, daughters and high officials were interred either in the existing elite Giza cemeteries, or in rock-cut tombs and mastabas to the south-east of his complex.

Menkaure was succeeded by his son Shepseskaf, 'Venerable is his Ka', a king whose name does not demonstrate any particular devotion to Re. Shepseskaf made a decisive break with tradition. He was to be buried in the new Sakkara south necropolis under a stone mastaba strongly reminiscent of the tombs of the 1st and 2nd Dynasty Abydos necropolis. 'Shepseskaf is purified', is known today by its Arabic name Mastabat Faraoun or 'pharaoh's bench'. Why the abrupt change in design? Is Shepseskaf returning to the royal mastaba and the Horus-based religion of his ancestors while retaining the custom of northern burial? Is he challenging Re's growing economic power by promoting a rival religious sect? Or are we in danger of over-analysing things? Has Shepseskaf, who has just been called upon to complete his father's unfinished pyramid complex, realized that he has neither the time nor the resources to complete a full pyramid project of his own? If this is the case, it would suggest that the pyramid, although desirable, is by no means theologically essential to a secure Afterlife. Shepseskaf was right to proceed with caution. He was to rule for a mere four to six years.

The Mastabat Faraoun is a gigantic rectangle (99.6 by 74 by 18 metres), oriented north–south and originally cased in fine limestone and red granite. Its entrance, on the northern face, leads downwards through the bedrock to meet in turn a horizontal passageway, an anteroom guarded by a portcullis system, and a granite-lined, curved-roofed burial chamber. Beside the entrance to the burial chamber are several storerooms. The mortuary temple was situated on the eastern face and included a false door and a courtyard decorated with niches. A causeway ran to the east, presumably towards the lost valley temple. Again there were no subsidiary tombs provided for the royal family or the bureaucratic elite. Although the remains of a carved basalt sarcophagus were found the burial chamber was never finished, and the tomb was unused. Wherever he was buried, Shepseskaf was worshipped at the Mastabat Faraoun during the Middle Kingdom, and his tomb was one of those 'restored' by the Ramesside prince-turned-archaeologist Khaemwaset.

Shepseskaf's mastaba served as the model for a large tomb built to the south of Khaefre's pyramid and connected to Menkaure's valley temple

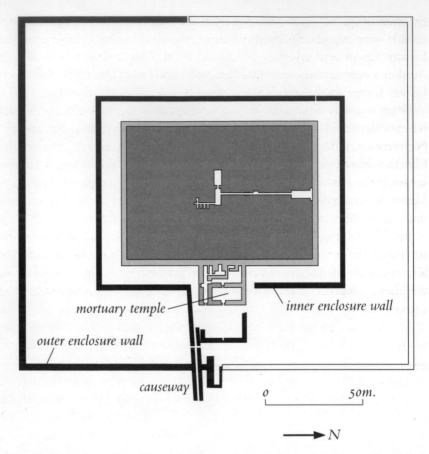

Figure 11.3   The 'Mastabat Faraoun' tomb of Shepseskaf at Sakkara.

by a causeway. This large and imposing tomb (45.5 by 45.8 by 17.5 metres and accompanied by a small 'pyramid village') was initially mis-classified as 'Lepsius Pyramid 100'. It is in fact a limestone mastaba-style superstructure perched on top of a natural rock base cased in Tura limestone and decorated with false-door style niches.[13] Inside, a granite-lined vestibule allows access to a descending passage leading to the antechamber, burial chamber and a series of storerooms. Here were found the fragments of a smashed alabaster sarcophagus but no other signs of burial. A vast granite doorway names the tomb's owner as Queen Khentkawes I, lists her impressive titles and then, in the tantalizing manner of so many Egyptological texts, adds a cryptic phrase which could, with equal validity, be translated either as 'King of Upper and Lower Egypt and Mother of the King of Upper and Lower Egypt' (Junker's translation) or as 'Mother of the Two Kings of Upper and Lower Egypt' (Vikentiev's interpretation).

Who was this influential lady? Initial opinion tended to the view that Khentkawes had given birth to two fifth Dynasty kings, Sahure and Neferirkare, who were preceded on the throne by the high priest Prince Userkaf. However, her gateway shows the queen seated on a throne, wearing the false beard and uraeus and carrying the sceptre of a king of Egypt. Khentkawes's name is not presented in a cartouche, but it seems that she is fully entitled to assume kingly regalia.

Just like Merit-Neith before her, she must have ruled Egypt as regent on behalf of an infant heir to the throne. As a temporary pharaoh Khentkawes would have been excluded from the king lists, but she might well have been rewarded with a grand tomb in Egypt's most prestigious cemetery.

12

Sun Temples and Pyramid Texts

Khufu quizzed Djedi concerning the number of secret chambers in the sanctuary of Thoth. But the magician could not satisfy his pharaoh: he did not know the number, only that it was written inside a flint chest hidden in the ancient city of Heliopolis. 'And will you bring it to me?'

But this even Djedi could not do. The chest could only be brought by the eldest of the triplet sons now in the womb of the lady Reddjedet.

On the fifteenth day of the first month of winter Reddjedet, wife of a priest of Re, went into labour and found herself in difficulties. Four goddesses set out to help her. Disguised as dancing girls Isis, Nephthys, Meskhenet, and Heket offered their services. In a locked room Isis stood in front of Reddjedet, Nephthys behind her, and Heket hastened the birth. As three sturdy sons were safely delivered, each with limbs of gold and headdresses of lapis lazuli, Meskhenet prophesied 'A king who will rule the whole land'. The three sons were Userkaf, Sahure and Neferirkare. They had been fathered by the sun god, Re, and were destined to replace the descendants of Khufu.[1]

Things were changing. The chain of kingship which had stretched unbroken from Snefru to Shepseskaf had snapped and Egypt's next pharaoh, Userkaf, is a mystery man who tells us nothing of his parentage and who dies after a mere seven years on the throne leaving only his monumental architecture as testimony to his reign. It seems likely, given his sudden rise to prominence, that he is a member of the wider royal family, possibly a grandson of Djedefre or a son of Menkaure. The Westcar Papyrus, summarized above, is obviously applying a fantastic explanation to actual events, but some of its exaggerated characters are semi-real; its pivotal female character, Lady Reddjedet, may be read as a distorted version of the powerful queen mother and queen regent, Khentkawes I.

15. The Sphinx peers down into his own temple. Khaefre's pyramid
is in the background.

16. The Great Pyramid of Khufu, photographed by Felix Bonfils in the 1880s. In the foreground is the Valley Temple of Khaefre.

17. Khaefre's pyramid, instantly recognizable by its surviving upper casing, photographed in 1900.

18. A shattered block, once part of the now derelict mortuary temple of Khaefre.

19. *(above)* Fragment of a head, possibly from a statue of Khaefre, found at Giza.

20. *(right)* Khaefre protected by the god Horus.

21 Khaefre's valley temple showing the empty floor-niches provided for multiple statues of the king.

22. The third Giza pyramid, that of Menkaure.

23. Menkaure with the goddess Hathor and one of the nome deities, taken from the Valley Temple of the Pyramid of Menkaure.

24. Standing on a modelled knoll of rock, the impressive tomb of Queen Khentkawes.

25. Granite door jambs mark this pyramid as belonging to King Unas.

26. Interior of the pyramid of King Unas.

27. The causeway of King Unas, lined with the tombs of his own
and later courtiers.

28. The collapsed pyramid of King Userkaf at Sakkara.

29. The ruined pyramid
of Amenemhat III at
Dahshur.

30. *(above)* And its still magnificent
black granite pyramidion,
c. 1850–1800 BC.

31. *(left)* The last great pyramid builder
of Egypt, King Amenemhat III.

Userkaf inherited a very different country to that which Djoser ruled. Two centuries of pyramid building had changed the face of Egypt for ever. Physically the pyramids dominated the northern cemetery skylines. Economically they dominated the whole land with vast numbers now employed either directly or indirectly in their construction and many others employed in servicing the extensive farming operations, trade networks and military campaigns which underpinned their finances. The pyramid estates owned vast tracts of land and had 'colonized' much of the previously untamed region on the outskirts of the Delta. The higher ranking officials, who for many centuries had been rewarded with estates by their kings, owned a small but growing percentage of the remainder. As the pyramids and state temples acquired more and more the crown owned less and less and grew correspondingly poorer. For the time being this was not a great problem, Egypt being a large and relatively underpopulated land, but there were other changes in the air. The moist climate enjoyed by the 4th Dynasty pyramid builders was slowly evaporating. Egypt was shrinking at the margins, the oases were drying and the people who occupied these marginal zones were being drawn towards the fertile valley and Delta.

Society, too, was changing, and the once rigid social distinctions had started to blur. The civil service had grown strong and efficient with revenue collection a speciality. Now it was threatening to become too large, and too independent, for one family to control. The elite still guarded access to the most prestigious positions but literacy was spreading and a new, economically empowered middle class was emerging. Scribes and accountants found themselves in demand. Well rewarded for their efforts, they were for the first time able to develop their own ambitions. The vast gulf which separated the semi-divine pharaoh from his mortal people had narrowed; pharaoh now appeared more human, not so very different after all, while his people had gained unprecedented access to resources. At the opposite end of the social scale farmers still supported the social pyramid, using age-old techniques to farm the traditional crops. With thousands regularly drawn off the land to work on the national projects they were fewer in number and had to work harder and harder to produce the surpluses required by their king.

Egypt's new pharaoh was a dedicated follower of Re. Userkaf reinstated the pyramid as the royal tomb, but the age of the massive pyramid was well and truly over and he was happy with a scaled-down version which allowed him to divert resources towards the building of a sun temple. The two were physically separate entities – Userkaf's sun temple was built in line of site of Heliopolis at Abu Gurob just to the north of Abusir while his pyramid sat close by the north-east corner of Djoser's mortuary enclosure – but they were both part of the king's mortuary provision and, as such, shared strikingly similar architecture. The tradition of the diminished pyramid and the prominent sun temple would be followed by six of the nine 5th Dynasty kings although so far only two sun temples have been discovered. Re now reigned king of heaven while his beloved daughter, Hathor, became richer and more influential than ever before. Meanwhile, as temple records testify, the lower-profile state and regional gods continued to benefit from royal generosity, retaining and even increasing their share of offerings.

Given the question mark that hangs over Userkaf's legitimacy, it is difficult not to see his choice of a site beside Djoser's Step Pyramid as a calculated move designed to confirm his right to rule. 'Pure are the Places of Userkaf' was relatively small (49 metres high, with a square base of 73 metres and an angle of 53°) and, beneath its polished limestone exterior, so badly made that today, minus its casing blocks, it has reverted to a shapeless mound known locally as the 'Ruined Pyramid'.[2]

The pyramid substructure had once again been built in an open trench with the superstructure subsequently erected on top. The entrance, located in the courtyard pavement on the north side of the pyramid, descended through masonry and bedrock to a horizontal corridor equipped with a large granite portcullis. Continuing past a T-shaped storage area, the corridor opened into an antechamber which led, via a short westerly passage, to the burial chamber. This, limestone-lined with an angled slab roof, held a plain basalt sarcophagus which was empty when discovered.

While there was a small offering chapel with a quartzite false door resting against the eastern face, Userkaf's mortuary temple was, most unusually, erected to the south of, and at an angle to, his pyramid. This innovation may be read as a proof of Userkaf's slightly different religious convictions as a southern temple would effectively catch the sun's rays all year long, while the southerly statue niches would allow their occu-pants to look towards the pyramid. But it may also represent a practical response to an architectural problem. Userkaf had built so close to Djoser's complex that he may not have had the room to site his temple on the approved eastern side.

The entrance to the mortuary temple led into a vestibule and then, via a wide passageway, to a large open court with granite pillars. Here were found many fragments of hard-stone statues plus one colossal head, the remains of the largest known 5th Dynasty sculpture. We may guess from its context that this piece, originally some 5 metres high, showed Userkaf seated on his throne. The king wears the simple *nemes* headcloth and uraeus, and his is a simplified, rounded face designed to be seen from below. Today this head is displayed in Cairo Museum. To the south of the court a columned hall allowed access to five statue niches and a sanctuary which was itself orientated south rather than towards the pyramid.

Userkaf's causeway leads away from the entrance to the mortuary temple but is soon lost; his valley temple has never been discovered. There is a small, ruined satellite pyramid situated within the enclosure wall behind the mortuary temple on the south-west corner of the main pyramid, and the remains of a third, queen's, pyramid beyond the wall. This, once one of the largest queen's complexes ever built, is today an unreconstructed ruin, the name of its occupant unknown.

Userkaf called his sun temple *Nekhen Re* or 'Stronghold of Re', a name which brings to mind the once-glorious southern city of Hieraconpolis, *Nekhen*, and in so doing suggests that Userkaf may have adopted some of the architectural elements found in the ancient temple of Horus. In form the sun temple resembled a pyramidless mortuary complex, with an upper temple sited in the desert and linked, via a causeway, to a valley temple lying on the shore of the Abusir lake.[3]

The upper temple is today completely ruined, but there is sufficient archaeological evidence to suggest four development phases: phase one, an enclosed mound; phase two, the erection of a squat, almost truncated composite granite obelisk on top of a pedestal building plus the dedication of two statue shrines; phase three, the rebuilding of the mud-brick area around the obelisk in limestone; phase four, the erection of a mud-brick altar to the east of the pedestal building, the building of five benches in the courtyard, and the casing of the exterior faces in mud-brick and plaster. It is difficult to determine just how far Userkaf was responsible for his temple's final form, as both his son Neferirkare and his grandson Niuserre tampered with their forebear's design.

Within the wide causeway low mud-brick walls defined a central road, perhaps used to drive animals for slaughter, and a path on either side. We know, from the Palermo Stone, that two geese and two oxen were slaughtered every day in the sun temple, and indeed the upper temple was provided with a slaughterhouse which fed both the sun cult and the nearby pyramid complex.

The valley temple, completed and/or remodelled by Niuserre, is badly damaged, its frontage now completely lost. Rectangular in shape, it is roughly orientated towards Heliopolis and includes an open court with a colonnade of sixteen granite pillars and a series of statue niches that appear to be a new version of the statue niches found in the pyramid mortuary temples.

Although papyri name the other 5th Dynasty sun temples, only one, the 'Delight of Re' built by Niuserre, has been discovered.[4] Delight of Re had a simplified valley temple, but it followed the same broad plan as Userkaf's monument and it too was reworked in three distinct building phases which saw it transformed from mud-brick to stone. Outside the upper temple enclosure, within a pit, was moored a 30-metre long, mud-brick boat. Inside the temple a remarkable chamber, the 'Room of the Seasons', depicted with delightful naturalism the three seasons and their principal agricultural activities. While the artistic repertoire was expanding, the ancient and more formal scenes of rejuvenation were still extremely important and so near the innovative 'Room of the Seasons' we also find images of Niuserre's traditional *heb-sed* celebrations.

Userkaf's successors – his son Sahure, a second son, Neferirkare, his grandson Raneferef, a second grandson Niuserre – were to build their pyramids at Abusir, about a mile to the south of Userkaf's sun temple. Now for the first time in our lengthy history pyramid evolution slows down as these four surviving pyramids show an unprecedented degree of standardization, a standardization which must surely have been helped by the decision to adopt one pyramid cemetery for four or five consecutive reigns. The brevity of the reigns, too, must have contributed to their architectural consistency. From the start of Sahure's rule to the end of Niuserre's was no more than seventy-five years, with Niuserre accounting for twenty-five to thirty of those years. East facing, each pyramid

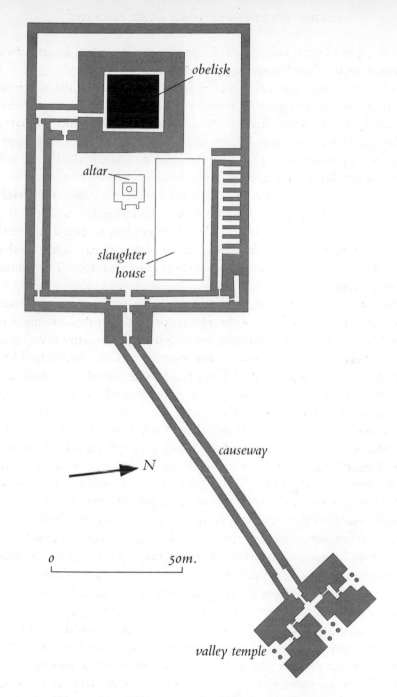

Figure 12.1 *The sun temple of Niuserre at Abu Gurob.*

was relatively small, with a simplified internal structure and a satellite pyramid on the south-east corner. The mortuary temple included a vaulted, decorated hall and a pillared courtyard leading to the five statue niches and the offering hall. A causeway linked the mortuary temple to the valley temple built on the Abusir lake front. All the complexes included extensive storage facilities and all were, naturally, already robbed when re-discovered.[5]

The decrease in pyramid size went hand-in-hand with an increasing emphasis on detailed carved and painted scenes on the interior walls,[6] which is already apparent in Userkaf's monuments. With the older pyramids already tending to ruin, it had finally been admitted that carved relief, impossible to steal (at least by ancient thieves), offered the only hope of preserving the function of the pyramid for eternity. The decorative function of the scenes was clearly important, and they could be very jolly; Sahure's valley temple, for example, employed colourful bands of black basalt, red granite and white limestone, its walls were carved and painted with images of the king as a sphinx, and its limestone ceiling was in places a deep blue sky which shimmered with carved, golden stars. But the scenes were strictly controlled to convey the correct theological message, and we find the same images appearing again and again in the same locations to tell the same tale.

The most obvious message is that of deliberate royal aggression; the complex is used to promote, and is being protected by, the age-old propaganda of pharaoh as warrior, vanquisher of chaos and upholder of *maat*. Thus we find, included amongst the surviving scenes from Sahure's causeway, images of the gods leading despised foreign prisoners to their awful fate while Sahure appears as a sphinx, crushing Egypt's enemies beneath his weighty paws. In his mortuary temple the theme continues with more conventional military victories; Sahure smites his traditional enemies and Seshat, goddess of writing, is kept busy counting a vast pile of booty. Small-scale statues of bound and kneeling foreigners, found in several of the Abusir mortuary temples, lined the walls of these rooms and corridors to emphasize the role of pharaoh triumphant. Less obvious, but still aggressive in intent, are the images of hunting, fishing and fowling which decorate the temple courtyard and which show the king imposing his own order on uncontrolled nature.

Other scenes, found throughout the Abusir complexes, emphasize the

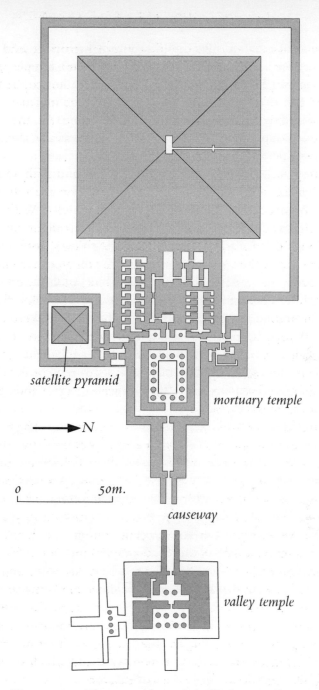

satellite pyramid

mortuary temple

►N

0   50m.

causeway

valley temple

Figure 12.2   The pyramid complex of Sahure at Abusir.

practical side of pyramid life; the bringing of the offerings and tribute which will sustain the dead king and maintain his priesthood, and the building and provisioning of his complex. Trade was particularly important. Sahure was already importing timber from Byblos, while regular expeditions were sent trekking across the arid desert to reach the turquoise and copper mines of Sinai, and sailing south into deepest Nubia to retrieve precious diorite. Now he financed a successful sea mission to the land of Punt, a trading centre somewhere along the east coast of Africa, famed for its luxury goods, its incense, wild animals, ebony, ivory and gold. A journey to Punt was no mean undertaking; it required seaworthy ships which had to be transported overland to the Red Sea, good navigational skills and a large element of luck as the Egyptians, skilful beyond compare on their own river, were neither experienced nor enthusiastic sea sailors. Only the most successful, divinely inspired pharaoh could hope to pull off such a spectacular mission.

Sahure's pyramid, 'The Rising of the Ba Spirit', stood on a small hill, had a square base of 79 metres and stood 47 metres high with an angle of just over 50°. His mortuary temple, famous for its reliefs, included an impressive amount of plumbing; rainwater flowed down from the roof through pipes whose spouts were carved with lion heads, while the basins used for libations were connected via copper pipes to a central drainage system almost 400 metres long which allowed the impure water to vanish from the sacred temple precincts.

Sahure was to be succeeded by his brother Neferirkare rather than his young son, Netjerirenre; a sideways jump which was to leave two parallel blood-lines with a strong claim to the throne. We can see the pre-promotion Neferirkare on the wall of Sahure's mortuary temple, where his unmistakably non-royal figure has been hastily embellished with a uraeus, false beard and cartouche. Neferirkare's own pyramid was an ambitious project. Built on higher ground, and started most unusually as a six-step pyramid, it was eventually filled in to form a true pyramid which would have stood approximately 70 metres high with an angle of 54°. Unfortunately 'Kakai [Neferirkare] is a soul' was never finished and is today an ill-defined mass with a badly damaged substructure.

Nearby, Neferirkare's widow, Khentkawes, owned a pyramid complex built of blocks discarded from her husband's building site. Once standing about 17 metres high with a base angle of 52°, cased in white limestone and capped with a grey granite pyramidion, today her pyramid is a low, shapeless mound. Its simple substructure consists of a corridor leading through a granite portcullis to a burial chamber housing the remains of a pink granite sarcophagus, shreds of mummy linen and fragments of hard stone vessels. Casual inscriptions scrawled on the masonry show that the pyramid had an interrupted history, being temporarily abandoned on the Year 10 death of the king. Originally built for Queen-Consort Khentkawes as a part of her husband's wider funerary complex, the pyramid was completed for Queen-Mother Khentkawes as an independent monument built by her son.

Khentkawes's mortuary temple stood to the east side of her pyramid. Started in stone, it was extended and completed in mud-brick. We know from contemporary papyri that it included at least sixteen statues of the queen although these are now lost. The queen featured on the walls, too, which were decorated not with images of military victory, but with more conventionally feminine scenes of offerings and family. Included amongst these is one remarkable image which shows Khentkawes sitting on a throne holding a sceptre and wearing the uraeus, although she does not have a false beard. Furthermore, she bears the ambiguous title 'Mother of Two Kings of Upper and Lower Egypt' or 'King of Upper and Lower Egypt and Mother of the King of Upper and Lower Egypt' which we have already encountered in the Giza necropolis. For many years this led to the misidentification of the Abusir Khentkawes with Khentkawes I, 4th Dynasty regent. Now it is realized that two formidable queens bore the same name. Here we have Khentkawes II, mother of Raneferef and Niuserre who, it seems, was also called upon to act as temporary regent. Khentkawes II was worshipped at her pyramid until the end of the Old Kingdom.

Khentkawes's elder son, Raneferef, started to build a pyramid complex to the south-west of Neferirkare's complex, aligned with the pyramids of Sahure and Neferirkare. Dying before his pyramid could take shape, he was buried in the completed burial chamber in a granite sarcophagus equipped with a set of alabaster Canopic jars. Human remains found in the burial chamber suggest that the king was in his early twenties when he died. Hastily finished in mud-brick, his aborted complex served as a functioning cult centre for the dead king while his partially cased incomplete pyramid, which resembled a low, square mastaba, was completed with a layer of clay decorated with stones – a form of ancient pebble-dash – so that it might serve as a version of the primeval mound.

Today the pyramid superstructure has completely vanished and the stone which once lined its subterranean chambers has been stolen. The valley temple and the causeway were never built. But the brick mortuary temple, which had little to tempt the stone robbers, remains substantially complete, its architecture complicated by three discernible building phases. The first phase, undertaken soon after the king's death, saw the building of a small limestone temple orientated north–south. The next two phases, both conducted during Niuserre's reign, saw large-scale remodelling so that the temple became an impressive structure with an entrance portico, boat sanctuaries, and extensive storage facilities. Within the temple we find two innovations. A hypostyle hall, Egypt's first, housed four rows of five wooden columns shaped like bundles of six lotus stems; here, papyri tell us, there stood a large wooden statue, the focus of the mortuary cult, and here the deep blue sky once again sparkled with golden stars. The appropriately named 'Sanctuary of the Knife' was a butcher's yard, a place of ritual slaughter where animals could be penned, killed, and dismembered. The flat roof served as a drying area; the dried meat was then stored in the temple.

Raneferef was probably succeeded by Shepseskare, an ephemeral king whose pyramid was barely started at his death and whose very position in the succession must be questioned, as some Egyptologists would place him a reign earlier, between Neferirkare and Raneferef. This left the next king, Niuserre, to complete the pyramids of his predecessor, his father, his mother and his brother while of course starting work on his own complex.

Although Niuserre enjoyed a lengthy and successful reign – his funeral complex shows the king active in the near east, in Libya and Sinai, while his cartouche has been recovered from Byblos in Lebanon and from Buhen in Nubia – it is not surprising, given this drain on resources, that Shepseskare's complex was left unfinished while his own pyramid, 'The Places of Niuserre are Enduring', was relatively unambitious (52 metres high, a square base of 79 metres and a base angle of 51° 50'). Logically, in order to preserve the cemetery alignment with Heliopolis, this pyramid should have been built out in the desert, beyond that built by Raneferef. Instead, wary of increased costs, Niuserre squeezed his pyramid alongside

Neferirkare's mortuary temple while, to save time and resources, his causeway and valley temple were built over foundations originally prepared by Neferirkare. This plan worked well although to make the causeway meet its new temple it was necessary to incorporate a fairly sharp bend.

Niuserre was succeeded by Menkauhor, who ruled for eight years but whose pyramid, 'Divine are the Places of Menkauhor' has vanished and whose reign is an historical blank.

Next came Djedkare-Isesi, a monarch whose reign of at least thirty-two years confirms what we have already suspected; an almost imperceptible but unstoppable decline in royal authority matched by an increase in the power of the civil service and the priesthoods, and the development of local rather than central loyalties. For many centuries government had been focused on the north. Local rulers had been permitted to run their own departments but only, it seems, after a period of indoctrination at the capital. Otherwise northern officials had been sent southwards to run Upper Egyptian affairs. Political reform – the creation of an administrative department for Upper Egypt with a bureaucratic capital based at Abydos parallel to that at White Walls, and headed by a 'Governor of Upper Egypt' – went some way towards addressing this last problem. Now the elite who govern the provinces will live in the provinces and, as their positions quickly become hereditary, a provincial aristocracy bordering on royalty will develop. From this time on the cultural difference between the capital and the provinces diminishes, and the local graveyards grow rich.

The wider royal family had always provided Egypt's top officials. But now the old way was abandoned as government ceased to be the sole responsibility of one family. Princes dropped from public view and the highest positions were thrown open to men of proven ability regardless of birth although, if we are realistic, the uneducated lower classes had no chance at all of a prestigious administrative post. The educated elite may have become a wider and slightly more democratic group, but they were still very much a minority.

As wealth and power radiated beyond the tight royal circle, as Osiris offered an Afterlife to all, individuals started to invest in their own tombs. No longer the gift of a grateful king, and so no longer controlled by the royal architects, the privately built mastabas show a relaxing of the uniformity which has hitherto characterized the elite cemeteries. At Abusir, Ptahshepses, Vizier, Overseer of Construction Projects and son-in-law of King Niuserre, built himself a tomb which was gradually extended, in three building phases, from a simple if large mastaba to the largest known private funerary monument of his age; measuring 80 by 107 metres, in its final version his mastaba was equipped with porticoes, a twenty-pillared courtyard, two large offering chambers and a boat-shaped shrine designed to hold two wooden boats. Clearly Ptahshepses was comfortable in assuming some of the architectural forms and many of the building materials hitherto reserved for royalty. Others – not necessarily those of obvious high rank but often those with control over local resources – were happy to follow his precedent.

The new-style elite tombs have multiple chambers whose smooth stone walls are richly illustrated with scenes of daily life. More importantly, from the Egyptologist's point of view, they contain lengthy texts. Individuals have been recording their increasingly complex titles for many decades. Now these abrupt lists are embroidered into fluent autobiographies which, although highly stylized and of course strongly biased in favour of their authors, tell us something of the lives of the tomb builders. Autobiography is still in its infancy, and will only truly come to life during the 6th Dynasty, but meanwhile we are able, to take just one example, to meet the official Hetepherakhet, and learn how he built his tomb 'in a pure place, where there was no earlier tomb ... I made this tomb because I was honoured by the king who gave me a sarcophagus'.

Officially Djedkare's was a highly successful reign, but then all reigns were officially successful. There were glorious military campaigns to the east; in the tomb of Inti, at Deshasha, we see Egyptian bowmen, troops using ladders to scale the town walls and foreign, desperate women fighting in the street. A policy of vigorous trade certainly paid dividends, climaxing with a successful expedition to Punt, from whence the King's envoy returned with a much-prized dancing dwarf. Back home arts and crafts flourished, and literature was starting to take form. It was during Djedkare's reign that Ptah-hotep, 'Prince, Eldest Son of the King, Mayor of the City and Vizier' penned a series of rules which, in revised form, were to become a respected and much-copied part of Egypt's cultural tradition. The Egyptians had a great fondness for texts which set out to teach the uneducated and socially gauche how to lead a good life. In *The Maxims of Ptah-hotep*[7] the vizier advised his readers to avoid the sins of pride and greed, to follow their hearts, to have good table manners, and to love yet restrain their wives, for 'if you listen to my words all your affairs will progress'.

Hand in hand with political reform went theological development. While Re remained supremely important and the pyramid remained the royal tomb of choice, Djedkare's reign saw the end of the sun temple as the doctrine of Osiris gained strength. Although some of his officials, his daughters and his son would continue the tradition of burial at Abusir, Djedkare chose to establish his own mortuary complex at South Sakkara. 'Beautiful is Isesi', today known as the Sentinel Pyramid, was badly damaged in antiquity and although investigated many times[8] has never been properly published; its causeway remains unexcavated and its valley temple is today represented by some sad granite blocks and a few mud-brick walls.

The pyramid originally stood some 52 metres tall, with a base length of 79 metres and an angle of 52°. Its stepped core was built from small limestone blocks bound with mortar, and was cased in fine white limestone. The entrance, signposted for the first time by a limestone chapel, was situated at ground level, slightly off-centre, in the pavement which ran alongside the north face of the pyramid. A granite-lined corridor led to a limestone chamber which has yielded a series of smashed pots; beyond this came three granite portcullises and a lengthy passageway leading past a blocking stone to an antechamber, three storage rooms and, opening out of the west wall, a burial chamber equipped with a grey basalt sarcophagus and a pit designed to hold the Canopic chest. When discovered the sarcophagus and the alabaster Canopic jars had been smashed to smithereens; the king's body, retrieved from a pile of rubbish, was represented by most of his left side including his still fleshy face, head, neck, spine, and limb parts.

The mortuary chapel stood against the east side of the pyramid and, elaborately decorated, grew darker and more private as the visitor passed from the impressive masonry pylon, through the colonnaded open court, towards the five statue niches and sanctuary. The satellite pyramid was in a south-easterly courtyard between the mortuary temple and the pyramid; a larger queen's pyramid equipped with mortuary chapel and satellite pyramid was in a separate compound to the north-east.

Djedkare, son, brother or perhaps even cousin of Menkauhor, may have owed his ascent to his royal-born wife. Queens, shadowy and often anonymous beings throughout the 3rd and 4th Dynasties, are starting to assume prerogatives hitherto reserved for pharaoh. The queen consort, like all the royal family, owed her position to her intimate relationship with the king. She was the 'King's Wife' who, with luck, would go on to become a 'King's Mother'; often she was also a 'King's Sister', a title which she would retain all her life. Now for the first time it is admitted that the queen herself is touched with divinity. Queens appear alongside kings and deities as colossal statues which serve as the focus for worship, and they are entitled to hold the *ankh*, the divine symbol of life and authority, which is rarely carried by private individuals. The vulture headdress adopted by the 5th Dynasty queens is the headdress of Nekhbet, goddess of Upper Egypt. In art and statuary, queens have started to resemble goddesses; they will do so until the end of the Dynastic Age. The confusion in the eye of the uneducated is deliberate.

Prominent, politically active royal women suggest some form of crisis; a regency on behalf of a minor, civil unrest, or a king seeking to rely on his wife to justify his position.[9] Djedkare never reveals his consort's name, but a substantial, anonymous pyramid complex built to the north-east of his own complex has been attributed to this lady. If this identification is correct, the sheer size of the complex suggests that his queen was a woman of great importance and economic power.

Unas, who never reveals his parentage, became the last king of the 5th Dynasty. He too enjoyed a lengthy reign of fifteen to thirty-plus years, but at just 43 metres in height (base 58 metres) 'Perfect are the Places of Unas' is the smallest king's pyramid yet attempted and his two consorts, Nebet and Khentu, had to be satisfied with mastaba tombs. With the benefit of hindsight we know that Unas was not short of time. Was he, then, short of resources, his pyramid a symptom of widespread economic malaise? Egypt, growing drier by the year, was effectively shrinking, and there were problems over the southern trade networks which saw pharaoh travelling to Elephantine to take matters in hand. Unas's pyramid was raised at Sakkara between Djoser's and Sekhemkhet's partially ruined monuments, close by Userkaf's pyramid and, unfortunately, directly on top of the substructure excavated by the 2nd Dynasty Hetepsekhemwy.[10]

The pyramid entrance lay in the floor of the northern pyramid court. It sloped down to a horizontal passageway which then opened into a corridor chamber followed by three granite portcullis slabs. Beyond this came an antechamber which allowed access to the east to three storage rooms, and to the west to a decorated burial chamber. Here were discovered a greywacke sarcophagus, a pit designed to hold a Canopic chest, and a few fragments of human bone and skin – an arm and hand, a fragment of shin and pieces of skull – which are now stored in Cairo Museum. Around the sarcophagus the alabaster walls had been carved and painted to allow the defunct Unas to lie in a reed and wood tent and gaze upwards into a night-blue sky ablaze with golden stars.

The remaining walls, and the walls of the antechamber and part of the passageway, are covered in carved and green-blue painted hieroglyphs which echo the blue-green tiles found in Djoser's subterranean chambers. This is our first sight of the Pyramid Texts, a collection of potent incantations and utterances chosen from a corpus of magical spells which has developed over many centuries as a means of helping the deceased. Over 700 spells are known; Unas's pyramid preserves 228, including some of the most ancient. The spells name the king and, as they are carved into the very fabric of his pyramid, will ensure that he is protected for ever, even if his cult fails and robbers manage to steal his grave goods and desecrate his mummy. They offer us, for the first time, the opportunity of looking into the Egyptian mind and understanding, or at least appreciating, the complexities of a theology which we have hitherto had to extrapolate from mute stone and mud-brick.

The texts, strongly biased towards Osirian and solar belief but with a significant element of stellar doctrine, tell the exciting but extremely complex and frequently contradictory story of the dead king, his burial, his life within the closed tomb, and his daily journey with Re. We read how the king, at sunset, becomes an unsetting star. At night his mummy sleeps in the tomb, where it is able to commune with Osiris, king of the Afterlife. At daybreak the king is reborn from the mother-goddess Nut and, as the young and vigorous Re-Khepri, hurries to join the solar barque of Re. The entire cycle is to be repeated for all eternity, so that even today, if we look very carefully towards Egypt's blazing sun, we might just catch a glimpse of Unas sailing in triumph across the blue sky.

A couple of examples will serve to give the flavour of these most complicated of writings:[11]

Excerpt from Utterance 217, carved on the south wall of Unas's burial chamber:

> Re-Atum, Unas comes to you, an indestructible spirit, lord of the place of
>   the four pillars.
> Your son comes to you, this Unas comes to you.
> May you cross the sky, being united in the darkness.
> May you rise on the horizon, in the place where it is well with you.
>
> Horus go and proclaim to the souls of the east and their spirits 'This Unas
>   comes, an imperishable spirit.
> Those whom he wishes to live will live, those whom he wishes to die will
>   die.'
>
> Re-Atum, your son comes to you.
> Unas comes to you.
> Raise him up, enfold him in your embrace, for he is the son of your body
>   for ever.

Excerpts from Utterance 273–4, the so-called Cannibal Hymn, a very ancient, dark spell which would be reused in Teti's pyramid and then dropped from the repertoire:

> The sky is overcast and the stars are darkened,
> The celestial expanses quiver as the bones of the earth-gods tremble,
> And the planets are stilled.
> For they have seen Unas appearing in power,
> As a god who lives on his fathers,
> And feeds on his mothers . . .
>
> The king is one who eats men and lives on the gods . . .
> Unas eats their magic and swallows their spells.
> Their big ones are for his breakfast,
> Their medium-sized ones are for his dinner,
> Their little ones are for his supper,
> Their old men and their old women provide his fuel.
>
> Unas has risen again in heaven.
> He has been crowned as the lord of the horizon.
> He has smashed their bones and marrow, and seized the hearts of the gods.

He has eaten the Red Crown [Lower Egypt], swallowed the Green One
   [Upper Egypt].
Unas feasts on the lungs of the wise,
And is satisfied living on hearts and their magic . . .

Unas may have built a small pyramid, but he made up for it with a
splendid causeway, 750 metres long, roofed with a central slit to admit
light, and carved and painted with wonderfully vibrant reliefs showing
scenes of craftsmen, farmers, and barges transporting the palm-topped
granite columns which were included in his temples. Less peaceful are
the scenes of fighting, of enemies, prisoners and wild animals – lions,
giraffes and leopards. Frankly disturbing are the images of emaciated
people apparently starving to death. Not Egyptians, these are the nomads
and Bedouin who inhabit the increasingly dry marginal zones and who,
deprived of their own natural territory, are starting to threaten the
security of the settled farmlands. They may well be included in the
decoration to form a pleasing contrast to the well-fed, well-rounded
Egyptians. A similar scene had already been incorporated in Sahure's
causeway, suggesting that starvation amongst Egypt's nearest neighbours
is an accepted part of life.

   At one end of his causeway Unas's mortuary temple, entered via an
immense granite doorway provided by his successor, Teti, followed the
plan employed by Djedkare. At the other end his valley temple fronted
on to a lake which provided him with a harbour. To the south of the
upper part of the causeway lay two limestone-lined boat pits. In the New
Kingdom the ruined complex was restored by Prince Khaemwaset, who
recorded his own noble deeds in an inscription on its south side. Later
still the buildings were thoroughly plundered, and Unas's precious carved
palm columns were felled so that they might be re-erected in the new
Delta city of Tanis.

13

The Ending of an Era

The Count, Governor of Upper Egypt, Chamberlain, Warden of Nekhen, Mayor of Nekheb, Sole Companion, honoured by Osiris Foremost-of-the-Westerners, Weni, says: I was a fillet-wearing youth under the majesty of King Teti, my office being that of Custodian of the storehouse, when I became Inspector of tenants of the palace . . . When I had become Overseer of the robing-room under the Majesty of King Pepi, His Majesty gave me the rank of Companion and Inspector of priests of his pyramid town . . .[1]

Teti, first king of the 6th Dynasty, was the son of Queen Sesheshet and the son or son-in-law of Unas. He had married Iput, daughter of Unas, and his Vizier, Kagemni, had already served under both Unas and Djedkare. It is therefore clear that there was no significant break in bloodline or tradition between the 5th and 6th Dynasties, yet both Manetho and the author of the Turin Canon separate the two. The king himself adds to the confusion by choosing the Horus name 'He Who Reconciles Both Lands', a name which certainly hints at the quashing of civil unrest. In the absence of any further evidence of internal conflict, the most likely explanation for the dynastic split is the southerly shifting of the administrative capital and royal residence from White Walls first of all to Djed-isut and finally to Mennefer, which lay close by, and took its name from, 'Mennefer Pepi' or 'The Splendour of Pepi is Enduring', the South Sakkara pyramid built by Pepi I. Sakkara would remain the royal necropolis and Memphis the administrative capital until the end of the Old Kingdom.

The problems that were becoming apparent towards the end of the 5th Dynasty continue into the 6th and are made clear through the increasing literacy of the age. However, all was not gloom and doom. Sixth

Dynasty missions departed for Sinai and returned laden with copper and turquoise, while vast amounts of stone were transported from Hatnub and Wadi Hammamat. Ships set sail for Byblos and, although the permanent Egyptian trading post at Buhen was long gone, caravan trails still led across the desert to the oases and to Nubia.

Teti built his pyramid in the North Sakkara necropolis, to the north-east of Userkaf's complex and close by his capital, Djed-isut. Here he followed the basic plan of Unas's pyramid, which he adapted to the dimensions of Djedkare's. Originally measuring 52.5 metres tall with a base length of 78 metres and an angle of 53°, 'The Places of Teti Endure' has not in fact endured, but has been stripped of much of its stone so that it now appears as a large, ill-defined rubble mound. The entrance chapel lay on the north side of the pyramid, and the mortuary chapel, now badly denuded, was on the east, but so far there is no sign of either Teti's causeway or his valley temple.[2]

Inside the pyramid a granite-lined descending passageway leads to a corridor chamber and then past three granite portcullises to the now usual arrangement of three storage rooms, an anteroom and a burial chamber carved with (now) badly damaged Pyramid Texts and, around the sarcophagus, a stylized palace façade. Teti's sarcophagus was inscribed on the inside with gilded words spoken by the goddess Nut. When discovered the sarcophagus was of course empty; ancient robbers had managed to smash their way through its heavy basalt lid and had torn the mummy apart, leaving behind an embalmed shoulder and arm.

In the cemetery which surrounded his pyramid Teti provided a mastaba tomb for Queen Iput. Later Iput's son, Pepi I, was to convert his mother's tomb into a small, steep pyramid which completely covered the vertical access shaft of her original mastaba, leaving the pyramid itself entranceless. A fake entrance chapel was provided on the northern side of the pyramid, while the mortuary temple on the eastern side housed statue niches, the false door and offering altar. Although her tomb was robbed in antiquity, Iput's bones were discovered lying in the remains of a cedar-wood coffin within her limestone sarcophagus; the queen was still wearing a gold bracelet and necklace, and there were five Canopic jars and an alabaster headrest close by. Iput had died a middle-aged woman blessed with large eyes and a narrow nose.

A second consort, Khuit, was given a mortuary enclosure beside Iput's complex. Today this ruin stands only 7 metres high, and it was not until 1997, when Zahi Hawass investigated the site, that it became obvious that it was the remains of a 20-metre high pyramid plus mortuary temple. Below ground the pyramid incorporated a descending passageway, a storage room and a burial chamber housing a granite sarcophagus. Queen Khuit was obviously a woman of importance but as yet we do not know who she was. As her tomb was originally conceived as a pyramid, while Iput's tomb was designed as a mastaba and only converted into a pyramid when her son became king, may we assume that Khuit was the mother of Teti's acknowledged heir? Manetho tells us that Teti was assassinated by his bodyguard, a startling, unconfirmed statement. The next king, Userkare, was an ephemeral ruler – Teti's murderer, perhaps? Or simply his elder son born to Khuit? – whose route to the throne is uncharted and whose burial place is unknown. With the disappearance of Userkare the crown passed to Pepi I, son of Teti and Iput.

By now everyone who was anyone aspired to include an autobiography in their tomb. Thus, when the retired politician Weni came to build his single-room tomb-chapel at Abydos, he naturally dedicated an entire wall to his own story. And, as Abydos was far from any official censorship, he told his story in full. The beginning of Weni's autobiography is quoted at the start of this chapter. It tells how, having commenced his service under Teti and having served as part of his bodyguard – though making no mention of any assassination – Weni became one of Pepi's most trusted officials. So trusted, indeed, that he acted as a judge alongside the vizier, hearing all manner of secret cases:

When there was a secret charge in the royal harem against Queen Weret-yamtes, his majesty made me go in to hear it alone. No chief judge and vizier, no official was there, only I alone . . . Never before had one like me heard a secret of the king's harem; but his majesty made me hear it, because I was worthy in his majesty's heart beyond any official of his . . .

Unfortunately, Weni is too discreet to tell what dreadful deed has been committed in the harem. Was the queen guilty of attempted regicide or murder – perhaps to put her own son in line to the throne – or was this 'merely' a case of adultery? Was the vizier excluded from proceedings for reasons of secrecy or because he, too, was implicated in the plot? We do know that one of Pepi's viziers, Rawer, left his post in deep disgrace over some unspecified misdeed, but we cannot be certain that the two cases are contemporary. Weni provides no further details and we learn neither the outcome of the investigations nor the fate of the unfortunate queen. However, the very fact that there was a serious problem in the harem, the very heart of the king's private world, bodes ill for the security of Egypt. From this time onwards we find Egypt's Old Kingdom viziers, and indeed all her top officials, buried in smaller tombs suggestive of a loss of status and/or economic power.

Weni's story continues with a dramatic, poetic account of a successful series of punitive campaigns against the Asiatic Sand Dwellers in an unspecified region to the east of Egypt. Pepi musters an army of tens of thousands led, of course, by the faithful Weni – 'I was the one who commanded them, while my rank was merely that of overseer of the royal tenants, because of my rectitude. I ensured that no one attacked his fellow, or seized a loaf or sandals from a traveller, or took cloth from any town, or a goat from anyone.' Within Pepi's ruined mortuary temple were found a series of limestone statues of kneeling, bound prisoners with their heads snapped off; it seems that Pepi, too, chose to line his corridors with three-dimensional reminders of his own superiority. A less ebullient view of 6th Dynasty life, an indication of the extent of the loss of royal authority, is offered by the Dahshur Decree, issued by Pepi to protect Snefru's pyramid estate which was being eroded by officials who had dared to divert estate lands and assets for their own ends.

With the Central and North Sakkara necropolis uncomfortably full, Pepi built Mennefer Pepi at South Sakkara. This pyramid, which has suffered from centuries of intensive stone quarrying, is now a spreading, doughnut-shaped mound with a devastated mortuary temple attached. Its true significance was only realized in the 1830s, when:[3]

. . . a fox managed to penetrate into a cavity situated in the rubbish surrounding a ruined pyramid, and the animal was followed by an Arab head-workman who, passing into the cavern, arrived at the funerary chamber of King Pepi I. The walls of the tomb were covered with hieroglyphic text . . . Mariette did not hear of this until a long time afterwards, when he was on his deathbed. He authorized excavations to be carried out near this pyramid, and on January 4th, 1881, sent Heinrich Brugsch and his brother Emile – his German assistants – to verify the Arab's statement. It is doubtful whether, before he drew his last breath, the illustrious archaeologist wished to credit the statement of his assistants.

These were the first Pyramid Texts to be discovered. They caused Gaston Maspero, newly appointed director of the Egyptian Antiquities Service, great joy, but left his predecessor, the elderly and frail Auguste Mariette, with a conflict of mixed emotions. Throughout his life Mariette had maintained that there were no inscriptions within the pyramids, and that to open up the pyramids in order to search for non-existent texts would be a complete waste of resources. It was only on his deathbed that he finally realized his error and admitted that the pyramids were indeed worthy of examination.[4]

Today his pyramid stands little more than 12 metres high, but in its prime Pepi's pyramid reached a respectable 52 metres, with a base angle of 53° and a side length of 79 metres.[5] We know that its collapse must have happened some time after the 19th Dynasty, as a restoration text commissioned by the archaeologist-Prince Khaemwaset details a series of relatively minor improvements, carved into a piece of the original limestone casing which can now be found only at the lowest levels of the pyramid. Pepi had followed the pattern set by his predecessors, and his substructure differs from Teti's only in having a greater number of carved, green-painted texts (green, *wadj*, being the colour of fertility and renewal) so that Pepi's writings extended into the access corridor. The false funerary bower of the burial chamber yielded a wrapped parcel of Pepi's viscera lying close by his empty granite Canopic chest. The black stone sarcophagus, carved with writing from the Pyramid Texts, was also empty, but it is rumoured that a mummified hand was recovered from the burial chamber.

As the provincial elite grew increasingly influential, Pepi embarked on a series of diplomatic marriages designed to strengthen his links with the regional aristocracy. The best known of these, made relatively late in his reign, was his marriage with the two daughters of Khui of Abydos. Confusingly, both sisters were named Ankhesen-Merire or its variant, Ankhesen-Pepi, although, as the name literally means 'She lives for King Merire/King Pepi', it seems likely that the sisters assumed a new name at the time of their marriage. The policy of multiple marriages is reflected in the necropolis where, in addition to his satellite pyramid, Pepi built at least six queen's pyramids outside, and to the south of, his enclosure wall. Pyramids, of course, were only built for the most influential royal women; clearly Pepi is suffering from an unprecedented superabundance of powerful ladies and this, while not necessarily a cause of political unrest, may certainly be counted amongst its symptoms.[6]

Each sister bore the king a son, and so after fifty years of rule the elderly and experienced Pepi was succeeded by a youth and a baby whose deeds were guided by the sisters from Abydos and their brother Djau, Egypt's new vizier. Pepi's elder son Merenre, born to Ankhesen-Merire I, ruled for no more than nine years during which the indefatigable Weni served as governor of Upper Egypt, the first non-elite to hold this important position. He applied himself to his role with gusto, taxing the people, overseeing the digging of canals and the building of barges, and organizing missions to Hatnub and Nubia, returning with vast quantities of stone which were incorporated in Merenre's pyramid: 'His majesty sent me to Ibhat to bring the sarcophagus, the chest of the living, together with its lid, and the costly pyramidion for the pyramid "Merenre Appears in Splendour".' Later he would acquire the granite false door and lintels and a great alabaster altar for the pyramid.

Leaving these domestic duties aside, Weni was occupying an increasingly important diplomatic position. Once complaisant Nubia, perhaps sensing weakness, was becoming a cause of some concern and already Pepi had been forced to send Merenre south to reinforce his rights. Now matters were being made worse by an influx of new settlers, the so-called Nubian C Group, who had arrived from further south to settle in Lower Nubia, and who were seen as a potential threat to Egyptian interests. Weni's fellow bureaucrat, Harkhuf, included an autobiography in his Aswan tomb which tells of trading in Upper Nubia, and intermittent campaigning in Lower, under Merenre and his successor Pepi II.

Merenre had planned to build the now standard pyramid 450 metres to the south-west of his father's complex, but he never completed his project so that today we are again faced with an indistinct mound atop a relatively well-finished substructure. Anyone who wonders how a pyramid can be 'lost' should take a look — if they can find it — at the heap of sand and rubble which was once 'Merenre Appears in Splendour', Merenre's hope of eternal life. The pyramid was examined by Perring in the 1830s, and re-explored by Maspero and the Brugsch brothers who

inched their way down an ancient robbers' tunnel to enter the danger-
ously unstable burial chamber and discover a black basalt sarcophagus –
the sarcophagus retrieved by Weni – whose lid had been pushed back
to reveal a well-preserved mummy. Later a granite Canopic chest was
found, empty, at the foot of the sarcophagus. The body was taken to
Cairo where it was examined by Grafton Eliot Smith. Smith found it to
be that of a male still young enough to wear the 'sidelock of youth'
hairstyle, and classed it as an intrusive 18th Dynasty burial. Some Egyptologists have argued against his conclusion, believing these to be the
remains of the young Merenre, but as the body had never been properly
published we must simply file the remains under 'unidentified', and
move on.

Manetho tells us that Pepi II inherited the throne at approximately six
years of age and reigned for an extraordinary ninety-four years, dying in
his centenary. However, as Merenre had already ruled for approximately
nine years, it seems that either Manetho was misinformed, or that Pepi
served as co-regent alongside his half-brother. We do know that Pepi
II's early years were heavily influenced by his mother, the queen regent
Ankhesen-Merire II, and her family. The queen mother was a person of
considerable importance; an alabaster statue now housed in the Brooklyn
Museum shows Ankhesen-Merire with the young king sitting on her
knee, while a rock carving at Wadi Maghara, Sinai, makes Ankhesen-
Merire's status clear, as the queen is shown wearing a uraeus, the preroga-
tive of the king and the gods. Queens will not normally start to wear the
uraeus until the Middle Kingdom. The Pyramid Texts included within
her tomb, and her huge basalt sarcophagus, offer further confirmation of
Ankhesen-Merire's entitlement to kingly privileges.

It was during this early part of Pepi's reign that Harkhuf, now governor of Upper Egypt, returned from Nubia with an almost unimagin-
able prize, 'a dwarf of the god's dances from the land of the horizon
dwellers, like the dwarf whom the god's seal bearer Bawerded brought
from Punt in the time of King [Djedkare-] Isesi'.[7] Pepi, with all the
eagerness of a child, demanded that the dwarf be guarded night and day
– particularly on the boat, where he might fall overboard and drown –
and that he be brought immediately to the palace, as 'My majesty desires
to see this dwarf more than the gifts of the mine-land [Sinai] and
of Punt.'

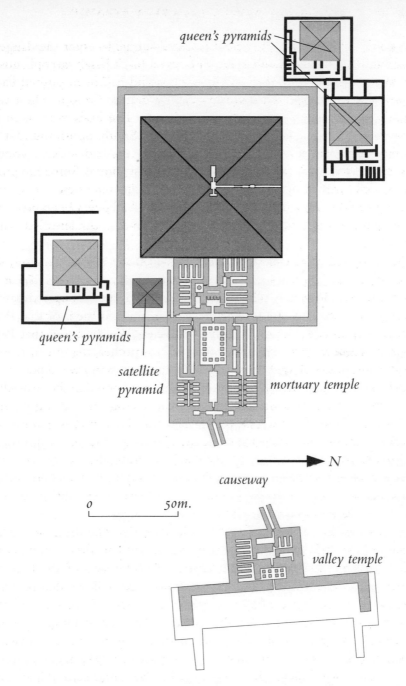

queen's pyramids

queen's pyramids

satellite pyramid

mortuary temple

N

causeway

0   50m.

valley temple

Figure 13.1   The pyramid complex of Pepi II at Sakkara.

'Pepi is Established and Living' was built close by the mastaba tomb of Shepseskaf. Again Pepi followed the standard design and despite his long reign his pyramid was of the usual dimensions (52 metres high; a side length of 79 metres and an angle of 53°);[8] again it was badly constructed around a five-step core so that the removal of its limestone outer casing reduced it to a low mound. One curious feature was a wide band or belt of brick added around the pyramid after its completion; the consistent rebuilding which once characterized the pyramid sites had by now been abandoned, suggesting that this enlargement may have had a personal significance for Pepi, perhaps as a commemoration of one of his jubilees.[9]

Inside the pyramid were the now-usual Pyramid Texts, star-spangled ceiling, and engraved granite sarcophagus resting in a stone-carved reed booth. Outside, the mortuary temple included an open court, sanctuary and statue niches, and was decorated with scenes of royal triumph and the defeat of animal and human foes copied from Sahure's complex. Despite its imposing entrance, the mortuary chapel was not well built; it employed limestone rather than granite or alabaster, and several walls were left blank. Given the king's extreme longevity this neglect can hardly be attributed to time-pressure; we must assume that Pepi's builders lacked the resources to complete their task to a satisfactory standard. The valley temple had a slightly different plan; visitors entered the central doorway via two ramps leading on to a rectangular terrace, and made their way through a pillared hall decorated with scenes of the king hunting, the king conquering and the king before his gods, into a vestibule and thence into the causeway.

Pepi's resources stretched far enough to build pyramid complexes for three queens: Neith, Iput II and Wedjebten. Neith was the daughter of Pepi I and Ankhesen-Merire I, and therefore the half-sister of Pepi II; her name and titles are preserved on the two limestone obelisks which mark the entrance to her enclosure, while the queen herself appears conventionally beautiful on the walls of her court. Her pyramid is the oldest, the largest and the most carefully built of the three; standing 24 metres square, it has an entrance chapel on the north side and a mortuary chapel equipped with offering hall, statue niches and false door on the east. The satellite pyramid, built in the south-east corner, has yielded many pottery sherds; the remains of vessels smashed during the funeral rituals. Between the main and the satellite pyramid were buried sixteen wooden model ships, provided to help the queen's soul sail to the sky.

Underground, a descending passageway leads past a single granite portcullis and a small storeroom into the star-spangled burial chamber. While the west wall of the burial chamber is an intricate, stylized palace façade the remaining three walls are carved with Pyramid Texts which, no longer exclusive to the king, are to be allowed to all of Pepi's queens. Neith's granite sarcophagus, discovered beside her empty Canopic chest, was empty but a headless and battered mummy with some remaining soft tissue, attributed to Queen Neith, is stored in Qasr el-Aini Hospital, Cairo.

Iput II was buried in a similar but smaller complex to the south-west of Neith's. This has almost entirely vanished but, as we have the obelisks which once flanked the entrance, we can read the queen's titles and see that although a queen, she was never a queen-mother. It is therefore a sign of the more relaxed approach to protocol – or the loss of control – during Pepi's reign, that she too is accorded the honour of burial within a pyramid. The remains of Iput's western storeroom yielded a granite sarcophagus carved for Ankhesen-Pepi IV (the name is correct; the number is speculative), a wife of Pepi II whose son, Neferkare Nebi, was to rule during the 8th Dynasty. This is clearly a secondary burial made some time after Iput's own death, most probably during the First Inter-mediate Period. Intrusive burials are commonplace at the pyramid sites; the real interest of this piece lies in its lid, which is carved with a series of almost unintelligible royal annals which seem to confirm the story of civil unrest and royal bloodshed at the end of Teti's reign.[10]

Wedjebten, also a daughter of Pepi I and a wife of Pepi II, had a small complex incorporating a pyramid, mortuary temple and subsidiary pyramid ringed by a double enclosure wall. The secondary enclosure thus formed included offering chapels dedicated to the priests of the queen's estates.

We have been well prepared for the ending of the Old Kingdom, but its suddenness still comes as a shock; a shock which is intensified by the shortage of written accounts of this traumatic time. Our facts are once again drawn from archaeology rather than texts. We can pinpoint no one specific cause for the collapse of central authority. Rather, it was a combination of causes – the enormous bureaucracy, the declining power of the ageing king, disunity in the royal household – made worse by the ever-increasing dryness and a series of disastrously low Nile levels. It was clear that pharaoh could no longer fulfil his divine obligation to provide for his people; the impoverished, perhaps even starving people in turn lost faith in their king. Pepi had outlived his controlling mother, his contemporaries and his immediate descendants; he left no obvious heir and far too many grandchildren and great-grandchildren eager to succeed. He was to be preserved in legend as a homosexual whose voracious appetites demeaned him.[11]

Pepi II was followed on the throne by Merenre II and then by Queen Nitocris who ruled as king. Female pharaohs were an aberration, but they could be tolerated if it was perceived that they were acting for the good of Egypt. Thus Manetho praises Nitocris as 'the most noble and lovely woman of her time', while Herodotus tells a story intended to prove her passionate dynastic loyalty:[12]

They said that she succeeded her brother; he had been king of Egypt, and had been put to death by his subjects, who then placed her upon the throne. Bent on avenging his death, she devised a cunning scheme by which she destroyed a vast number of Egyptians. She constructed a spacious underground chamber, and, on pretence of inaugurating it, contrived the following: – Inviting to a banquet those of the Egyptians whom she knew to have had the chief share in the murder of her brother, she suddenly, as they were feasting, let the river in upon them by means of a large, secret duct. This, and only this, did they tell me of her, except that, when she had done what I have said, she threw herself into an apartment full of ashes, that she might escape the vengeance whereto she would otherwise have been exposed.

Nitocris left no known monuments, and no tomb. Her reign (two years one month and one day according to the Turin Canon; twelve years according to Manetho) marked the end of the 6th Dynasty.

Dynasties 7 and 8 were a series of ephemeral kings. Only one of these, Qakara Ibi, has left a pyramid; built at Sakkara, near the pyramid of Pepi II, his was a tiny affair, only 21 metres high and 31.5 metres square at the base, with a rudimentary mortuary temple on the north-east face. Fragmented, Egypt was governed by the provincial rulers who each, simultaneously, claimed the title of pharaoh. City-state once again fought city-state for dominance. The Old Kingdom, the glorious pyramid age, was well and truly over.

SECTION FOUR
Variation and Imitation: Distant Echoes

Soldiers, consider that from the summit of these pyramids, forty centuries look down on you.

From Napoleon's speech before the Battle of the Pyramids, 1798; this stirring phrase was subsequently engraved on a bronze medal decorated with fierce soldiers and steep-sided pyramids.

14

Mud-bricks and Golden Treasure

Beside the eternal Nile
The Pyramids have risen.
Nile shall pursue his changeless way;
Those pyramids shall fall;
Yea! Not a stone shall stand to tell
The spot whereon they stood.[1]

The First Intermediate Period was a time of decentralized control: of feeble northern kings, strong provincial rulers and fierce local rivalries. Trade ceased, the mines and quarries were abandoned and, although the increasing aridity which characterized the 5th and 6th Dynasties had halted, there was crop failure and hunger. The scribe Ipuwer famously tells a gruesome tale of violence, starvation, blood and emptied graves. Although he, writing from the golden prosperity of the late Middle Kingdom, aims to paint the *maat*-less Intermediate Period as black as possible, contemporary records do lend partial support to his account. Ankhtifi, semi-autonomous nomarch (a governor) of the 2nd and 3rd Upper Egyptian provinces, owed nominal allegiance to the 9th/10th Dynasty kings of Herakleopolis. He built himself a splendid tomb cut into a small pyramid-shaped mountain, or *gebel*, close by the modern town of Mo'alla. This, as yet only partially excavated, included a courtyard and causeway, and faced west. Here, amid the splendid illustrations, he carved a detailed auto-biography.[2] From this we learn how Ankhtifi, a self-confessed 'hero without equal', was called upon to subdue the rebellious Theban nome – a somewhat inglorious battle as the enemy ran away – and to pacify Edfu:

The god Horus called me to the nome of Edfu for life prosperity and health to re-establish it . . . I found the House of [the administrator] Khuu inundated like a marsh neglected by its keeper, in the grip of a rebel and under the control of a wretch. I made a man embrace the slayer of his father, the slayer of his brother, so as to re-establish the nome of Edfu . . .

Ankhtifi tells us how he, rather than the king, 'gave bread to the hungry and clothing to the naked . . . All of Upper Egypt was dying of starvation and people were eating their children, but I did not allow anyone to starve to death in this nome . . .' His vigorous, optimistic text lacks the bleak desolation of Ipuwer's world and he treats the twin terrors of famine and cannibalism with such a light touch that we are tempted to believe he is exaggerating the crisis as a means of proving his own worth.

Occasional food shortages apart, this was far from a time of universal poverty. While the quality of life at Memphis suffered a steep decline, life in the provinces improved for many. Technology continued to advance – the potter's wheel, first developed during the 5th Dynasty, was now revolutionizing the southern ceramic repertoire – and the provincial cemeteries speak of prosperity and social levelling. Here we find increasing numbers of inscribed funerary stelae telling the stories of self-made men. The richer tombs now include painted and moulded cartonnage mummy masks, and model figures which will work for the deceased beyond death. For the first time, hesitantly at first, Coffin Texts, magical spells and utterances are found on the wooden coffins of the provincial elite:[3]

Spell 227 Becoming the counterpart of Osiris. I am indeed Osiris, I indeed am the Lord of All, the Radiant One, the brother of the Radiant Lady. I am Osiris, brother of Isis. My son Horus and his mother Isis have protected me from the foe who would harm me; they have put cords on his arms and fetters on his thighs because of what he has done for me . . .

After a century of weak northern rule two power centres emerged: a series of northern kings based at Herakleopolis, and a series of southern princes based at Thebes. The Theben princes were the product of a strong line of local administrators, while the northern kings formed the 9th and 10th Dynasties. Both claimed sovereignty over the whole land; neither could dislodge the other. They were enemies forced into an uneasy alliance.

The northern kings continued the tradition of pyramid burial but they lacked the resources to make a grand statement and their small-scale monuments are almost entirely lost. One exception stands in the desert at Dara, Middle Egypt.[4] This, now a sad 4-metre-high heap of rubble, was once an impressive mud-brick pyramid; its ground plan suggests that it would have been almost the size of Djoser's Step Pyramid. The entrance was on the north face and led downwards to a simple burial chamber whose limestone lining had been stolen from nearby 6th Dynasty tombs. A second devastated pyramid, Lepsius XXIX or the 'Headless Pyramid' in the Sakkara necropolis, may also belong to this period.

Meanwhile the southern rulers had started to build what are today known as *saff*-tombs in the Theban necropolis of el-Tarif. *Saff*-, literally 'row', refers to the ranks of pillars and doors that decorate their fronts. Ideally suited to the local geography, the tombs were constructed by driving a flat court into the sloping desert terrace until the rock-face attained the necessary height to serve as a façade. The pillars and doorways were carved directly into the face, the tomb chapel was cut into the rock and a shaft dropped down to the simple burial chamber. Finally, perhaps, a small mud-brick pyramid was erected nearby (there is no archaeological evidence for this but the New Kingdom Abbott Papyrus uses the pyramid sign to describe these tombs).

The two courts indulged in a hundred years of intermittent civil war until the Theban Nebhepetre Montuhotep II defeated his northern rivals to reunite his country and establish a capital city at Thebes. He founded what was, at first glance, an entirely traditional kingship modelled on the glorious days of the Old Kingdom; there were Nubian campaigns and impressive trade missions to Lebanon and Punt. But two centuries of turmoil could not be easily forgotten. No matter how much Montuhotep stressed his personal divinity – he was the 'Son of Hathor' who wore the two feathers of Amen – everyone knew that pharaoh was vulnerable, and pharaoh himself had to admit this fact.

Montuhotep introduced a full programme of monumental building works. There were new temples and restorations at many sites, but his most impressive, innovative project was his tomb, built in the shelter of a natural bay at Deir el-Bahari, Thebes. This did not follow either the strict pyramid or *saff*-tomb format but included elements of both. Montuhotep's tomb is today reduced to one tier, but 'Glorious are the

Places of Nebhepetre [Montuhotep]' originally rose as a layered mastaba which the Abbott Papyrus again suggests was topped by a pyramid. The complex incorporated terraces (seen for the first time in Egypt), verandahs, a hypostyle hall and an inner sanctuary cut directly into the Theban cliff. The granite-lined burial chamber lay at the end of a 150-metre sloping passageway, and included a massive alabaster shrine which served as Montuhotep's sarcophagus. Out in the sunshine the wider complex encompassed groves of trees and flowers, and a series of tombs for Montuhotep's wives and daughters. An open causeway linked the complex to the valley temple and the river. The complex was decorated with scenes of pharaoh hunting, fishing and harvesting crops plus, inevitably, images of fighting and the trampling of enemies.

After fifty-two years of strong rule Montuhotep II died and was replaced by his son Montuhotep III. There were continuing missions to the quarries, and a large-scale tomb was started to the south of Deir el-Bahari. Montuhotep III, however, reigned for only twelve years, and his ambitious tomb was never finished. His successor, Montuhotep IV, proved a weak ruler and the 11th Dynasty stuttered to a halt with his death.

The 12th Dynasty was founded by the ex-vizier Amenemhat I, an altogether more vigorous king who piously honoured the dynasty he had usurped. Amenemhat took the important decision to relocate the court to the new city of Amenemhat-Itj-Tawy (Amenemhat seizer of the two lands). The new capital, now lost, lay not far from Memphis and conveniently near the entrance to the economically important Faiyum. Now Amenemhat undertook a series of political reforms designed to reduce the influence of the nomarchs whose provincial powers still posed a threat to his authority. It was due in great part to his political acumen that the 12th Dynasty would recover from a bumpy start to become a time of internal peace and external adventure. Literature and the arts flourished, there was increased foreign trade and a series of successful military campaigns. Now the royal sculptors subtly adjusted their style and the official image of the king changed from the imperious living god of the Old Kingdom to a more human, compassionate king burdened with the responsibility of caring for his people.

Amenemhat I built 'Cult Places of Amenemhat's Appearance' in the Lisht cemetery, close by his new capital. This would be the last royal pyramid built entirely of stone blocks. His complex included some

Theban features but was essentially a replica of the Pepi II pyramid and would have been instantly recognizable to his illustrious predecessors, some of whom, indeed, would have recognized it far too well, as it incorporated stone stolen from Giza and Sakkara. The pyramid, today a 20-metre-high ruin, originally stood 55 metres high, with a base length of 84 metres and an angle of 54°. A northern entrance chapel allowed access to the descending corridor which led to a Theban-style deep burial shaft. This must have been uncomfortably close to the water table when it was built; today it is completely submerged.

Amenemhat's mortuary temple is a ruin, but we know that it was situated on a low Theban-style terrace to the east side of his pyramid, and that it led via an open causeway to a now vanished valley temple. Outside his immediate enclosure, but within an outer mud-brick wall, were twenty-two burial shafts for the significant royal women, and a series of mastaba tombs for his high-ranking courtiers.

After thirty years on the throne Amenemhat met an untimely end. The *Instruction of King Amenemhat*[5] purports to be a posthumous letter addressed by the deceased king to his co-regent and successor Senwosret I, but is actually written by the scribe Khety. Despite its fanciful format it tells of real-life drama:

As I began to drift into sleep, the very weapons which should have been used to protect me were turned against me while I was like a snake of the desert. I awoke with a jump, alert for the fight, and found that it was a combat with the guard. Had I been able to seize my weapon I would have beaten back the cowards single handed, but no one is strong at night. No one can fight alone and no success can be achieved without a helper . . .

The Middle Kingdom *Story of Sinuhe*, an epic tale of travel and adventure (and a cynical piece of royal propaganda) offers partial confirmation of this tale. Prince Senwosret is returning from a campaign against the Libyan tribes when messengers arrive from the palace. The king is dead! Senwosret abandons his troops and rushes to claim his inheritance. Meanwhile Sinuhe suffers a disproportionate reaction to the news; his senses are disturbed and he trembles all over. Most unaccountably – unless, perhaps, he knows something of the murderous plot – Sinuhe runs away to spend many years in exile, pining for Egypt.

Senwosret I embarked upon a series of military campaigns designed to strengthen his eastern and southern borders. Nubia, colonized as far as the second cataract, was endowed with a series of temples and forts designed to protect the interests of the Egyptian traders now engaged in a vigorous exploitation of her resources. Back home there were political reforms designed to define the provincial boundaries. Senwosret built his pyramid, 'Senwosret Appears', just over a mile to the south of his father's complex. Once an impressive 61 metres tall, with a base length of 105 metres and an angle of 49°, Senwosret's pyramid is today a low, block-studded hill. It again replicated the features of the Old Kingdom pyramids, but it had not been constructed in the same labour-intensive way. Beneath the concealing casing the core had been built as a honeycomb of thick limestone walls whose thirty-two chambers were packed with rubble and sand. This proved only a qualified success. The foundations were weak and not properly levelled, and cracks soon marred the pyramid face. Again the entrance chapel opened on the north face and allowed access to a descending corridor; again the burial chamber is lost under water. The valley temple too is lost, while the mortuary temple is a ruin.

Senwosret's inner enclosure, defined by a limestone wall decorated with *serekh* niches, included a subsidiary pyramid. His outer enclosure, surrounded by a mud-brick wall, incorporated an unprecedented nine queens' pyramids, each with its own enclosure. These were not all planned from the outset, but were added over the years, with the last pyramid perhaps being built several years after Senwosret's death. Outside this circle again were the tombs of Senwosret's most prominent officials. His causeway, originally wide and open to the sun, was eventually narrowed and roofed. Here in a series of statue niches stood the divine Senwosret, almost life-sized, mummiform like the god Osiris, and wearing the red crown of Lower Egypt along the northern wall, and the white crown of Upper Egypt along the southern wall.

Senwosret's successor, Amenemhat II, built his pyramid to the east of the Red Pyramid at Dahshur. Abandoning all attempts to replicate the Old Kingdom complex, 'Amenemhat is Well Cared For' sat within a simplified rectangular enclosure opening on to a wide, open causeway. Unfortunately it has been so severely robbed that we cannot estimate its original size although we do know that it re-employed the compart-

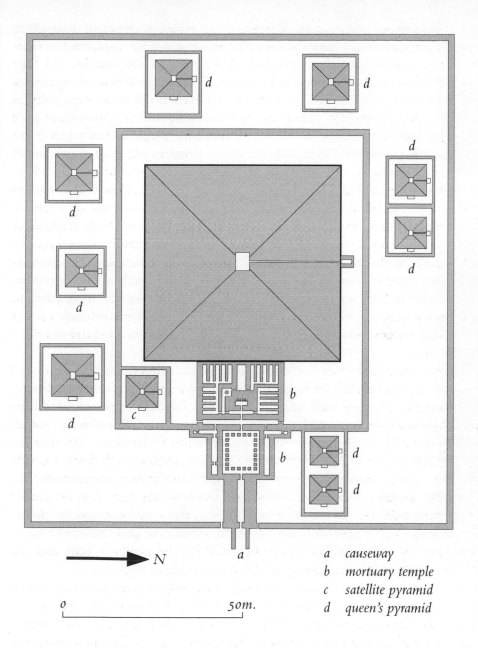

a causeway
b mortuary temple
c satellite pyramid
d queen's pyramid

N

0   50m.

Figure 14.1   The pyramid complex of Senwosret I at Lisht.

mental core technique, the voids in this instance being filled with sand rather than stone. The valley temple is now lost, and there is little trace of the mortuary temple. However the underground structure has survived tolerably well; we know that the pyramid was entered on the northern face, and that a descending corridor led past two portcullises to a burial chamber equipped with a sandstone sarcophagus.

Senwosret II moved the royal necropolis south west to Illahun [Lahun], close by the opening to the Faiyum. Here he raised a mud-brick pyramid, 'Senwosret Shines', with a casing of fine limestone, a height of 48 metres, an angle of 42° and a base length of 106 metres. The core of his pyramid was centred on a naturally occurring outcrop of limestone; from this, limestone walls and cross walls formed compartments which were filled with mud-brick. The entire pyramid was surrounded by a rubble-filled trench which may have had a symbolic meaning, but which also served as a useful rainwater drain.

Although the north face was provided with an entrance chapel the entrance to the pyramid was, for the first time, sited on the south side – a deliberate denial of tradition which was, we must assume, intended to foil thieves. It certainly foiled Flinders Petrie, who spent months hunting for a northern doorway. From this the entrance shaft dropped to a wider horizontal corridor before opening into a room furnished with a vaulted ceiling and a deep well sunk down to the water table. A second, wider 'service shaft' was situated to the south of the official entrance; this, used while the pyramid was under construction, was eventually hidden beneath the tomb of an anonymous princess. Beyond the room with the well, past a storage room, the horizontal corridor led through an antechamber and short corridor into the burial chamber. This held a red granite sarcophagus of exceptionally precise construction, a white alabaster offering table, and, in a side room, a gold uraeus and some portions of leg bone. A second, winding passageway led from the corridor between the antechamber and the burial chamber and passed around the burial chamber to enter it in the north-west corner, close by the sarcophagus.

Again there were two enclosure walls, an inner stone wall decorated with *serekh* panelling and an outer mud-brick wall. Within the inner enclosure there was a mortuary chapel – now vanished – and within the outer enclosure there were a series of mastaba tombs and a queen's pyramid. To the south of the outer wall there were four shaft tombs, one of which, that of Princess Sit-Hathor-Iunet, yielded the 'Illahun treasure': five boxes of jewellery and toiletries which, hidden in a plastered recess, had survived the looting which had otherwise wrecked the burial. The treasure was completely coated in a hard, thick mud. Guy Brunton was to spend a week living in the tomb, extracting the objects from the recess and handing them to Petrie who, suffering from 'a strain', had to content himself with cleaning the finds in pure water using a camel-hair brush. This revealed a delicate gold diadem, an inlaid gold pectoral with the cartouche of the princess's father Senwosret II, a second pectoral with the cartouche of her nephew, Amenemhat III, a beautiful polished mirror with an obsidian handle and a jumble of necklaces, bracelets, razors and cosmetics jars.[6]

Senwosret's causeway remains unexcavated, while his valley temple is a ruin. However, the town built to service his mortuary complex has survived remarkably unscathed.[7]

Senwosret III was a strong and confident king; it was under his rule that Nubia was finally defeated in a series of hard-fought military campaigns. Closer to home political reforms attacked the powers of the nomarchs; the resultant re-centralization of authority is apparent in the provincial cemeteries which lose their most expensive burials and acquire ranks of middle-class tombs. Senwosret returned to Dahshur to build a limestone-cased mud-brick pyramid constructed around a mud-brick core whose cracks and crevices were filled with sand. Again, what was once an impressive pyramid (78 metres high; side length 105 metres; base angle 56°) situated within a rectangular double enclosure and accompanied by seven subsidiary pyramids and an innovative south temple, is today reduced to a collapsed hillock in a barren landscape. This time the entrance lay in the courtyard on the west side of the pyramid and led, via a sloping corridor, into an antechamber and granite-lined burial chamber.

Although there was a niched granite sarcophagus within the chamber, there was no sign that it had ever been occupied. And, as we know that this was not Senwosret's only tomb, we must question whether he was ever interred here. We do know that some of the royal women were buried within the pyramid complex, as an underground gallery of graves has yielded sarcophagi inscribed for the Princesses Ment and Senetsenebti, and jewellery belonging to the Princesses Merit and Sit-Hathor.

Senwosret's second tomb was built at Abydos, necropolis of the most ancient pharaohs now gaining additional kudos as the burial place of the god of the Underworld, Osiris. Senwosret built a tomb which combined elements of the northern pyramid enclosure, the southern *saff*-tomb and the archaic Abydene complex. Against the cliff a large T-shaped enclosure allowed access to a lengthy curving passage leading to several chambers. A causeway led across the desert to a chapel on the edge of the cultivation. To all intents and purposes this was a cenotaph. However, below ground the architects had installed a sophisticated system of anti-theft devices which suggest that this may, after all, have been intended as a functioning tomb. Behind a quartzite façade a once-hidden room has yielded a granite sarcophagus and Canopic chest. Did Senwosret prefer security over tradition, to the extent that he was prepared to abandon his pyramid and all that it stood for? Could he have ever hoped to have a secret burial, given the pomp and circumstance which would have attended his death?

Senwosret's son, Amenemhat III, inaugurated irrigation and land reclamation schemes in the Faiyum. He too invested in two tombs, both pyramids and both situated in the north. His Dahshur pyramid, 'Amenemhat is Beautiful' was a mud-brick limestone-cased structure raised within a conventional later Old Kingdom style complex with a mortuary temple, causeway and valley temple, but it incorporated archaic elements, most obviously the palace façade design carved on the king's sarcophagus. The internal structure of the pyramid was unexpectedly complicated and constructed on several levels. The king's own limestone-lined burial suite could be entered via both the eastern and the western face. A series of corridors and stairways led to rooms, storerooms, a Ka-chapel and the burial chamber which housed a granite sarcophagus carved with the king's unblinking eyes. On the south face of the pyramid two separate entrances led to two queens' tombs built within the pyramid mass. One, belonging to Queen Aat, has yielded a sarcophagus, Canopic chest, sundry burial equipment and human bone. The other, built for an anonymous lady, has provided the remains of a once rich burial. The queens' tombs were linked via a corridor to each other and to the king's suite.

Amenemhat had started his pyramid early, and by Year 15 it was substantially complete. The granite pyramidion had been carved, and was waiting to be raised to the peak. Things were not, however, going to plan. The pyramid had been sited too low in the valley and the unstable bedrock was not strong enough to support its weight. The pyramid was slowly settling. The multiplicity of corridors and rooms within the masonry did not help matters. As the walls cracked and sank, as the door frames buckled and the ceilings bowed, the workmen employed cedar beams to make the corridors safe. Amenemhat, facing the inevitable, started to build again.

His second complex, built at Hawara close by his grandfather's pyramid, was in a style so different that it casts doubt upon our assumption that pyramid layout inevitably reflects religious belief. This too was to be a mud–brick, stone–lined structure. But while the old pyramid had enjoyed a slope of 57° and a height of approximately 75 metres the architects had grown cautious, and the new pyramid was smaller, with a slope of 48° and a height of approximately 58 metres. Internally the pyramid was different, yet equally complex. With only one entrance, on the southern side, there were far fewer stairways, corridors and chambers, but far more portcullises, trapdoors and hidden doorways. The entire emphasis had shifted from display to secrecy.

A long corridor led downwards from the entrance through a small room and then came to an abrupt halt. Hidden in the ceiling, however, was the entrance to a second chamber. This chamber gave access to a blind northern passageway, while beyond a wooden door a second passageway ran eastwards to a third empty chamber. Here the right–angled turn and hidden entrance were repeated, and repeated again under the north–east corner of the pyramid. The visitor to the burial chamber, having entered the pyramid on the south side, finally entered the ante–chamber from the east. Petrie was the first archaeologist to make this journey:[8]

By January 6, we got through into the upper chamber. There I wriggled head down into a forced hole which opened into the actual burial, and saw two sarcophagi in the water; I had to be dragged out by the heels. After enlarging the hole a little, I could enter. The chamber was one solid block of quartzite, twenty–two feet long, eight feet wide, and six feet deep inside, polished and cut so clean at the corners that I did not realize that it was not built, until I searched for a joint and found none. The water was up to one's waist, so the chips could only be searched by pushing them with the feet on to the blade of a hoe, and

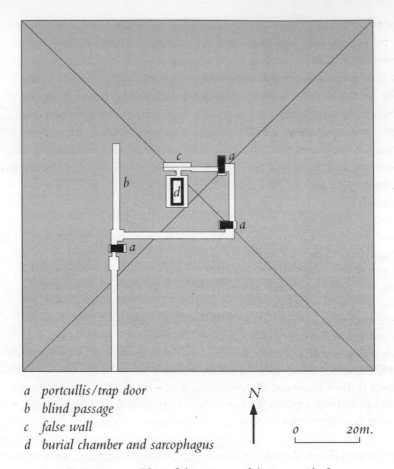

a   portcullis / trap door
b   blind passage
c   false wall
d   burial chamber and sarcophagus

N

0   20m.

Figure 14.2   Plan of the interior of the pyramid of
Amenemhat III at Hawara.

so lifting them up. I promised half a piastre for every hieroglyph found, and a dollar for a cartouche. This ensured a thorough search. The next day the name appeared, Amenemhat III, as was expected; the surface being half decayed by the water there could not be any doubt of its age.

The burial chamber had been hollowed from one massive block of quartzite, and it was roofed with three large granite slabs so that the entire door-less room served as a gigantic stone sarcophagus. Above the roofing slabs, an angled ceiling and mud-brick vault prevented the weight of the pyramid from crushing the burial chamber. Such a chamber could only be sealed after the burial, when the ceiling blocks, which rested temporarily on pillars supported by sand, would be lowered mechanically by draining away the supporting sand.

The pyramid was surrounded by a large, north–south orientated enclosure and connected via an open causeway to a valley temple. The mortuary temple, now a sorry ruin, stood to the south of the pyramid and was of such complex design, with a multiplicity of courts, chapels and statues, that it served as the inspiration for the tale of the Labyrinth of Knossos, home of the Minotaur. Herodotus, for one, was very impressed:[9]

I visited this place and found it to surpass description; for if all the walls and other great works of the Greeks could be put together in one, they would not equal either in labour or expense, this Labyrinth ... The pyramids likewise surpass description, and are severally equal to a number of the greatest works of the Greeks, but the Labyrinth surpasses the pyramids. It has twelve courts, all of them roofed, with gates exactly opposite one another, six of them to the north and six to the south. A single wall surrounds the entire building. There are two different types of chambers throughout – half underground, half above ground, the latter being built upon the former; the whole number of these chambers is three thousand fifteen hundred of each kind ... At the corner of the Labyrinth stands a pyramid, forty fathoms high, with large figures engraved on it; which is entered by a subterranean passage.

Amenemhat III was the last powerful king of the Middle Kingdom. Why such a vigorous monarchy should so suddenly fail is something of a mystery, although the accession of a female pharaoh suggests that the dynasty may have been damned by the lack of a male heir. We have a few 'spare' anonymous 12th Dynasty pyramids – there is a badly damaged specimen at Dahshur, and two elaborately designed but sadly unfinished examples at nearby Mazghuna – but the last, short-lived kings of the 12th Dynasty, Amenemhat IV and Queen Sobeknofru, left no named tomb.

Many of the numerous 13th Dynasty kings were equally incapable of leaving significant monuments, but we should not fall into the trap of underestimating the tenacity of this dynasty. There were continuing trade missions, and building works up and down the Nile. One king, Ameny-Qemau, started but never finished a mud-brick pyramid at

Dahshur; nearby two mounds/unfinished pyramids await investigation. Khendjer, a king with an intriguingly suggestive foreign name, was able to complete a 37-metre high pyramid with a relatively complex internal structure at Sakkara. To the south-west of his monument lay an ambitious but again unfinished and unoccupied pyramid.

The Middle Bronze Age was a time of turbulence and mass-migration throughout the eastern Mediterranean. The Delta was already uneasy. For centuries dispossessed 'Asiatics' had been arriving in ever-increasing numbers, attracted by the peace and prosperity of Delta life. Now they were forming semi-independent communities, so that it seemed to the native-born Egyptians that foreigners had effectively 'conquered' the north-eastern corner of their land. The atmosphere of intense political unease was exploited by the provincial governors who took the opportunity to kick against their loss of inherited authority. To make matters worse, a series of high Nile levels was causing floods, hunger and economic disruption. A strong ruler might have overcome these difficulties but the royal family was incapable of taking action. Merneferra Ay, the last pharaoh of the 13th Dynasty, fled his responsibilities and the Middle Kingdom was over.

The Second Intermediate Period started with the Nubian kingdom of Kerma ruling in the extreme south, an Egyptian dynasty ruling from Thebes and the Hyksos, Palestinian invaders, ruling the north from Avaris. The Hyksos were strong, rich, cosmopolitan arrivistes who adopted the titles and regalia of the Egyptian king, but who have left no royal tombs. The contemporary Theban kings were isolated and impoverished but, considering themselves the true inheritors of the double crown, they clung to the old traditions. Denied access to the royal cemeteries, they buried their kings in the Dra Abu el-Naga cemetery, opposite the Karnak temple of Amen. Here they built the pyramids which, in defiance of local tradition, they felt appropriate to their royal status. These were not the massive structures of the Old Kingdom, but elegant, steep (angles of 60° or more; heights of approximately 10 metres) mud-brick edifices coated with plaster and paint and capped with inscribed stone pyramidions.[10]

After many generations of struggle the Theban Ahmose managed to expel the Hyksos, subdue Nubia and capture part of Palestine. In tribute to his achievement he is acknowledged as the first pharaoh of the New

Kingdom, and the first pharaoh of the 18th Dynasty. The newly unified and peaceful Egypt, with its eastern and southern territories restored and its trade networks reactivated, grew steadily richer. The mines and quarries were reopened and craftsmen again picked up their tools. Ahmose was deeply grateful to Amen, 'the Hidden One', of Thebes who had supported him in his victorious campaign. Amen became the happy recipient of a host of valuable offerings until he emerged the most significant non-royal landowner in the Egyptian empire. His Karnak temple became the focus of national religious life and, although Memphis continued to serve as the northern administrative base, Thebes effectively became Egypt's capital city.

Ahmose died after twenty-five years on the throne, and was buried in a small-scale pyramid at Dra Abu el-Naga. He had also provided himself with a cenotaph plus pyramid at Abydos, where he built a complex highly reminiscent of that built by Senwosret III. The tradition of Abydene cenotaphs would continue throughout the New Kingdom. But the tradition of royal pyramid building had ended.

Amenhotep I, son of Ahmose, was almost certainly interred at Dra abu el-Naga. His tomb has never been found but his well-wrapped mummy, recovered from the Deir el-Bahari royal cache, today rests in Cairo Museum. Amenhotep's adopted successor, Tuthmosis I, was a southerner firmly devoted to Amen and the Osirid tradition. Confident, successful, with nothing to prove and no blood link to the ancient kings, Tuthmosis established a new tradition. His mortuary temple would be open and obvious to all. His tomb would be hidden, secret and, it was hoped, secure, cut into the rock of the remote Valley of the Kings. There would be no man-made pyramid to tempt thieves, and no vast gang of workers to betray the whereabouts of the royal treasure. But high above the rock-cut tomb the peak of the Theban mountain would serve as a natural, indestructible Stairway to Heaven.

15

Postscript: The Pyramid Legacy

*Year 47, 2nd month of winter, day 25 (January 1232 BC), the
Treasury-Scribe Hednakht, son of Tjenro and Tewosret, came to take
a stroll and enjoy himself in the west of Memphis, along with his brother
Panakht . . . He said: 'O all you gods of the West of Memphis . . .
and glorified dead . . . grant a full lifetime in serving your good pleasure,
a goodly burial after a happy old age, like yourself' . . .*[1]

Royal pyramids were out of fashion. The pharaohs continued to raise
obelisks – they had no quarrel with the theology of Re and the principle
of the sun's rays made solid in the *benben* stone – but the stairway to
heaven was no longer a literal necessity and they preferred the illusory
security of burial in tombs hidden beneath the natural pyramid of the
Theban peak.

With the withdrawal of the royal monopoly on pyramid building,
private individuals felt free to incorporate the form in their own tombs.
Small-scale New Kingdom private pyramids may be found at sites stretching from Sakkara to Nubia, but the best-known examples are those built
by the wealthy workmen and officials of Deir el-Medina, the village
associated with the Valley of the Kings. Here, as we might expect from
a well-resourced community of elite grave-diggers, the village cemetery
was a masterpiece of the tomb-maker's art. Outside the imposing village
wall the terraced hillside displayed ranks of mud-brick pyramids, each
plastered, painted and capped with a limestone pyramidion, perched on
top of colonnaded funerary chapels which allowed access to elaborately
decorated rock-cut burial chambers. The pyramids were hollow, to
reduce the weight on the chapel roof, and frequently included a niche
to display a statue of the deceased.

In the early 19th Dynasty, Tia, the commoner-born sister of Ramesses

*Figure 15.1 A New Kingdom funeral in front of a pyramid-topped tomb,
from the Book of the Dead of Hunefer.*

II, and her husband, a superintendent of the treasury also named Tia,
built a tomb in the Sakkara cemetery. Their superficially grand but
ill-built monument included a colonnaded courtyard, chapels, sunken
burial chambers and, as was then fashionable, a small stone pyramid
whose pyramidion showed the dead couple worshipping Re-Horakhty,
Osiris and Atum.

Tia's nephew, Prince Khaemwaset, shared his aunt's interests in pyramids. Living in Memphis, where he served as a priest in the great temple
of Ptah, Khaemwaset could not fail to notice that the Sakkara and Giza
cemeteries were in a disgraceful condition. Long-since robbed, the
pyramids lay open and empty, their stone blocks crumbling and their
temples covered in sand. Being a man of action, he embarked on a

mission to restore *maat* to this very obvious chaos. With Khaemwaset himself supervising, a gang of labourers worked their way through a series of pyramids, tombs and temples, cleaning, tidying and restoring as they went. Finally they carved huge labels into each monument. The labels preserved the essential details: the name of the original owner, the name of Ramesses II and, of course, the name of Khaemwaset.

The late New Kingdom was a time of economic uncertainty, unpredictable Nile levels and extensive population shift. Once again Egypt was acting as a magnet for the dispossessed and hungry of the eastern Mediterranean world. Ramesses III was able to repel the invaders who threatened the security of the Delta, but he almost bankrupted himself in the process. As eight further Ramesses succeeded to the throne Egypt plunged into crisis. The eastern empire was lost, Nubia broke free, and Thebes fell under the control of the High Priests of Amen. In what is becoming a familiar story the end of the New Kingdom saw Egypt divided, with a local dynasty ruling the north from Tanis and the High Priests ruling the south from Thebes. A confusing period followed – confusing, that is to historians; as with the First and Second Intermediate Periods, life for the majority of the population continued more or less as normal – with various local chieftains, many of Libyan descent, simultaneously proclaiming themselves king.

Meanwhile Nubia was fully independent with her own ruling family, her own impressive military machine and her own dreams of expansion and empire. The first independent kingdom of Kush had developed during Egypt's Second Intermediate Period but had collapsed with Nubia's re-absorption into the Egyptian empire. Now a second Kushite kingdom emerged. In 770 BC Kashta of Napata marched northwards to Thebes. Kashta was proclaimed King of Upper and Lower Egypt but it was his son and successor, Piye, who eventually reached the Nile Delta and founded the 25th Dynasty. Piye was crowned at Heliopolis where he worshipped before Re and the ancient *benben* stone.

Egypt's ancient pantheon flourished in Nubia and the pious Piye, considering himself the true heir of the lost dynasties, was shocked by the lack of religious propriety he found throughout his new land. Like the Hyksos before them, the Nubian pharaohs immediately adopted the obvious trappings of Egyptian kingship becoming more Egyptian than the Egyptians themselves. They expressed their thoughts in hieroglyphs, were depicted in Egyptian-style art performing typically Egyptian actions, wore pharaonic regalia (subsequently modified to include Nubian elements) and worshipped Egyptian gods in long-established Egyptian temple rituals. However, they shunned the Egyptian cemeteries and returned home to be buried under pyramids, a tradition not native to Nubia but imported from Egypt.

Piye's family cemetery was situated at el-Kurru, close by the as yet undiscovered Napatan royal palace. Here may be found the badly decayed funerary complexes of Piye, his father, three of his successors (Shabako, Shebitku and Tantamani), five generations of ancestors and fourteen queens.[2] These complexes, highly reminiscent of Egypt's New Kingdom private pyramid-tombs, were essentially subterranean burial chambers topped by pyramids, with mortuary chapels on the eastern side. The pyramids, with bases measuring roughly 8 metres square (less for the queens), and with slopes of 68°, were both small and steep. We have fragments of Piye's Canopic jars, which suggest that he was embalmed, Egyptian-style, yet within his tomb his mummy rested on a bed rather than in a sarcophagus. Close by was a curious and most un-Egyptian animal cemetery housing twenty-four chariot horses and two dogs, the property of the dead kings. The animals had been decapitated and buried headless and ornamented, in a standing position.

Taharka crossed the river to erect his pyramid in the Nuri cemetery. This he built on a grander, more obviously Egyptian scale. Taharka's pyramid, first conceived as a smallish, sandstone-clad monument, would be expanded until the original pyramid and mortuary chapel were totally concealed within a pyramid standing over 40 metres high with a base length of 51 metres and a steep angle of 69°. Underground, his pyramid was equally complex, incorporating a pillared antechamber and a trough cut to hold his now lost Egyptian-style sarcophagus.

In 671 BC Assyrian invaders captured the Nile Delta, forcing King Tantamani southwards into Nubia. Here his dynasty would flourish for a further 350 years, using the el-Kurru and Nuri cemeteries until Nuri held the pyramids of twenty-one kings and fifty-two lesser royals. The Egyptian influence, if anything, grew stronger with time, so that the tomb of King Aspelta included a massive granite sarcophagus carved with

Pyramid Texts and images of Egyptian gods. Eventually, the burial site moved upriver to Meroe where the Nubian royals continued to build steep, stone pyramids until their empire collapsed in *c.* AD 350.

While Nubia prospered, Egypt had become a province, her Delta ruled by the Assyrian-appointed Saite puppet kings. The beginning of the Late Period saw the country once again independent under the now autonomous Saite 26th Dynasty. The Saite kings revered the builders of the three Giza pyramids, and burial close to the royal tombs was considered beneficial for the elite. The kings themselves were buried in hidden tombs within the courtyards of their major temples, but private individuals built small-scale pyramids in the cemeteries of Abydos and Thebes.

In 525 BC the Persian army conquered Egypt, installing their own dynasties which were interspersed by a brief period of local rule. Finally, in 332 BC Alexander the Great arrived. Greece, and later Rome, would be profoundly influenced by their Egyptian connections. While in Egypt, both Greeks and Romans adapted to local customs, local gods and, perhaps most surprising given the tendency of societies to cling to long-held funerary rituals, local traditions of mummification. At the same time these ideas were exported so that Egyptian elements entered the classical architectural and artistic repertoire. Some Egyptian gods – Osiris (Serapis), and to a lesser extent Ptah, Hathor and Horus – gained international recognition while Isis, remodelled as a classical maiden, attained supergoddess status. Isis was worshipped in temples throughout the Roman world. She had a particular appeal to the imperial families: Caligula, who built the Aula Isiaca on the Palatine Hill, was so impressed by her tale of brother–sister incest that he, too, married his sister. As Christianity eventually replaced paganism, the legend of Isis and Horus would survive to make an important contribution to the developing cult of the Virgin Mary.

The Romans collected genuine antiquities, Augustus being the first to ship an obelisk to Rome. Where they could not collect, they copied. The pyramid – the small, steep-sided pyramid of New Kingdom Egypt, el-Kurru and Meroe rather than its massive Old Kingdom predecessor – was adopted by not only Graeco-Romans living in Egypt, but by Romans living in Rome. The best known and best preserved of these is the pyramid erected by Caius Cestius in *c.* 12 BC, which now towers over

Rome's Protestant cemetery. This pyramid, small, steep and built of marble-covered concrete, was by no means the only one of its kind; pyramids were rising in cemeteries across the empire.

The Arab conquest of Egypt in AD 640 left Egypt isolated and mysterious. The land of the pharaohs had effectively vanished, accessible to Europeans only through the Bible and the classical authors. During the Renaissance, as Egypt gradually reopened to outsiders, these works were studied anew, sparking a new wave of interest in Egyptian-style architecture. In Rome Gian Lorenzo Bernini (1598–1680) not only incorporated a genuine Egyptian obelisk within his Fountain of the Four Rivers, he designed pyramid-inspired funerary monuments for the papal tombs in St Peter's Basilica. These in turn inspired imitations throughout Europe. The ready acceptance of the pagan pyramid as an entirely suitable Christian tomb would survive until the present day, and the new, large, neat and sanitary public cemeteries which appeared across Europe, America and India at the start of the 19th century all had their share of pyramids, sphinxes and obelisks.

In more recent times the pyramid, once a symbol of death, has come to stand for ancient Egypt herself; a glamorized, sanitized Egypt which the pharaohs themselves would be hard-pressed to recognize. Thus we find modern architects adapting the pyramid to serve the living as an Egyptian-style house, as a shopping mall or even, as seen at Las Vegas, as a hotel and casino decorated with meaningless hieroglyphs and fake Egyptian statuary. More appropriately, perhaps, a glass pyramid now serves as the entrance to the Louvre Museum, Paris.

Chronology

The dating and even the ordering of Egypt's earliest kings has been the subject of much debate due to the lack of unequivocal archaeological evidence; dating generally becomes more accurate as the dynasties progress. The dates given here are broadly in line with those suggested by the *Oxford History of Ancient Egypt*, edited by Ian Shaw (Oxford, 2000).

The Egyptians themselves were not particularly interested in history for history's sake; they took a more cyclical view of events, regarding each new reign as a fresh start rather than a continuation of what had gone before. In consequence their years were dated, not consecutively from a single, fixed event as are our own, but with reference to the current king. Thus a particular event would be assigned to regnal Year X of King Y (or even simply to Year X). Year numbers would naturally start again with each successive reign so that, in a very real sense, a new king brought a new beginning.

Naqada III/Dynasty 0 (*c.* 3200–3000 BC)	Various simultaneous local kings Scorpion? Iri-Hor Ka Narmer: first king of the unified land
1st Dynasty (*c.* 3000–2890 BC)	Aha Djer Djet (also known as Wadji or Uadji) Queen Merit-Neith Den Anedjib Semerkhet Qaa

2nd Dynasty (*c.* 2890–2686 BC)	Hetepsekhemwy Raneb (or Nebre) Ninetjer Weneg Sened Peribsen Khasekhem/Khasekhemwy
3rd Dynasty (*c.* 2686–2613 BC)	(Nebka: recorded by Manetho but otherwise unknown) Djoser: also known by his Horus-name Netjerikhet Sekhemkhet Khaba Sanakht Huni
4th Dynasty (*c.* 2613–2498 BC)	Snefru Khufu (Cheops) Djedefre (or Radjedef) Khaefre (Chephren) (Nebka: recorded in the Turin Canon) (Others?) Menkaure (Mycerinus) Shepseskaf
5th Dynasty (*c.* 2494–2345 BC)	Userkaf Sahure Neferirkare (Shepseskare?) Raneferef (or Neferefre) Shepseskare Niuserre Menkauhor Djedkare (or Djedkare-Isesi) Unas

6th Dynasty (*c.* 2345–2181 BC)	Teti Userkare Pepi I Meryre Merenre Pepi II Neferkare Nitocris
7th and 8th Dynasties	A confused jumble of kings called Neferkare The end of the 8th Dynasty signals the collapse of central authority and the end of the Old Kingdom.

FIRST INTERMEDIATE PERIOD (Dynasties 9–11)
A series of local rulers, the 9th and 10th Dynasties based at the Middle Egyptian city of Herakleopolis, the 11th Dynasty at Thebes only.

11th Dynasty – Local Rule (2125–2055 BC)	Montuhotep I Intef I Intef II Intef III

MIDDLE KINGDOM (Dynasties 11–14)

11th Dynasty – National Rule (2055–1985 BC)	Montuhotep II Montuhotep III Montuhotep IV
12th Dynasty (1985–1773 BC)	Amenemhat I Senwosret I Amenemhat II Senwosret II Senwosret III Amenemhat III Amenemhat IV Queen Sobeknofru
13th and 14th Dynasties (1773–1650 BC)	A confused series of local rulers

SECOND INTERMEDIATE PERIOD (Dynasties 15–17)

15th Dynasty (1650–1550 BC)	A series of foreign 'Hyksos' rulers based in the Delta
16th Dynasty (1650–1580 BC)	A series of local Theban rulers contemporary with the Hyksos
17th Dynasty (1580–1550 BC)	A series of Theban rulers growing increasingly strong Sekenenre Taa II Kamose

NEW KINGDOM (Dynasties 18–20: 1550–1069 BC)

THIRD INTERMEDIATE PERIOD (Dynasties 21–25: 1069–664 BC)

LATE PERIOD (Dynasties 26–31: 664–332 BC)

Notes

Introduction

1 R. Talbot Kelly (1902), *Egypt Painted and Described*, London: 69–70.
2 Those in search of accurate descriptions of the fabric and construction of the pyramids should turn to the three classics of the genre. I. E. S. Edwards's 1947 masterpiece *The Pyramids of Egypt*, and Mark Lehner's heavily illustrated 1999 *The Complete Pyramids* are invaluable guides to pyramid building. More recently (2002), there is Miroslav Verner's *The Pyramids: their archaeology and history*, revised and translated into English from the Czech. With these three publications the internal structure of the pyramids is laid bare for all to see.
3 A fuller chronology is provided for reference on pages 227–30.

Chapter 1   The First Egyptians

1 M. and C. H. B. Quennell (1921), *Everyday Life in the Old Stone Age*, London: viii–ix.
2 At the same time increasing numbers of pregnancies decrease female life expectancy; women live longer as hunter-gatherers.
3 Brunton, G. and Caton-Thompson, G. (1928), *The Badarian Civilization and Prehistoric Remains near Badari*, London.
4 Petrie, W.M.F. (1931) *Seventy Years in Archaeology*, London: 155–6.
5 'Whatever we left was sure to be lost for ever, as any cemetery known to the natives is completely grubbed out very soon. The hundreds – thousands – of open tomb-pits all along the desert, rifled and refilled in recent years, show this only too plainly.' Petrie, W.M.F. and Quibell, J.E. (1896), *Naqada and Ballas*, London: x.

Chapter 2   River of Life

1 Diodorus Siculus *Histories* I; Diodorus is expanding on Herodotus's often quoted comment 'Egypt is the gift of the Nile.'
2 'Of the sources of the Nile no one can give any account, since the country through which it passes is desert and without inhabitants . . . It enters Egypt from the parts beyond . . .': Herodotus *Histories* 2: 34.
3 Moorehead, A. (1960), *The White Nile*, London: 37.
4 Herodotus *Histories* 2: 19.
5 From the Middle Kingdom *Satire of the Trades*: for a full translation of this text see Lichtheim, M. (1973): 184–92.
6 A stone building required an unfaltering supply of large blocks which were hard to cut, heavy to transport and difficult to erect. It therefore demanded precise architecture and good coordination: a large, well-trained workforce at the quarry, a fleet of strong barges, a network of canals and an experienced crew at the building site. More specifically, intensive quarrying demanded reliable supplies of copper (to make tools which would cut through stone and shape wood), good quality timber (to make tools, levers, sledges, boats and barges), and mile upon mile of rope. Supplies of wood, and to a lesser extent copper, were dependent upon trade. These difficulties merely enhanced the attraction of stone. A stone building became the ultimate proof of efficient kingship, only available to those who had total control over their country's resources.

Chapter 3   The Horus Kings

1 Herodotus *Histories* 2: 99.
2 Hieraconpolis has long been recognized as a prime archaeological site and has been excavated by, amongst others, Petrie's sparring partner de Morgan, his protégés Quibell and Green, the British archaeologist John Garstang, and the Americans Walter Fairservis and Michael Hoffman.
3 The most recent excavation has been conducted by a team led by Gunther Dreyer of the German Institute of Archaeology (D.A.I.).
4 A jumble of carved ivories, palettes and vases dating to the very end of the Naqada age was deliberately buried and subsequently forgotten within the

sacred precincts of the Horus temple. Whether they were hidden from looters during the civil unrest of the First Intermediate Period, or merely tidied away by temple-proud priests, is uncertain. They were rediscovered in the ill-defined 'Main Deposit' by James Quibell in his 1897–8 season of excavation.

5 The principal surviving fragments of this palette are now housed in the Ashmolean Museum, Oxford and the British Museum, London.

6 A suggestion first put forward by Gunther Dreyer.

Chapter 4   Archaic Abydos

1 Mrs Arthur Bell (1897), *The Story of Early Man*, London: 7–8.

2 Petrie, W.M.F. (1931), *Seventy Years in Archaeology*, London: 175.

3 *Histories* 2: 86.

4 This cemetery was principally excavated by Bryan Emery, from 1936–56.

5 *Seventy Years in Archaeology* 1931: 172–3; *The Royal Tombs of the First Dynasty Part 1*, 1900: 2. It is hard to imagine any contemporary excavator feeling free to publish his thoughts in this uninhibited way, no matter what the provocation.

6 These are today assigned to Dynasty 0 (Iri-Hor, Ka, and Narmer), Dynasty 1 (Kings Aha, Djer, Djet, Den, Anedjib, Semerkhet, Qaa and Queen Merit-Neith), and Dynasty 2 (the last two kings: Peribsen and Khase-khemwy).

7 Petrie, W.M.F. (1900), *The Royal Tombs of the First Dynasty Part 1*, London: 4.

8 Similar mounds were found in Sakkara Tombs 3507, 3111 and 3471.

9 *Histories* 1: 88.

10 Arnold, D. (1998), 'Royal cult complexes of the Old and Middle Kingdoms', in B.E. Schafer (ed.) *Temples of Ancient Egypt*, London and New York: 31–85: 32.

11 Working with the combined Yale University and Pennsylvania University Museum expedition.

12 And similar benches surrounding the slightly later tombs 3506, 3507 and 3505.

13 O'Connor, D. (1989), 'New funerary enclosures (Talbezirke) of the Early Dynastic period at Abydos', *Journal of the American Research Centre in Egypt* 22: 51–86: 82.

Chapter 5   The Rising of the Sun

1 The Legend of Osiris, as told in Graeco-Roman times.

2 If not already flattened during the construction of the Step Pyramid, they must have been demolished during the building of the 5th Dynasty causeway of King Unas which runs close by.

3 Coffin Text 335. Discussed in Quirke, S. (1992), *Ancient Egyptian Religion*, London: 23.

4 The Legend of the Destruction of Mankind as told in New Kingdom times.

5 John Greaves (1646), *Pyramidographia, or a description of the pyramids in Egypt*.

6 Pyramid Text 1688; 6th Dynasty sarcophagus text of the Vizier Khentika Ikhekhi. Both these texts are discussed in Edwards, I. E. S. (1994), 'Do the pyramid texts suggest an explanation for the abandonment of the subterranean chamber of the Great Pyramid?', in Grimal *et al* (eds.) *Homages à Jean Leclant* I: 159–67.

7 This difference was, of course, nowhere near as obvious as it would have been in a country 600 miles wide; long, thin Egypt has only one time-zone.

8 Simpson, W. K. (1963), *Papyrus Reisner I: the records of a building project in the reign of Sesostris I*, Boston: 57.

9 Reworded after Gardiner, A. H. (1927), 'An Administrative Letter of Protest', *Journal of Egyptian Archaeology* 13: 78.

10 Posener-Krieger, P. (1976), *Les Archives du temple funéraire de Neferirkare-Kakai, les papyrus d'Abousir, traduction et commentaire*, Cairo and Paris.

11 *Laws* 7: 819.

12 Arithmetic is, however, today a specialist taste, and here a brief summary will suffice to confirm the ancient expertise. Those requiring further explanation, together with worked examples, are referred to Sir Alan Gardiner's *Egyptian Grammar* (Oxford 1957; chapter 20).

Chapter 6   Djoser's Step Pyramid

1 Amelia B. Edwards (1877), *A Thousand Miles up the Nile*, London: 52. The door lintel and frame had been discovered in 1842–3 by a German mission under the leadership of Karl Richard Lepsius.

2 According to the Turin Canon, rather than the twenty-nine years given by Manetho and the thirty plus years accepted by some Egyptologists.

3 *Natural History* Book 36: 14.

4 Pyramid Text Utterance 245; after Faulkner, R. O. (1969), *The Ancient Egyptian Pyramid Texts*, Oxford.

5 Napoleon's soldiers, von Minutoli and Segato (1821), John Shae Perring and Colonel Vyse (1837), Richard Lepsius (1842), even Amelia B. Edwards (1877) all ignored the surrounding ruins. It was not until 1924, when Pierre Lacau and Cecil M. Firth started to excavate around rather than beneath the Step Pyramid, that the true complexity of the site was recognized.

Chapter 7   A Brief History of Failed Step Pyramids

1 Thomas Fuller (1608–61), *Holy State* 3: 14.

2 Goneim worked at the site until his untimely death in 1957; after a six year pause, the excavation was continued by his friend and colleague Jean-Philippe Lauer.

3 No pyramid has yielded an intact or even partially intact burial. Why? If we accept that the pyramids are tombs (and there are some who, in spite of the evidence for the development of the pyramid complex already discussed, cannot accept this) we should be asking what happened to the bodies. The answer is provided by the Egyptians themselves: 'Those who were entombed are cast on high ground and the embalmers' secrets are thrown away.' Here Ipuwer, a Middle Kingdom scribe, is lamenting the fate of the vulnerable dead as law and order collapse at the end of the Old Kingdom. He is exaggerating, but his account holds more than a grain of truth. The pyramid complexes had survived for many centuries as successful economic units. But with the loss of central authority, with the advent of civil unrest and perhaps even famine, they made very obvious targets. And the thieves made straight for the royal bodies. They ripped open the mummies, snatched their jewellery and amulets, set fire to the coffins to melt the precious metals, and fled. As the New Kingdom dawned, the pyramids lay empty and forlorn.

4 While Hans Stock has suggested that the entire site was converted into a gigantic mastaba by filling in the area within the enclosure walls – somewhat as Djoser's complex may have been buried in sand – others believe that the pyramid alone was converted into a mastaba.

5 The last, incomplete, investigation into the pyramid occurred before the

First World War, and was led by George Reisner and Clarence Fisher. The pyramid had previously been investigated by Perring (1839) and Barsanti (c. 1900).

Chapter 8   Snefru, Master Builder

1 The story of Snefru's court, as told in the Middle Kingdom Westcar Papyrus.
2 New Kingdom graffito found in Snefru's Meidum mortuary temple.
3 A ruin which has attracted the great and the good of Egyptology, it has been investigated by, amongst others, Captain Frederick Norden (1737); W. G. Browne (1793); V. Denon (1799); John Shae Perring (1839); Richard Lepsius (1843); Auguste Mariette (1871); Gaston Maspero (1890: the date that the entrance was discovered and the nearby mastabas opened); the ubiquitous Flinders Petrie (1891 and 1909–10: the discovery of the mortuary temple and causeway); G. A. Wainwright (1911–12); Ludwig Borchardt (1926); Alan Rowe (1929–30); Ali el Khouli and the Egyptian Antiquities Organisation (1983).
4 (1974), *The Riddle of the Pyramids*, London.
5 This involved carving figures into the limestone and then filling them with coloured plaster-paste and polishing them.
6 Amelia B. Edwards (1877), *A Thousand Miles up the Nile*, London: 485–6.
7 After nineteenth-century investigation by Perring, Lepsius and Petrie, it has been studied by Abdel Salam Hussein and Alexandre Varille (1940s), Ahmed Fahry (1950s) and Maragioglio and Rinaldi (1960s).
8 Fakhry, A. (1961), *The Pyramids*, Chicago: 94.
9 A suggestion first made by Rainer Stadelmann, long-term excavator of Snefru's third pyramid.

Chapter 9   Khufu's Great Pyramid

1 The story of Khufu's court, as told in the Middle Kingdom Westcar Papyrus. The Westcar Papyrus, written at a time when scribes were challenging the highly centralized authority of the Old Kingdom, is by no means an unbiased document.
2 *Histories* 2: 126.

3 'Khnum is his protection'; Khnum being the ram-headed creator god of Elephantine.

4 The dating of this piece is, however, uncertain, and it may be considerably younger than the Old Kingdom.

5 Quoted at length in the appendix to Vyse R. Howard. and Perring, J. S. (1840–42), *Operations Carried on at the Pyramids of Giza*, London.

6 1866, 4th edition 1880; later reissued as *The Great Pyramid; its secrets and mysteries revealed*. See also Smyth's *Life and Work at the Great Pyramid* (1867).

7 Petrie, W. M. F (1931), *Seventy Years in Archaeology*, London: 12–3.

8 *ibid*: 34–5. Following Petrie's survey Gaston Maspero, Director of the Egyptian Antiquities Service, invited Egyptologists to apply for the Giza concession. Three teams responded, an Italian team led by Ernesto Schiaparelli of Turin, a German team led by Ludwig Borchardt working under Georg Steindorff of Leipzig, and an American team under George Reisner who was initially funded by Phoebe Apperson Hearst but who from 1905 became part of the Joint Expedition of Harvard University and Boston Museum of Fine Arts. The Italians received Khufu's pyramid, the Germans Khaefre's and the Americans Menkaure's. Eventually the Italians gave Reisner their concession, while Steindorff donated his concession to Hermann Junker of Vienna. Today archaeological attention is concentrated less on the pyramids and more on the surrounding structures which have or are being explored by, amongst others, Jean-Patrice Dormion and Gilles Goidin, Herbert Ricke, Mark Lehner, Zahi Hawass and James Allen.

9 See Troy, L. (1994), 'Painting the Eye of Horus', in Grimal *et al* (eds.) *Homages à Jean Leclant* I: 351–60.

10 Solid volume was measured by the *hekat*, with one *hekat* equalling just over a modern gallon. Liquid volume was measured in *hin*, with 1 *hin* measuring one tenth of a *hekat*. A very important measurement, for a society that traded by barter, was the *pefsu* or 'baking ratio', a measure of quality which indicated the number of produce (standard loaves, or measured jugs of beer) obtained from a given amount of grain. The higher the *pefsu* of a loaf of bread, the more loaves had been made from a single measure of grain.

11 A suggestion first made by the late pyramid expert I. E. S. Edwards.

12 Spence, K. (2000), 'Ancient Egyptian Chronology and the Astronomical Orientation of the Pyramids', *Nature* 408: 320–24.

13 A method suggested by Mark Lehner who has conducted experiments to test his theory.

14 Suggested by Miroslav Verner, in Verner, M. (2002), *The Pyramids: their archaeology and history*, London: 74.

15 *Histories* 2: 125.

16 Identified by Mark Lehner.

17 A suggestion put forward by Craig Smith, a construction project manager who has employed modern management theories and three-dimensional computer graphics in his analysis of the Great Pyramid (discussed in Tyldesley, J. A. [2000], *Private Lives of the Pharaohs*, London, Section 1).

18 Petrie, W. M. F. (1883), *The Pyramids and Temples of Gizeh*, London: 214.

19 *Histories* 2: 124.

20 The pyramid was rediscovered by Zahi Hawass beneath a modern road in 1991.

Chapter 10   The Pyramid Builders

1 James Baikie, *A Century of Excavation in the Land of the Pharaohs*, 1922: 67.

2 References for the following two paragraphs are as follows: Edwards, A. B. (1877), *A Thousand Miles up the Nile*, London: 15–16; Clarke, S. and Engelbach, R. (1930, reprinted 1990), *Ancient Egyptian Construction and Architecture*, Oxford and New York, frontispiece; Goyon, G. (1990), *Le Secret des Bâtisseurs des Grandes Pyramides*, Paris; Baines, J. and Malek, J. (1984), *Atlas of Ancient Egypt*, Oxford: 140; Gardiner, A. H. (1961): *Egypt of the Pharaohs*, Oxford: 79; Edwards, I. E. S. (1961 revised), *The Pyramids of Egypt*, London: 117; James Baikie *op. cit.* 52.

3 *Histories* 2: 124; his wording is unfortunately unclear; did he imagine 400,000 working on the pyramid in any given year, or four teams of 25,000?

4 *Histories* 1: 5.

5 *Histories* 2: 125.

6 Following Reisner's numbering system cemeteries 1200, 2100 and 4000 are collectively known as the Western Cemetery; cemetery 7000 is the Eastern Cemetery.

7 Basil Stewart, *History and Significance of the Great Pyramid*, 1936: 93.

Chapter 11   Khufu's Descendants

1 Diodorus Siculus *Histories* 1: 5.
2 This site was excavated by the French Institute of Near Eastern Archaeology from 1901–24, and has recently been re-examined by the French Institute working in association with the University of Geneva under the direction of Michel Valloggia.
3 *Histories* 2: 127.
4 It was discovered and subsequently excavated by the gunpowder-happy Auguste Mariette in 1853 and then re-explored with considerably more restraint by German archaeologist Uvo Holscher 1909–10.
5 *Narrative of the Operations and Recent Discoveries within the Pyramids, Temples, Tombs, and Excavations in Egypt and Nubia* (1820).
6 The Great Sphinx is nowhere labelled and dated, but as it is included within Khaefre's larger pyramid enclosure, and as some of the stone removed during its carving was incorporated in his temple, it can be accepted as part of Khaefre's funerary provision and dated to approximately 2500 BC. Those who have suggested a far earlier date of somewhere between 7000–5000 BC, and who believe that the Sphinx was built by a lost civilization rather than by the indigenous prehistoric peoples, base their date solely upon a highly speculative identification of 'water erosion' on the body of the sphinx.
7 This pyramid, approximately a mile to the north of Khaba's 3rd Dynasty Layer Pyramid, was excavated by Alexandre Barsanti (1904–12) and by George Reisner (1910–11) but is today inaccessible.
8 *Histories* 2: 133.
9 Quoted in Cottrell, L. (1956), *Mountains of Pharaoh*, London: 64–5.
10 The pyramid was first properly investigated by Vyse and Perring in 1837, while its temples were thoroughly excavated and published by Reisner in the early twentieth century.
11 Battiscombe Gunn, writing in Winifred Brunton's *Illustrated Great Ones of Egypt*, 1929: 66.
12 This curious coffin is today displayed in the British Museum.
13 It has most recently been excavated by Selim Hassan (1931–2).

Chapter 12 Sun Temples and Pyramid Texts

1 The continuation of the tale of Khufu's court in the Westcar Papyrus.
2 It has been investigated in modern times by a variety of workers, principally Marucchi (1831), Perring (1839), Firth (1928), Lauer (1948–55) and el-Khouli (1970s), but its substructure has been inaccessible since Perring's day.
3 Herbert Ricke, excavator of Userkaf's sun temple 1955–7, first proposed its four developmental phases.
4 The others are: Sahure, 'Re's Offering Field'; Neferirkare, 'Place of Re's Pleasure'; Raneferef, 'Re's Offering Table'; Menkauhor, 'The Horizon of Re'.
5 Abusir has been investigated by a number of experts including Perring, Lepsius, and Borchardt; the most recent work is being conducted by the University of Prague under the leadership of Miroslav Verner.
6 But not the exterior walls and not within the pyramid.
7 For a full translation consult Lichtheim, M. (1973), *Ancient Egyptian Literature 1: The Old and Middle Kingdoms*, Berkeley and Los Angeles: 61–80.
8 Principally by Perring, Lepsius, Maspero, Varille and Hussain, Fakhry, Razek and Mursi.
9 Strong queens occasionally flourished in times of peace and tranquillity – Tiy, wife of the New Kingdom Amenhotep III is the best example of such a consort – but this was rare.
10 It has been explored by, amongst others, Perring, Lepsius, Maspero, Barsanti, Firth, Lauer, Hassan, Goneim, Hussain and Mussa.
11 For a full translation of the pyramid texts consult Faulkner, R. O. (1969), *The Ancient Egyptian Pyramid Texts*, Oxford.

Chapter 13 The Ending of an Era

1 The autobiographical inscription of the bureaucrat Weni. This and all subsequent extracts after Lichtheim, M. (1973), *Ancient Egyptian Literature 1: The Old and Middle Kingdoms*, Berkeley and Los Angeles: 18–23.
2 The pyramid has been investigated by the now familiar experts: Perring, Lepsius, Maspero, Emile Brugsch, Bouriant, Wilbour, Quibell, Lauer and Leclant.

3 Jacques de Morgan (1894), *Fouilles à Dachour*: translation after Cottrell, L. (1956), *Mountains of Pharaoh*, London: 159.

4 Maspero was inspired by the discovery. Within three years he had copied the texts in the pyramids of Unas, Teti, Pepi I, Merenre and Pepi II, and published them with a translation. Subsequently Kurt Sethe published *The Pyramid Texts* (1908), the foundation stone of Pyramid Text studies and the basis of Faulkner's *Ancient Egyptian Pyramid Texts* (1969), which will only be superseded when all the fragmented Sakkara texts have been restored, collated and translated.

5 Decades of dedicated work by the French Archaeological Sakkara Mission, under the leadership of Jean Leclant since 1966, have brought this badly damaged pyramid, its fragmented texts and ruined mortuary temple back to life, although the causeway is as yet only partially cleared and the valley temple has yet to be excavated.

6 The pyramids were dedicated to Queens Nebwnet, Inenek-Inti, Princess? (an anonymous 'elder daughter of the king'), Meretites, Ankhesen-Pepi II and Ankhesen-Pepi III. A broken relief mentioning Nedjeftet, 'who belongs to the pomegranate tree' [i.e. the 13th and 14th nomes] suggests that she, too, may once have had a pyramid, and we may reasonably expect to find at least one more, that of the missing Ankhesen-Pepi I.

7 After Lichtheim (1973) *op. cit.*: 26.

8 The pyramid has been investigated by, amongst others, Perring, Maspero, and Jequier.

9 A suggestion first put forward by Mark Lehner; I. E. S. Edwards believed that it was built to protect the pyramid against earthquake damage.

10 Painstakingly translated by Michel Baud and Vasil Dobrev, this text is as yet unpublished; discussed in Verner, M. (2002), *The Pyramids: their archaeology and history*, London: 370.

11 This was less a criticism of a lifestyle choice (we have absolutely no idea about the king's sexual orientation), more a veiled means of attacking a king whose reign was perceived as weak and ineffectual.

12 *Histories* 2: 100.

Chapter 14   Mud-bricks and Golden Treasure

1 Percy Bysshe Shelley, 'Queen Mab' (1813).
2 Lichtheim, M. (1973), *Ancient Egyptian Literature 1: The Old and Middle Kingdoms*, Berkeley and Los Angeles: 85–6.
3 After Faulkner, R. O. (1973), *The Ancient Egyptian Coffin Texts 1*, Warminster: 179.
4 Excavated in 1911 by Ahmed Kamal who classified it as a square mastaba tomb attributed, on the basis of an inscribed brick, to King Khui.
5 Lichtheim, M. (1973) *op. cit.*: 135–9.
6 Today the diadem, one pectoral and the mirror are part of the Cairo Museum collection, while the remainder of the treasure is housed in the Metropolitan Museum, New York.
7 Much of the material recovered from Petrie's excavations is today housed in Manchester Museum, while the papyri, woefully underpublished, are currently being reviewed by Mark Collier of Liverpool University and Stephen Quirke of the Petrie Museum, London.
8 Petrie, W. M. F. (1931), *Seventy Years in Archaeology*, London: 95. With internal measurements of 7 by 2.5 by 1.83 metres, Petrie estimated the weight of the gigantic stone block used to make the burial chamber at an impressive 110 tons.
9 *Histories* 2: 148.
10 Today these pyramids and their associated chapels have virtually vanished; a team under the leadership of Daniel Polz of the German Archaeological Institute in Cairo is currently re-investigating their remains.

Postscript   The Pyramid Legacy

1 Graffito left at Djoser's complex by the New Kingdom tourist Hednakht; Egyptian graffiti tended to be longer and more meaningful than our own.
2 Excavated by George Reisner, 1918–19.

Bibliography and
Further Reading

I have avoided the use of extensive references and footnotes throughout this book as these are of interest to the minority of readers and tend to interfere with the flow of ideas. Where possible I have also avoided references to articles published in academic journals, as these may be difficult for the non-specialist reader to obtain. For similar reasons, and with apologies to my foreign colleagues, I have here given preference to books published in English. All the books listed below contain extensive and more specialized bibliographies. This bibliography, although itself lengthy, should merely be regarded as a preliminary reading list.

The translations of ancient writings presented in the book are free translations based on published works included in the list below. There are many published translations of ancient Egyptian texts, but perhaps the most accessible, and most poetic, are those given by Miriam Lichtheim (1973–80). These make an excellent introduction to Egyptian literature. Egyptian texts are included in this bibliography under the names of their translators, classical texts under the names of their authors.

Some of the older excavation reports have been superseded by more recent academic works and syntheses. However, the older reports are well worth reading. Not only are they beautifully presented, they offer glimpses of a vanished, more personal archaeological world which today's determinedly scientific works deliberately omit. Where else, apart from the fluent pen of Flinders Petrie himself, would we learn of, for example, his loathing of the 'writhing and wriggling of this maggoty world' (1931: 126) or, of more immediate archaeological interest, how the bulk of his Naqada collection was donated to the Ashmolean Museum in Oxford simply because he had taken an intense dislike to the curator at the British Museum?

Abd el-Gelil *et al.* (1996), 'Recent excavations at Heliopolis', *Orientalia* 65: 136–46.
Adams, B. (1995), *Ancient Nekhen: Garstang in the City of Hieraconpolis*, Surrey.

Adams, B. (1996), 'Elite Tombs at Hieraconpolis', in A. J. Spencer (ed.) *Aspects of Early Egypt*, London: 1–15.

Adams, B. and Cialowicz, K. M. (1997), *Protodynastic Egypt*, Princes Risborough.

Amelineau, E. (1899–1905), *Les Nouvelles Fouilles d'Abydos (1885–98)*, Paris.

Arnold, D. (1979), *The Temple of Mentuhotep at Deir el-Bahari*, New York.

Arnold, D. (1991), *Building in Egypt: pharaonic stone masonry*, Oxford and New York.

Arnold, D. (1998), 'Royal Cult Complexes of the Old and Middle Kingdoms', in B. E. Schafer (ed.) *Temples of Ancient Egypt*, London and New York: 31–85.

Arnold, D. and Ziegler, C. (eds.) (1999), *Egyptian Art in the Age of the Pyramids*, New York.

Assmann, J. (1970), *Der König als Sonnenprieste*, Gluckstadt.

Assmann, J. (1989), 'Death and Imitation in the Funerary Religion of Ancient Egypt', in J. P. Allen *et al.* (eds.) *Religion and Philosophy in Ancient Egypt*, New Haven: 135–59.

Assmann, J. (1996), 'Preservation and Presentation of Self in Ancient Egyptian Portraiture', in P. Der Manuelian (ed.) *Studies in Honour of William Kelly Simpson* 1: 55–81.

Baer, K. (1960), *Rank and Title in the Old Kingdom: the structure of the Egyptian administration in the fifth and sixth dynasties*, Chicago.

Bard, K. (1994), *From Farmers to Pharaohs: mortuary evidence for the rise of complex society in Egypt*, Sheffield.

Bard, K. (ed.) (1999), *Encyclopedia of the Archaeology of Ancient Egypt*, London and New York.

Borchardt, L. (1907), *Das Grabmal des Königs Ne-user-re*, Leipzig.

Borchardt, L. (1910–13), *Das Grabmal des Königs Sa-hu-re I–II*, Leipzig.

Borchardt, L. (1928), *Die Entstehung der Pyramide an der Baugeschichte der Pyramide bei Mejdum Nachgewissen*, Berlin.

Borchardt, L. (1932), *Einiges zur dritten Bauperiode der Grossen Pyramide*, Berlin.

Brunton, G. and Caton-Thompson, G. (1928), *The Badarian Civilization and Prehistoric Remains near Badari*, London.

Butzer, K. (1976), *Early Hydraulic Civilization in Egypt*, Chicago.

Caton-Thompson, G. and Gardner, E. W. (1934), *Kharga Oasis in Prehistory*, London.

Claessen, J. M. and Shalnik, P. (eds.) (1978), *The Early State*, The Hague.

Clarke, S. and Engelbach, R. (1930, reprinted 1990), *Ancient Egyptian Construction and Architecture*, Oxford and New York.

Cottrell, L. (1956), *The Mountains of Pharaoh: 2,000 years of pyramid exploration*, London.

Curl, J. S. (1994), Egyptomania, *The Egyptian Revival: a recurring theme in the history of taste*, Manchester.

David, A. R. (1986), *The Pyramid Builders of Ancient Egypt: a modern investigation of pharaoh's workforce*, London, Boston and Henley.

Davis, W. (1992), *Masking the Blow: the scene of representation in late prehistoric Egyptian art*, Berkeley and Los Angeles.

Diodorus Siculus, *Bibliotheca Historica*, translated by C. H. Oldfather and C. L. Sherman (1933–67), New York.

Dodson, A. (1994), 'From Dahshur to Dra Abu el-Naga; the decline and fall of the royal pyramid', *KMT* 5:3: 25–39.

Dunham, D. (1956), 'Building an Egyptian Pyramid', *Archaeology* 9: 159–65.

Dunham, D. (1978), *Zawiyet el-Aryan: the cemeteries adjacent to the Layer Pyramid*, Boston.

Edwards, I. E. S. (1961 revised), *The Pyramids of Egypt*, London.

Edwards, I. E. S. (1994), 'Chephren's Place Among the Kings of the Fourth Dynasty', in C. J. Eyre *et al.* (eds.) *The Unbroken Reed: studies in the culture and heritage of ancient Egypt in honour of A. F. Shore*, Liverpool: 97–105.

Edwards, I. E. S. (1994), 'Do the Pyramid Texts Suggest an Explanation for the Abandonment of the Subterranean Chamber of the Great Pyramid?', in Grimal *et al.* (eds.) *Homages à Jean Leclant* I: 159–67.

Emery, W. B. (1949), *Great Tombs of the First Dynasty I*, Cairo.

Emery, W. B. (1954), *Great Tombs of the First Dynasty II*, London.

Emery, W. B. (1958), *Great Tombs of the First Dynasty III*, London.

Emery, W. B. (1961), *Archaic Egypt*, Harmondsworth.

Eyre, C. J. (1994), 'Weni's Career and Old Kingdom Historiography', in C. J. Eyre *et al.* (eds.) *The Unbroken Reed: studies in the culture and heritage of ancient Egypt in honour of A. F. Shore*, Liverpool: 107–24.

Fakhry, A. (1959), *The Monuments of Snefru at Dahshur*, 2 vols., Cairo.

Fakhry, A. (1961), *The Pyramids*, Chicago.

Faulkner, R. O. (1969), *The Ancient Egyptian Pyramid Texts*, Oxford.

Faulkner, R. O. (1973–8), *The Ancient Egyptian Coffin Texts 1–3*, Warminster.

Firth, C. M. and Quibell, J. E. (1935), *The Step Pyramid* (2 vols.), Cairo.

Fodor, A. (1970), 'The Origins of the Arabic Legends of the Pyramids', *Acta Orientalia Academiae Scientiarum Hungaricae* 23:3: 335–63.

Friedman, F. D. (1996), 'Notions of Cosmos in the Step Pyramid Complex', in P. Der Manuelian (ed.) *Studies in Honour of William Kelly Simpson* 1: 337–51.

Friedman, R. (1996), 'The Ceremonial Centre at Hieraconpolis Locality HK29A', in A. J. Spencer (ed.) *Aspects of Early Egypt*, London: 1–35.

Friedman, R. and Adams, B. (eds.) (1992), *The Followers of Horus: studies dedicated to Michael Hoffman*, Oxford.

Gardiner, A. H. (1927), 'An Administrative Letter of Protest', *Journal of Egyptian Archaeology* 13: 78.

Gardiner, A. H. (1957: 3rd Edition), *Egyptian Grammar*, Oxford.

Gomaa, F. (1973), *Chaemwese; Sohn Ramses' II und Hoherpriester von Memphis*, Wiesbaden.

Goneim, M. Z. (1956), *The Buried Pyramid*, London.

Goneim, M. Z. (1957), *Horus Sekhemkhet. The Unfinished Step Pyramid at Sakkara*, Cairo.

Goyon, G. (1990), *Le Secret des Bâtisseurs des Grandes Pyramides*, Paris.

Greaves, J. (1646), *Pyramidographia, or a description of the pyramids in Egypt*, London.

Griffiths, J. G. (1948), 'Human Sacrifices in Egypt: the classical evidence', *Annales du Service des Antiquités de l'Egypt* 48: 409–23.

Habachi, L. (1977), *The Obelisks of Egypt: skyscrapers of the past*, London, Toronto and Melbourne.

Hassan, F. A. (1988), 'The Predynastic of Egypt', *Journal of World Prehistory* 2: 135–85.

Hawass, Z. (1996), 'The Discovery of the Satellite Pyramid of Khufu (Gi-d)', in P. Der Manuelian (ed.) *Studies in Honour of William Kelly Simpson* 1: 379–98.

Hawass, Z. (1996), 'The Workmen's Community at Giza', in M. Bietak (ed.) *Haus und Palast in Alten Agypten*, Vienna: 53–67.

Hawass, Z. and Lehner, M. (1994), 'The Great Sphinx at Giza: who built it and why?' *Archaeology* 47:5: 30–41.

Hawass, Z. and Lehner, M. (1994), 'Remnant of a Lost Civilization?', *Archaeology* 47:5: 44–7.

Hendrickx, S. (1996), 'The Relative Chronology of the Naqada Culture: problems and possibilities', in A. J. Spencer (ed.) *Aspects of Early Egypt*, London: 36–69.

Herodotus, *The Histories*, translated by A. de Selincourt, revised with Introduction and Notes by A. R. Burn (1983), London.

Hodges, P. and Keable, E. B. J. (1989), *How the Pyramids were Built*, Shaftesbury.

Hoffman, M. A. (1980; revised 1991), *Egypt Before the Pharaohs: the prehistoric foundations of Egyptian civilization*, London and Austin, Texas.

Hoffman, M. A. et al. (1982), *The Prehistory of Hieraconpolis: an interim Report*, Cairo.

Isler, M. (1989), 'An Ancient Method of Finding and Extending Direction', *Journal of the American Research Centre in Egypt* 26: 191–206.

Jeffreys, D. (1998), 'The Topography of Heliopolis and Memphis: some cognitive aspects', in *Stationen. Beitrage zur Kulturgeschichte Agyptens, Rainer Stadelmann gewidmet*, Mainz-am-Rhein, 63–71.

Jenkins, N. (1980), *The Boat beneath the Pyramid*, London.

Jequier, G. (1928), *Le Mastabet Faraoun*, Cairo.

Jequier, G. (1936–40), *Le Monument Funéraire de Pepi II*, 3 vols., Cairo.

Jequier, G. (1940), *Douze ans de fouilles dans la necropole Memphite*, Neuchâtel.

Kadish, G. E. (1996), 'Observations on Time and Work-Discipline in Ancient Egypt', in P. Der Manuelian (ed.) *Studies in Honour of William Kelly Simpson* 2: 439–49.

Kanawati, N. (1977), *The Egyptian Administration in the Old Kingdom*, Warminster.

Kemp, B. J. (1967), 'The Egyptian 1st Dynasty Royal Cemetery', *Antiquity* 41: 22–32.

Kemp, B. J. (1980), *Ancient Egypt: anatomy of a civilization*, London and New York.

Labrousse, A. (1999), *Les Pyramides des reines: un nouvelle nécropole à Saqqara*, Paris.

Lauer, J-P. (1962), *Histoire Monumentale des Pyramides d'Egypt*, Cairo.

Lauer, J-P. (1976), *Saqqara: the Royal Cemetery of Memphis. Excavations and Discoveries since 1850*, London.

Lauer, J-P. (1991), *The Pyramids of Sakkara*, Cairo.

Leclant, J. (1979), *Recherches dans la pyramide et au temple haut de Pharaon Pepi Ier à Saqqarah. Scholae Adriani De Buck memoriae dicatae 6*, Leiden.

Leclant, J. (1984), 'Recent Researches in the Pyramids with Text at Saqqarah', in H. I. P. Prince Takahito Miskasa (ed.), *Monarchies and Socio-religious Traditions in the Ancient Near East*, Wiesbaden: 51–4.

Lehner, M. (1985), *The Pyramid Tomb of Hetepheres and the Satellite Pyramid of Khufu*, Mainz.

Lehner, M. (1996), 'Z500 and the Layer Pyramid of Zawiyet el-Aryan', in P. Der Manuelian (ed.) *Studies in Honour of William Kelly Simpson* 2: 507–22.

Lehner, M. (1997), *The Complete Pyramids*, London.

Lehner, M. (2000), 'Lost City of the Pyramids', *Egypt Revealed*, Fall 2000: 42–57.

Lichtheim, M. (1973–80), *Ancient Egyptian Literature*, 3 vols., Berkeley and Los Angeles.

Lloyd, A. B. (1970), 'The Egyptian Labyrinth', *Journal of Egyptian Archaeology* 56: 81–100.

Malek, J. and Forman, W. (1986), *In the Shadow of the Pyramids: Egypt during the Old Kingdom*, London.

Maragioglio, V. and Rinaldi, C. (1965), *L'Architettura delle Piramidi Menfite IV*, Rapallo.

Mathieson, I. J. and Tavares, A. (1993), 'Preliminary Report on the National Museums of Scotland. Saqqara Survey Project 1990–91', *Journal of Egyptian Archaeology* 79: 17–31.

Midant-Reynes, B. (2000), *The Prehistory of Egypt*, translated by I. Shaw, London.

O'Connor, D. (1989), 'New Funerary Enclosures (Talbezirke) of the Early Dynastic period at Abydos', *Journal of the American Research Center in Egypt* 22: 51–86.

O'Connor, D. and Silverman, D. (eds.) (1995), *Ancient Egyptian Kingship*, Leiden.

Partridge, R. (1996), *Transport in Ancient Egypt*, London.

Peden, A. J. (1994), *Egyptian Historical Inscriptions of the Twentieth Dynasty*, Jonsered.

Peet, T. E. (1914), *Cemeteries of Abydos II: 1911–12*, London.

Petrie, W. M. F. (1883), *The Pyramids and Temples of Gizeh*, London.

Petrie, W. M. F. (1892), *Meidum*, London.

Petrie, W. M. F. (1900), *The Royal Tombs of the First Dynasty I*, London.

Petrie, W. M. F. (1901), *The Royal Tombs of the First Dynasty II*, London.

Petrie, W. M. F. (1920) *Prehistoric Egypt*, London.

Petrie, W. M. F. (1931), *Seventy Years in Archaeology*, London.

Petrie, W. M. F. and Quibell, J. E. (1896), *Naqada and Ballas*, London.

Petrie, W. M. F. Wainwright, G. A. and Mackay, E. (1912), *The Labyrinth, Gerzeh and Mazghunah*, London.

Plutarch: *De Iside et Osiride*, translation and commentary J. Gwyn Griffiths (1970), University of Wales.

Posener-Krieger, P. (1976), *Les Archives du temple funéraire de Neferirkare-Kakai, les papyrus d'Abousir, traduction et commentaire*, Cairo and Paris.

Posener-Krieger, P. and de Cernival, J. L. (1968), *Hieratic Papyri in the British Museum, Series V: The Abu Sir Papyri*, London.

Quibell, J. E. and Petrie, W. M. F. (1900), *Hieraconpolis I*, London.

Quibell, J. E. and Green, F. W. (1902), *Hieraconpolis II*, London.

Quirke, S. (1992), *Ancient Egyptian Religion*, London.

Quirke, S. (2001), *The Cult of Ra: sun-worship in Ancient Egypt*, London.

Reisner, G. A. (1927), 'Hetepheres, Mother of Cheops', *Boston Museum Bulletin*, supplement to volume 30.

Reisner, G. A. (1931), *Mycerinus: the temple of the third pyramid at Giza*, Cambridge Mass.

Reisner, G. A. (1936), *The Development of the Egyptian Tomb Down to the Accession of Cheops*, Cambridge Mass.

Reisner, G. A. (1942), *A History of the Giza Necropolis I*, Cambridge Mass.

Reisner, G. A. and Smith, W. S. (1955), *A History of the Giza Necropolis 2: the tomb of Hetepheres, the mother of Cheops*, Cambridge Mass.

Robins, G. and Shute, C. (1987), *The Rhind Mathematical Papyrus: an ancient Egyptian text*, London.

Saleh, A. (1981), *Excavations at Heliopolis I*, Cairo.

Saleh, A. (1983), *Excavations at Heliopolis II*, Cairo.

Sandford, K. S. and Arkell, W. J. (1928–39), *Reports of the Prehistoric Survey of Egypt*, 4 vols., Chicago.

Shaw, I. (ed.) (2000), *The Oxford History of Ancient Egypt*, Oxford.

Siedlmayer, S. J. (1996), 'Town and State in the Early Old Kingdom: a view from Elephantine', in A. J. Spencer (ed.) *Aspects of Early Egypt*, London: 108–27.

Simpson, W. K. (1963), *Papyrus Reisner I: the records of a building project in the reign of Sesostris I*, Boston.

Smith, E. Baldwin (1938), *Egyptian Architecture as a Cultural Expression*, New York.

Spence, K. (2000), 'Ancient Egyptian Chronology and the Astronomical Orientation of the Pyramids', *Nature* 408: 320–24.

Spencer, A. J. (1982), *Death in Ancient Egypt*, London.

Spencer, A. J. (1993), *Early Egypt: the rise of civilization in the Nile Valley*, London.

Stadelmann, R. (1985), *Die Agyptischen Pyramiden: vom Ziegelbau zum Weltwunder*, Mainz.

Stadelmann, R. (1990), *Die Grossen Pyramiden von Giza*, Graz.

Stadelmann, R. (1996), 'Origins and Development of the Funerary Complex of Djoser', in P. Der Manuelian (ed.) *Studies in Honour of William Kelly Simpson* 2: 787–800.

Strudwick, N. (1985), *The Administration of Egypt in the Old Kingdom*, London.

Trigger, B. G. *et al.* (1983), *Ancient Egypt: a social history*, Cambridge.

Troy, L. (1994), 'Painting the Eye of Horus', in Grimal *et al.* (eds.) *Homages à Jean Leclant* I: 351–60.

Tyldesley, J. A. (2000), *The Private Lives of the Pharaohs*, London.

Vermeerch, P. *et al.* (1998), 'A Middle Palaeolithic Burial of a Modern Human at Taramsa Hill', Egypt, *Antiquity* 72: 475–84.

Verner, M. (1985), *Abusir III: The Pyramid Complex of Khentkaus*, Prague.

Verner, M. (1985), 'Les statuettes de prisoniers en bois d'Abousir', *Revue d'Egyptologie* 36: 145–52.

Verner, M. (1986), *Abusir I: The Mastaba of Ptahshepses: Reliefs*, Prague.

Verner, M. (1994), *Forgotten Pharaohs, Lost Pyramids*: Abusir, Prague.

Verner, M. (2002), *The Pyramids: their archaeology and history*, London.

Vyse, R. Howard and Perring, J. S. (1840–42), *Operations Carried on at the Pyramids of Giza*, London.

Waddell, W. G. (1948), *Manetho*, Cambridge, Mass.

Watson, P. (1987), *Egyptian Pyramids and Mastaba Tombs*, Aylesbury.

Wells, R. A. (1996), 'Astronomy in Egypt', in C. Walker (ed.) *Astronomy Before the Telescope*, London: 28–41.

Wendorf, F. W. and Schild, R. (eds.) (1976), *The Prehistory of the Nile Valley*, New York.

Wier, S. K. (1996), 'Insight from Geometry and Physics into the Construction of Egyptian Old Kingdom Pyramids', *Cambridge Archaeological Journal*: 1: 150–63.

Wilkinson, T. A. H. (1999), *Early Dynastic Egypt*, London.

Wilkinson, T. A. H. (2000), 'What a King is This: Narmer and the Concept of the Ruler', *Journal of Egyptian Archaeology* 86: 23–32.

Zaba, Z. (1953), *L'orientation astronomique dans l'ancienne Egypt et la précession de l'axe du monde*, Prague.

Index